MANAGING LIBRARY
VOLUNTEERS

ALA GUIDES FOR THE BUSY LIBRARIAN

BE A GREAT BOSS: ONE YEAR TO SUCCESS
by Catherine Hakala-Ausperk

HIRING, TRAINING, AND SUPERVISING LIBRARY SHELVERS
by Patricia Tunstall

MENTORING AT THE LIBRARY
by Marta K. Lee

WRITING AND PUBLISHING: THE LIBRARIAN'S HANDBOOK
edited by Carol Smallwood

MANAGING LIBRARY VOLUNTEERS

SECOND EDITION

PRESTON DRIGGERS AND EILEEN DUMAS

AMERICAN LIBRARY ASSOCIATION
CHICAGO 2011

Preston Driggers is an affiliate faculty member of Regis University, Denver, Colorado, where he facilitates courses in human resources, organizational behavior, business research, and sociology. He has held managerial human resources positions in both public and private sectors, including a public library district. Driggers earned his PhD at Colorado State University and has master's degrees from Arizona State University and the University of Illinois, Urbana-Champaign. He is actively involved in local civic efforts to preserve open space land.

Eileen Dumas, special services librarian, worked for the Aurora Public Library, Aurora, Colorado, for eighteen years as volunteer and homebound services coordinator. During this period she was actively involved in several local volunteer management associations as well as the Colorado Association of Libraries. She coedited the journal *Colorado Libraries,* for which she also created and edited the column "Volunteer Line." Dumas earned her MLS from Indiana University, Bloomington. She recently retired but remains active in the Colorado Association of Libraries and the Sustainable Living Library, a Second Life virtual library supported by the Colorado Association of Libraries.

ALA Editions purchases fund advocacy, awareness and accreditation programs for library professionals worldwide.

© 2011 by the American Library Association. Any claim of copyright is subject to applicable limitations and exceptions, such as rights of fair use and library copying pursuant to Sections 107 and 108 of the U.S. Copyright Act. No copyright is claimed in content that is in the public domain, such as works of the U.S. government.

ISBN: 978-0-8389-1064-1

Printed in the United States of America
15 14 13 12 11   5 4 3 2 1

While extensive effort has gone into ensuring the reliability of the information appearing in this book, the publisher makes no warranty, express or implied, with respect to the material contained herein.

Library of Congress Cataloging-in-Publication Data
Driggers, Preston F. (Preston Franklin), 1940–
  Managing library volunteers / Preston Driggers and Eileen Dumas. -- 2nd ed.
     p. cm. -- (ALA guides for the busy librarian)
  Includes bibliographical references and index.
  ISBN 978-0-8389-1064-1 (alk. paper)
  1. Volunteer workers in libraries--United States. I. Dumas, Eileen. II. Title.
  Z682.4.V64D75 2011
  023'.3--dc22

                                                                    2010012522

Book design in Charis SIL and Soho Gothic by Casey Bayer.

♾ This paper meets the requirements of ANSI/NISO Z39.48-1992 (Permanence of Paper).

ALA Editions also publishes its books in a variety of electronic formats. For more information, visit the ALA Store at www.alastore.ala.org and select eEditions.

CONTENTS

PART I | VOLUNTEER SERVICES LIBRARY PROGRAM

PART II | VOLUNTEER RECRUITMENT

SAMPLE DOCUMENTS

PREFACE TO THE SECOND EDITION

IN THE NEARLY ten years since the first edition went to press, when home dial-up was the only access to the Internet, library technology and the virtual world of the Internet have undergone substantial changes.

During this period, hundreds of thousands of dollars were spent by libraries to increase interconnectivity between online catalogs and databases. Additionally, library staff spent countless hours providing workshops for adults on how to use library databases, place holds, request interlibrary loan materials, and monitor personal accounts. A direct result of this surge in technology and training is an increase in computer literacy among adults and an increase in technologically savvy volunteers.

As high-speed Internet and WiFi become the norm in libraries, so do increased expectations from library customers—such as faster uploads of pictures, text, and videos. Today, social networking sites such as MySpace and Facebook—along with YouTube, Twitter, blogs, wikis, podcasts, webinars, steaming videos, and flash videos—are commonly accepted parts of personal, business, community, and library virtual identities. Now, more often than not, we come to know individuals and organizations through the virtual world as we go online to "check them out."

This second edition is written through the kaleidoscope of ever-changing virtual library technology as viewed from vantage points of potential and current library volunteers and through the eyes of library volunteer services managers. How can libraries make use of the skills and interests of the "on-the-go," computer-literate potential volunteer? Are there opportunities for virtual volunteers in public libraries? How are various forms of current communications technology being used in public library volunteer programs, and with what success? With these questions in mind, we reviewed numerous public library websites. These websites were approached first from the naïve view of residents who might have moved to the library location and wanted to volunteer. What would they see, what knowledge would they gain, and would it be informative and inviting?

The second view was from the perspective of knowledgeable professionals assessing the information found on the websites. We found small libraries with excellent websites and large public libraries very lacking. In addition, we exchanged follow-up calls and e-mail with volunteer services managers to better inform ourselves about the relative success of various virtual ventures.

We thank the many unknown volunteer services managers and their respective libraries for allowing us to peek inside their volunteer departments and programs—a process that was not possible when we first started this endeavor over a decade ago. In our review, we gained new insights into how technology is or can be used in these programs.

Whether recruited or delegated, staff members who are in the position of public library volunteer services manager/supervisor/coordinator are a flexible group. As with the first edition, we hope this manual provides useful tools and ideas to the many who have recently entered this new realm of working with library volunteers and to those who have been in the field for a while. You serve your libraries and communities by your commitment and support for community volunteers. Hats off to all of you!

We owe a special acknowledgment to Adrienne Breznau for her review of library volunteer websites. Her work enabled us to gain a broad perspective and a glimpse into the world of libraries online. In addition, we'd like to thank colleagues who assisted us in the first edition, especially Veletta Hopes, Nancy Milvid, and Willo Auger. A special thanks to Chauna Wall of the Public Library of Charlotte and Mecklenburg County (Charlotte, NC) for her insightful comments about current trends in public library volunteer services.

We acknowledge and thank the following libraries, listed in alphabetical order, for their willingness to share their volunteer services forms. Although space and editorial requirements prevented the use of all the forms, we are still very appreciative of the cooperation shown to us by these organizations:

Alachua County (Fla.) Library District

Carlsbad City (Calif.) Library

City of Aurora (Colo.) Public Library

Denver (Colo.) Public Library

Keene (N.H.) Public Library

Kenton County (Ky.) Public Library

Louisville (Ky.) Free Public Library

Louisville (Colo.) Public Library

Mesa County (Colo.) Public Library District

Metropolitan Library System (Oklahoma City, Okla.)

Nashville (Tenn.) Public Library

Omaha (Neb.) Public Library

Pikes Peak (Colo.) Library District

Pima County (Ariz.) Public Library

Public Library of Charlotte and Mecklenburg County (N.C.)

Although we made extensive efforts to ensure accuracy at the time of publication, it is inevitable that public libraries will make changes to their websites, and active links cited in this edition will go dead. We encourage you to use this manual as an administrative resource and freely add online resources or update links on the pages to serve you in your important public library role.

PREFACE TO THE FIRST EDITION

THIS MANUAL DATES back to the fall of 1991 when Eileen Dumas of the Aurora Public Library and Terry Nelson of the Denver Public Library recognized a need to form a group of library staff who coordinated and managed volunteer programs. Among others, Dumas and Nelson felt that there was a lack of information available that directly addressed the unique role of library volunteer services managers.

A new group was organized in 1992, called "Metro Area Library Volunteer Coordinators Council." The group expanded over time to include representation from all the major libraries along the Colorado Front Range. (For a history of the group, see Catherine Childs and John Waite Bowers, "Introducing the Colorado Libraries Volunteer Managers Council," *Colorado Libraries* 23 (Summer 1997): 36–39.

During the second year of the group's existence, Preston Driggers of the Douglas Public Library District became a member, adding his knowledge of human resources and risk management to the group. As information accumulated on volunteer program activities, group members suggested that a manual be written based on their experiences. The idea seemed a natural extension of the group meetings and two authors agreed to take on the task.

However, the early drafts of this manual were not circulated until the summer of 1996. Both authors are grateful to the members of the now renamed "Colorado Volunteer Managers Council," for their open discussions on the finer points of managing successful programs. Without their contribution, this manual would not have been as complete.

Special acknowledgments are due (in alphabetical order) to Willo Auger, Darrell Chayne, Catherine Childs, Belinda Goelbel, Ann Keller, Mary Lou McNatt, C. Terry Nelson, Liesel Schmid, Ed Stephen, Ann Tomas, and Midge Trueman. We would also like to extend our appreciation to the volunteer managers who were part of our group in the past and have gone on to new positions. They too are contributors.

Although many individuals from large and small programs have contributed, the authors accept responsibility for any errors, omissions, or confusion that the reader may encounter.

Finally, as one volunteer manager stated, "I have the best of all jobs because I work with library volunteers. These are wonderful people." We hope that is your experience too.

We wish to offer special acknowledgment to the following libraries for the use of their materials as reproducible samples:

Adams Public Library

Arapahoe Public Library

Aurora Public Library

Boulder Public Library

Denver Public Library

Douglas Public Library District

HOW TO USE
THIS MANUAL

THIS MANUAL IS designed for multiple uses. For a library staff member suddenly placed in the role of volunteer services manager, this manual is a ready guide with samples, policies, and practical discussions on establishing a new volunteer services program. Topical sections allow quick access to those problems that must be addressed immediately. Each section covers options for small, medium, and large libraries.

For a staff member taking over an existing volunteer services program, the discussion points serve as ready reference for explaining the underlying basis for existing procedures. Individuals trained in library and information science are often unfamiliar with the human resource, legal, and risk management requirements involved in operating a successful volunteer services program. This manual provides information on these topics.

The numerous samples of volunteer job descriptions as well as administrative and report forms found throughout the manual can be photocopied and used as they are or used as templates from which to build one's own library-specific forms.

Setting up or operating a volunteer services program is a challenge. The overriding goal of this manual is to help you, the volunteer services manager, meet the challenge.

TERMINOLOGY

As an auxiliary duty to their regular library jobs, staff members usually coordinate library volunteers. Few libraries enjoy the luxury of having a paid staff member whose sole function is to manage a volunteer services program. When a staff member shifts hats and works with the volunteer program, that person's title may change to *volunteer coordinator, supervisor, manager, administrator,* or *director of volunteer services.* Titles and range of duties vary, but for consistency in this book we use the term *volunteer services manager* to represent staff members who are assigned the responsibility of managing a library volunteer services program.

There is an ongoing controversy within the professional library community about whether to use the term *customer* or *patron* when referring to a library user. There are good arguments for either word. For consistency, we use the term *customer,* reflecting growing usage among public libraries without suggesting any commitment for or against this particular terminology.

The generic terms *volunteer staff supervisor* and *paid staff supervisor* are interchangeable. These titles do not assume a management position in a library or an MLS degree. With the increasing use of paraprofessionals ("parapros") in libraries, the person who directs the work of volunteers can be at any level of the library organization.

INTRODUCTION

The Volunteer Program Cycle

THE VOLUNTEER SERVICES program cycle (figure 1) demonstrates how all the parts of a volunteer program are related. Recruitment is successful when library needs are assessed and job descriptions are written on the basis of those needs. Volunteers can be placed only after the volunteer services manager has matched skills and interests to the library's needs, thus beginning the volunteers' transition from "outsiders" to "insiders" as unpaid members of the library staff.

The number of volunteer positions at any one time is based on the staff's perceptions of volunteers. When staff are favorably impressed by the work accomplished by volunteers, the number of individuals who are willing to supervise or work with them increases. With more staff involvement, the number of volunteer positions or open task slots grows. The growth of volunteer positions is, in turn, influenced by the volunteers' task performances; the better the volunteers perform, the more likely staff are willing to want additional volunteers. And volunteer performance is positively correlated to selecting, matching, and training new volunteers.

Reward, recognition, and a verbal or written thank-you for a job well done enhance the volunteers' sense of fulfillment. When people are pleased with their library experience, they generally share these feelings with others,

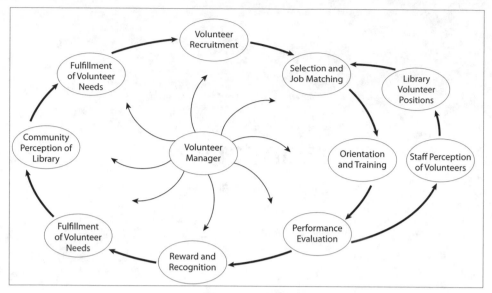

Figure 1. **Enhancing library services:**
The volunteer services program cycle

thereby encouraging positive community perceptions of the library. In turn, positive community perceptions may increase the number of individuals who want to become library volunteers. The program cycle continues ad infinitum.

In the day-to-day operation of the library, the role of the volunteer services manager is to find ways that volunteers can enhance library services. When the role of volunteer services manager is externally focused, the position becomes an integral part of library community relations. This manual is a practical guide to assist you in using the volunteer services program cycle to make your program a success.

PART 1 | **VOLUNTEER SERVICES LIBRARY PROGRAM**

SECTION 1 | THE VALUE OF LIBRARY VOLUNTEERISM

THE VALUE ASSOCIATED with volunteerism goes to the heart of our democratic society and the history of community libraries. In some instances, paid staff owe their library careers to the field of volunteerism. In many small towns today, public libraries remain open through the combined efforts of the Friends of the Library, volunteer trustees, and a small, dedicated group of community volunteers. Moreover, projects too costly to justify hiring extra staff are successfully carried out with the help of volunteers. In today's changing economy and probably that of the future, the importance of volunteers cannot be dismissed as a passing fad.

In the broadest sense, library volunteerism is one way of fostering the democratic ideal of community participation. It provides diverse individuals with an opportunity to work actively in their local government and serve the community. In the narrowest sense, volunteerism is one part of the total dialog between the community and the library. This dialog is enriched as meaningful volunteer opportunities emerge.

Community participation in local libraries, whether on-site or virtual, ensures a continuous flow of diverse ideas, skills, talents, heritages, ages, time, and energies that enable the library to continue to be a dynamic institution, a place where individuals and families choose to spend their time and give their support. With the increasing use of high-speed Internet access, there are evolving opportunities to provide new volunteer tasks that can be done from home, whether by people with physical disabilities or by caregivers who must of necessity stay home.

On an individual basis, recent studies point to volunteering as an important basis for physical and mental health. Experienced volunteer services managers know that some of their volunteers are using their library volunteer time as a way to reduce their personal stress, gain self-esteem with life losses, or gain a new perspective by feeling useful helping others. Although not often stated, library volunteer services contribute to the physical and mental health of the local community.

Keeping the library vital within the community requires hard work to connect all aspects of library services to community residents and visitors. Library volunteering underscores and supports this connection.

The following are thematic value statements that can be used in whole or in part to create a set of values for your program or to incorporate into your volunteer program mission statement.

Value Statements

> The library defines volunteerism as a resource for both the library and the community.
>
> Library volunteering supports the greater values associated with individual choice and participation that underlie a democracy.
>
> Volunteerism is a vital part of the enhancing dialog and social contacts between the library and the local community.
>
> The value of library volunteerism lies in the unique abilities and skills of each individual.
>
> When volunteers are placed in appropriate jobs, their personal contributions reflect and enhance the library's defined values as found in its mission and goal statements.
>
> The value of library volunteerism is to support the individual's need to be a productive and caring community member.
>
> The volunteer mission is to increase service provided by the library, extending the community ownership of the library through the skills and talents volunteered by individuals within the library jurisdiction.

SECTION 2 | VOLUNTEER SERVICES PROGRAM MISSION STATEMENT

WHY IS A mission statement important for a library volunteer program? It provides the purpose and goals, establishes a strong foundation, and offers consistent direction. A mission statement also ensures that your program is not working in isolation or in opposition to the library's mission. Therefore, the mission statement of your volunteer program must make reference to or include a part of the library's overall mission statement, plus have the support of the top administrator. Library branding needs to include community volunteers.

Although the term *mission* is used in this section, you may want to use the less lofty terms *purpose* or *goal* of your volunteer services program as a way of focusing on how your program is serving the library. One way to think through the process of writing a mission statement is to answer the following questions:

- What is the purpose of the library volunteer services program?
  (Purpose: To attract community volunteers who want to work with the paid staff to enhance library services and increase the success of the library within the community)
- Whom are you trying to attract to your program?
  (General Target Group: Community adults and youth)

- What do you want to achieve with the volunteer program?
  (Achievement: To provide enhanced library services to the community with volunteers and staff working as equals)
- What are the benefits of the volunteer program for the library, staff, community, and the volunteers?
  (Benefits: Opportunities for citizens to make positive contributions to library operations)

A mission statement needs to be broad enough to encompass diverse programs, even if these programs are still in the planning stages. For example, a general program directed toward volunteers assisting with the necessary, routine support tasks could complement a future program that is focused on serving the homebound or special needs populations. Ideally, the mission statement will not change with additional volunteer services. Below are examples of mission statements:

> The mission of the library's volunteer program is to encourage and expand the involvement of community volunteers, on-site and volunteering at a distance.

> Volunteers will work with the staff, as partners, to provide service to others by supporting, preserving, and promoting free and easy access to ideas and accurate and timely information.

> The library will provide opportunities so that all volunteers find satisfaction through their skills and talents in serving their community through their affiliation with this volunteer program.

> The library asks volunteers to give their talents and energy to supplement and complement the staff in order to free staff to initiate new and innovative programs. A successful program results in volunteers becoming public advocates for the library and its services.

> The library holds that volunteers are an important human resource. They have the right to be treated as coworkers, trained in a professional manner, and given richly deserved recognition.

> Library volunteers assist the library in achieving its mission of connecting a diverse community to resources that inform, enrich and entertain. The volunteer services program is a bridge, offering volunteer roles which provide opportunities for civic service, personal growth, building relationships, and assistance to the library.

SECTION 3 | VOLUNTEER SERVICES PROGRAM BENEFITS

AS THE VOLUNTEER services manager, you are responsible for "selling" and "reselling" the benefits of your program to the library staff. When a new program is set up or a previous program reestablished, the library staff may not appreciate the benefits of volunteers. Creating a volunteer-friendly library among staff can be a challenge. Staff may view your position as volunteer services manager and the use of community volunteers as an unwanted intrusion into library routines and somehow diminishing the professionalism of the library. Some staff see the volunteer services program as added work and hidden expenses for training, supervising, and evaluating the volunteers. Others view volunteers as more of a workplace hassle than a benefit, or as a way to replace professional staff. Still others—often highly focused librarians—do not like the "messiness" associated with the diversity of interests and backgrounds of community volunteers. Recognize that these are normal reactions in many public libraries.

If the benefits of community volunteers are weighed against the costs, then even the most questioning and negative employees can begin to appreciate the value of volunteers; this should be one of your goals. Establishing positive relationships between staff and volunteers is crucial to the long-term success of your program.

It is extremely important in building a successful volunteer services program to match supportive staff who are willing to supervise volunteers, regardless of their official library titles. Also, the more support expressed by the library director and the top administrators, the greater the number of library staff willing to give a volunteer a try. Over time you can gradually change some negative attitudes to positive ones by emphasizing program benefits at meetings of administrators, supervisors, and staff. You can use e-mail and print or electronic staff newsletters to outline particular benefits but remember to use your successes as supporting examples in your communications. In other words, demonstrate the usefulness of your volunteer services programs with real-life library examples that various staff members can relate to and might be willing to try. At every level of the library organization there are opinion leaders. If one or more of these people are willing to use volunteers in their areas of responsibility that is a great step forward.

Volunteer benefits must also be "sold" and "resold" to the potential and existing volunteers. Although the primary audience of announced benefits is the community pool of possible volunteers, the secondary audiences of existing volunteers and paid staff are also important. Existing volunteers may understand what volunteering means to themselves, but when family members or friends ask why they are spending time volunteering at the library, the volunteers can draw upon the volunteer benefit statements to articulate their reasons. Many of the same intrinsic benefits derived by volunteers also apply to lower-level paid staff. Most public library paid staff members receive tangible financial benefits; however, many of the intangible benefits identified through volunteer benefit statements also apply to these paid staff members.

In this section, we keep the intrinsic benefits of volunteering distinct from tangible benefits—awards, gifts, and perks. It is useful to distinguish these two categories of benefits when presenting the volunteer services program. There are community volunteers who are concerned about library budgets and want you, the volunteer services manager, to know that they are volunteering from their desire to give back to the community in a giving spirit. They do not want the library to spend money on recognition gifts and awards and do not want to attend public recognition ceremonies. Your skill as the volunteer services manager involves acknowledging the diverse desires of all volunteers in your program.

LIBRARY SERVICES

Volunteers can improve library services in the following specific ways:

- Expanding support for routine tasks and special library projects
- Enhancing the level and quality of customer services in the library
- Complementing the level and quality of off-site customer services
- Providing supplemental expertise

Expanding Staff Support

How can you develop volunteer job opportunities to help staff with routine tasks or special projects? First, send out a survey or ask specific staff members what tasks or programs are not getting adequate attention and need extra help. The responses will tell you how volunteers can best be used immediately or in the near future. For example, shelf reading, shelving, cleaning DVDs, and caring for indoor plants are tasks that need to be done, but often the staff does not have time to do them or cannot do them on a regular basis. Volunteers can be assigned to work in these areas with limited or no training.

Enhancing Customer Service

Volunteers can be trained to teach customers how to search the Internet or use the online catalog and databases. This training immediately improves customer service by providing customers with individualized help. It also enables the reference staff to concentrate their efforts on customers needing assistance with research or locating specific information in the reference area. In addition to teaching computer skills, volunteers can call customers about their reserve items, work on an information desk, give tours, and assist in technical services such as deleting items from a database or bar coding and stamping new books. All of these tasks improve the level and quality of service the library can provide.

Complementing Off-Site Customer Services

Off-site customer services include using library volunteers in the community (e.g., reading to seniors in nursing homes, delivering to the homebound) using virtual volunteers, who support the library by working from home or from wireless environments. The latter, a newly evolving group of volunteers, can beta test new library web links or flash videos or check on the connectivity of community information databases or the drop-down menus and web pages on the library website. When problems occur, they can e-mail designated librarians or web staff to reduce formal off-site customer complaints. Often these complaints may go unreported and increase the dissatisfaction off-site customers have when library website links do not work properly or information on web pages is out of date.

Providing Supplemental Expertise

Volunteers bring their skills, talents, and prior training to the library organization. Skills and training in computer hardware and specific software programs can help a department or small library set up database files, develop specialized reporting forms, or run mail merge programs. Retired elementary school teachers can volunteer their time to read or tell stories to young children during a morning storytime or at a local childcare center. Former department store "window dressers" are excellent resources for creating library displays. Graphic artists can design flyers or posters for special programs or recruitment advertisements. The library would have to pay hundreds or thousands of dollars to hire these experts for one day or several weeks. A volunteer services program gives the library an opportunity to recruit and benefit from the community pool of talent.

PERSONAL ENRICHMENT

Volunteering can provide an individual with opportunities for personal satisfaction, growth, and enrichment. Library volunteers can

- Acquire new marketable technical, office, administrative, or customer service skills that can be documented to enhance resumes and job interviews
- Gain a sense of personal achievement, self-esteem, and satisfaction by learning a new skill, successfully completing a project, or using existing skills in an organization that serves the whole community
- Give back to the community by making a difference in the lives of others within the library or enriching the lives of community members through library outreach programs
- Learn more about what is happening in the library and in the community through interactions with library staff and customers and the library community traditional and electronic bulletin boards

- Expand the circle of friends and acquaintances who enrich everyday life by sharing life experiences and interests
- Further the success of the library within the community

Volunteers are often surprised at the range of activities and skills required to run a library. At first, many volunteers are excited about learning a new skill, such as reading to seniors in nursing homes, presenting puppet shows for children, or preparing bibliographies, but at the same time they may be apprehensive about starting a new task and working in an unfamiliar environment. The strength of your volunteer program will lie in your ability to allay these apprehensions by ensuring that all new volunteers receive the necessary support from their immediate supervisors and adequate on-the-job training. This attention to volunteer needs encourages an atmosphere of success for everyone.

For young adults entering the job market for the first time, the benefits derived from learning skills such as word processing, operating a high-speed copying machine, or handling angry customers while working on the job are invaluable and useful for resumes and job interviews. More important, many will learn, often for the first time, the life skills of reporting to "work" on time, completing assigned duties, calling in when sick, and completing forms such as time records.

Adults returning to the job market after an extended absence also can gain marketable skills and self-confidence through library volunteering. The volunteer services manager or an assigned staff supervisor can document their experiences, enhancing their resume to show a level of competency in a particular skill area.

Individuals who become volunteers after losing a spouse or job or relocating from another city away from family and friends derive benefits from the structure of the tasks they perform and the friendships gained with library staff members and other volunteers. Libraries can keep people busy and allow their thoughts to shift from their losses to assisting others.

DIVERSITY

Volunteer programs can contribute to overall staffing diversity within the library. Although volunteers are not usually tallied on formal government Equal Employment Opportunity reports, they nevertheless add cultural diversity when viewed from the vantage points of customers, library staff, and the community.

Inclusiveness within the volunteer services program is an important goal so that potential volunteers can see themselves as a part of the library environment. If, for example, only married women were volunteers, then single women or men would believe they would not be welcomed, whether it was true of not. Similarly, if all the volunteers came from one church or one social club, then members of other local churches or social clubs might feel unwanted.

Cultural diversity statements raise awareness of those considering volunteering that they may be working with people who are different from them. Diversity statements also serve as administrative guidelines that can be used as part of the conflict resolution process if conflicts based on diversity issues among volunteers or volunteers and staff or customers arise. Here are some examples of cultural diversity statements:

> Our volunteers are special. They are parents, college students, teens, retired citizens, church groups, and scouts. They are our neighbors and our friends.

> The library volunteer program is open to all in the community regardless of cultural and financial background, sexual orientation, disability, caregiving responsibilities, or any other personal characteristic.

> The library provides volunteers the opportunity to work with diverse staff and volunteers, thereby increasing the cultural richness of the library and community.

Cultural diversity is not restricted to the usual set of characteristics—race, color, ethnicity, gender, age, nationality, religion, and disability—but includes others such as sexual orientation, income, skill, language, family status, veteran status, political affiliation, customs, and ideas. Depending upon jurisdiction under which the library operates, some of these attributes form protected classes by local employment laws and may be required on volunteer application forms and recruitment literature and brochures.

As a volunteer services manager, it is important that you ensure your forms and policy statements meet current jurisdictional requirements. This requires checking with the human resources department or legal department of the city, county, or other jurisdiction of the library. In some cities, the library volunteer program is part of the overall city volunteer program, which usually leads to more formalization of the library volunteer services program and more formal diversity statements.

Beyond legal requirements, inclusiveness should be an important goal of the volunteer program, for this can help increase awareness and usage among a library's diverse populations and underserved targeted community populations. Library volunteer programs provide opportunities in which individuals and diverse groups can work in an atmosphere of respect.

One final, useful point for a new volunteer services manager: Having a written diversity statement does not mean that everyone in the community has to be accepted as a library volunteer. Volunteer application requirements still must be met, and any placement of a volunteer into a position still must meet the requirements of the library.

COMMUNITY AND CITIZENSHIP VALUES

A public library is intimately linked to the community through its outreach efforts. By starting a volunteer services program, the library encourages a two-way dialog that supports local citizenship and community values that benefit and enhance all concerned.

Community Values

Create a positive image of the library in the community.

Promote community awareness of library services and programs.

Bring information about local ideas, issues, and concerns back to the library so that staff and administration can better meet community needs.

Demonstrate community support for the library as role models to encourage other local citizens to become shareholders in a local government agency.

Assist the community in providing a direct service.

Citizenship Values

Meet specific high school requirements for community service hours.

Allow youth and adults who have service commitments in civic, service, religious, and community groups an opportunity to volunteer.

Afford people the opportunity to make legal restitution back to the community through library service.

Provide seniors the opportunity to pay part of their property taxes by library volunteer services in certain jurisdictions.

Citizenship values vary from individual to individual. For some local residents, being a good citizen merely means paying property taxes. For others, it means giving something back to their community in terms of time, talents, or special expertise—as with the volunteer who organizes a fundraising effort, holds a book sale, or runs a library gift shop.

As a volunteer services manager, you will learn more about how your community feels about the library than the technical services administrator, who has little public contact. At the same time, volunteers are taking information about you, the volunteer program, and the library back to their family and friends. When this exchange is based on positive experiences, the results support an important component of the library's community public relations effort.

BENEFIT/PURPOSE STATEMENTS

You probably will not incorporate all of the aforementioned benefits at the beginning of a new volunteer services program, and they may not all apply in your library's prior practice. What is important is that by working with the staff and administrators you eventually develop benefit statements for your specific volunteer program. These may in fact be shorter variations or combinations of the above statements.

As you scan the sample benefit statements below, note that each one can be written from the perspectives of the volunteer or from that of the volunteer services program. In the latter form, individual "benefits" become program "purposes."

Do not throw your draft set of statements away when you have finished writing this document. You may well find them useful later when you construct your volunteer recruitment announcements, volunteer notices, or additions to the volunteer page on the library website.

Library Services

Our volunteers supplement, enhance, and support library staff by meeting the demands for high-quality public service.

Effective use of library volunteers can extend the value of every tax dollar by providing an increased pool of labor and a larger diversity of human resources.

Volunteers contribute to the success of the library program by providing enhanced customer service.

The library's use of volunteers helps us maintain high-quality children's services.

Personal Enhancement

Library volunteerism empowers individuals to reach their potential as productive members of the community and to make positive contributions to the quality of community life.

Library volunteering can serve as on-the-job training.

Our library volunteers gain a sense of personal achievement by being an important part of our library services program.

Library volunteers gain a sense of personal esteem by sharing their talents to help others through our "Reading to Seniors Program."

Cultural Diversity

The library volunteer program provides a diverse working environment and is open to all residents in the community regardless of cultural background, race, gender, family responsibilities, sexual orientation, or any other basis of personal diversity.

Volunteers have the opportunity to work with diverse individuals in an atmosphere of respect and tolerance.

Community/Citizenship Values

Our volunteer program provides an opportunity for citizens to volunteer and make positive contributions to the library.

Community volunteers bring good feelings and positive attitudes to the staff by freely giving their unique talents.

Volunteering encourages individuals in the community to appreciate the library.

Volunteering encourages citizens to become familiar with the library resources and services.

Volunteers reflect the ideas and concerns of the community and therefore bring special awareness to the library's planning and administrative processes.

The library provides volunteer hours for court-assigned community restitution.

Our volunteer program provides the opportunity for scouts and high school youth to complete their community service requirements.

VOLUNTEER ADMINISTRATION

THE OBJECTIVE OF this section is to provide an overview of the key areas you need to consider when setting up (or taking over) the administration of a volunteer program. Consider each of these areas as you develop general guidelines and a philosophy.

THE VOLUNTEER SERVICES MANAGER AND THE ORGANIZATIONAL CHART

Whether you are a full- or part-time volunteer services manager, you need to know where you fit into the organization as a whole. Does your volunteer program have its own budget, or are your funds part of someone else's budget? Whose approval do you need to develop and expand your program? For example, do you report to a library director, the human resources manager, a branch manager, adult services supervisor, or someone else? Do you have two supervisors, one for your regular library duties and another for your volunteer duties? Are you expected to coordinate volunteers for your library alone, or will you manage all the volunteers in the library system? Will you work with branch staff assigned as volunteer coordinators? When you have clear answers to these questions, you and the other staff members will understand how the volunteer program operates within the library system.

As a rule, the more departments your volunteer services program serves (e.g., circulation, reference, children's services, archives, grounds, facilities, administration), the higher up in the administrative hierarchy you should report if the program is to succeed. If, for example, you work with volunteers across library departments but you report to one department manager, it is unlikely that the other managers will accept your administrative efforts or suggestions. Regardless of how professionally you behave, how much you know about volunteerism, these managers are apt to perceive your coordination efforts as interference in their respective branches or departments. In these situations, you may reach a high level of frustration because you have neither the authority to assign or coordinate volunteers across multiple departments or library branches nor the feeling of being an integral part of the library team.

On the other hand, if you work with volunteers in a small library and report directly to the branch manager or library director, you are more likely to have the support of the full library staff because you have the authority to plan and use volunteers across a wide range of library services.

In a large library system, if you are the volunteer coordinator only within a children's department and report directly to the supervisor of children and youth services, you will probably find your work environment more consistent with the limited volunteer duties and authority.

It is always important to work with your key administrator to define your position within your particular library system.

THE VOLUNTEER SERVICES MANAGER'S JOB DESCRIPTION

Initially, you probably did not have a written job description, especially if you were the first person assigned to manage the volunteer services program. If you have taken over an existing volunteer program, it is important to make sure you have a written job description that is current at the outset to clarify your duties and explain how you will be evaluated or expected to evaluate your own performance. This is especially important for those whose duties are split between, for example, reference services and volunteer services. Because many volunteer positions are part-time, twenty hours or less, there is often less clarity about what are or are not reasonable job expectations and criteria of program success.

In a similar fashion, if you are hired as an experienced volunteer services manager coming from an agency that was primarily volunteer driven, you will immediately be challenged by the fact that most libraries are organized around paid staff, with volunteer programs of secondary importance. On one hand, this is a loss of personal status if you previously coordinated a large number of volunteers from a position of authority. Further, some library managers and librarians with their MLS degrees will not see you as a professional, regardless of your degrees and prior managerial experience. On the other hand, a library setting provides you the opportunity to use a wide range of personal and professional skills related to running a successful volunteer services program that might not have been available in your previous organizations. In this circumstance, a lot of two-way learning must go on; you have to learn about library operations and library jargon, and the staff need to learn how a professionally run volunteer services program can be valuable to the library and the community.

Clearly defined job expectations and job descriptions can reduce potential difficulties with administration and library staff. For example, if one of your duties is to visit local groups to recruit volunteers, does this mean "on your own time" without pay? Or are you expected to visit only groups that are available during your normal working hours? Can you juggle your hours so that you are able to visit groups whenever they meet? If you are performing two functions (e.g., reference librarian and volunteer services manager), do you have some leeway to shift or trade hours to administer the volunteer program?

In some large library systems, volunteer services managers have paid staff who report to them to help administer the program. But most volunteer services managers are one-person operations and get pulled in many directions at the same time. Depending on the number of volunteers, you may find it useful to assign yourself a volunteer administrative assistant who is highly organized, computer literate, and capable of handling many of your routine administrative duties. This gives you the opportunity to attend meetings, conduct interviews, place volunteers, and do higher-level program and project work without having all the routine work and telephone messages piling up while you are out of the office. This may require sharing space, sharing a computer, or finding a small niche where this part-time volunteer can work. Having such a person will make your position a lot more productive and will increase your job satisfaction—if you get the right person and if you learn to delegate tasks.

A job description for a full-time library volunteer services manager is shown in sample 4-1. This is a formal job description. Your library may use a simpler position description. Use this sample as a starting point to help you customize a job description for your specific position requirements that can be agreed upon with the library administration.

VOLUNTEER JOB DESCRIPTIONS

Volunteers want to be successful. A key to helping volunteers succeed is ensuring that they know at the outset what is expected of them. At the same time, you need stated standards in order to select and match the best volunteers for the available positions. That is why a position description is important for every volunteer job in the library.

Have written job descriptions available or post them to the volunteer services pages on the library website, allowing self selection among potential volunteers. Community residents can review job descriptions and requirements to make their own decisions about whether specific jobs and tasks fit their skills or interests.

A well-written position description allows you or other library staff to identify the people who do not fit the minimum standards and those who do. This process adds objectivity and professionalism to the interview, selection, and matching processes. Further, by reviewing the information about the job position in the beginning with applicants, you let them know that these jobs include expectations for time and work commitments along with standards for assessing performance.

Preparing written volunteer job descriptions is time consuming, but once done they can lead to improved productivity and a better sense of satisfaction. Volunteers like to know that they are meeting expectations, and this leads to fewer disagreements over what was or was not expected. In some libraries, volunteers must read the job descriptions and then sign off that they understand the duties identified. In these instances, the position description is more than just a document of information; it becomes a document of agreement. More specific information about volunteer job descriptions, with samples, is offered in section 13.

VOLUNTEER TRAINING AND ORIENTATION

For small programs, volunteer orientation and training may consist of nothing more than a one-on-one session with a tour of the library, followed by introductions to the staff and administrators, and ending with a quick explanation

Volunteer Services Manager

GENERAL STATEMENT OF DUTIES: The incumbent develops, administers, and coordinates the effective library-wide recruitment and use of volunteer talents as a community resource that supplements and complements those of the staff.

RESPONSIBILITY: Responsible on a daily basis for the implementation and administration of the Library Volunteer Services Program.

EXAMPLES OF DUTIES
[The following are intended to be illustrative only and not comprehensive]

Essential Functions:

Plans and coordinates, with library staff input, the effective use of volunteer talent and services for library branches, departments, and programs. Assesses volunteer staffing requirements and makes recommendations on volunteer staffing needs, new volunteer programs, or improvements in existing programs.

Actively recruits volunteers for all library branches, departments, and programs, including the design of recruitment materials; develops strategies; and coordinates with staff and volunteers in planning and implementing recruitment activities.

Works closely with any assigned branch coordinators to develop volunteer job descriptions and appropriate volunteer task assignments. Determines current and future needs for volunteers through staff interviews, Library Friends groups, Library Foundation members, and customer surveys.

Develops the library volunteer mission statement; policy and procedural manual; volunteer rules; staff supervision guidelines; and volunteer handbook. Stays informed about new volunteer approaches and legislative, legal, and risk management issues in the use of volunteers.

Responsible for content of volunteer services web pages on library Internet website. Makes recommendations on engaging style, content, and updates to recruit, market, and provide general information to community members about the volunteer services program.

Responsible for recommending updates on the web pages on the library Intranet site to ensure that accurate and timely information is provided to current volunteers.

Conducts training workshops in effective volunteer management principles for staff members supervising volunteers.

Reviews prospective volunteer application forms, conducts initial volunteer interviews, reference checks, background and/or driver's license reviews, and makes recommendations for placement. Provides new volunteers with preliminary library orientation.

Assesses volunteer/staff relationships, volunteer performance, and satisfaction levels. Works with the branch coordinators' requests for volunteer reassignments, problem-solving issues, and devolunteering.

Sample 4-1. **Position Description: Volunteer Services Manager**

Works with branch volunteer coordinators in designing appropriate volunteer awards and recognition programs.

Establishes communications through a newsletter, blog, bulletin boards, e-mail, newspaper articles, podcasts, and other media with volunteers, staff, Library Friends, customers, and the community about volunteer services activities and programs. Announces a calendar of volunteer events and publicizes volunteer accomplishments.

Utilizes social networking sites, when appropriate, to further communications with the community, current volunteers, and potential volunteers.

Establishes regular outreach efforts and serves as a liaison with local volunteer organizations and agencies. Provides talks and written information conducive to developing library volunteer interest and knowledge about library programs and services.

Maintains volunteer computer databases for human resources files, placement, hours, and performance records and submits regular statistical summaries of volunteer activities to the Library Director. Monitors volunteer services expenditures and budget items. Provides comparative value-added summaries of volunteer library-wide contributions.

Assists staff in marketing library volunteer services and programs throughout the library service area.

REQUIREMENTS: Extensive knowledge of volunteer administration principles and practices necessary to manage a volunteer services program, especially in a library environment. Knowledge of volunteer recruitment and program marketing techniques. Ability to establish and maintain effective working relationships with diverse staff, managers, volunteers, and representatives of outside agencies. Skilled in oral and written communication and demonstrated ability in making public presentations. Ability to exercise sound, independent judgment to find practical solutions in a variety of personnel and program situations. Able to work a flexible schedule.

DIFFICULTY OF WORK/CONSEQUENCE OF ERROR: Work is characterized by independent planning, originality, and imagination to devise, develop, and coordinate an effective volunteer services program. Errors in work or judgment can cause interpersonal conflicts between staff and volunteers, procedural errors and disruptions in providing library services, and negative impacts on patron and community relations.

RESPONSIBILITY: Works independently under general policy guidance and direction of the Library Director. Responsible for the overall administration of the volunteer services program. Must maintain high standards of ethics and public service. May direct work of volunteers.

WORKING CONDITIONS: Primary work is performed in an office environment with extensive e-mail and telephone contacts. Part of the workday is spent on a computer terminal. Usually works on multiple tasks, different software programs, and special projects during the course of a workday.

PERSONAL RELATIONSHIPS: Work involves daily contact with volunteers, staff, and representatives of community groups involving the exchange of routine and nonroutine information. Represents the library to various community groups that are interested in library volunteer services.

MINIMUM QUALIFICATIONS AND SPECIAL SKILLS REQUIRED AND RESTRICTIONS:

Physical: Position requires ability to work in an office environment and manage the stresses of numerous incoming communications, interruptions, and diverse demands.

Computer Knowledge: Requires knowledge of word processing and spreadsheet software and general knowledge about social networking sites.

Education: Minimum AA degree with preferred bachelor's degree;

AND

Experience: Nonprofit volunteer administrative experience in paid or unpaid positions or similar administrative experience;

OR

Equivalent combination of education and experience.

WEEKLY EMPLOYMENT HOURS: 40 hours a week.

Sample 4-1. **Position Description: Volunteer Services Manager** *(continued)*

of some specific task instructions. As your program expands to include more departments, or the tasks become more complex, you will need to develop more extensive orientation and training approaches (see part 3, "Training and Development").

If you cannot do all the training, then who can you assign to this task? What specific staff members have the interest, expertise, or patience to be good volunteer trainers? How will you get the cooperation of the department or branch manager to allow a staff member the time to train a volunteer?

As you set up the program, think about how volunteer training will be accomplished in a positive and productive manner.

VOLUNTEER COMMUNICATION AND FEEDBACK

Volunteers are as interested as staff in knowing what is happening in the library. Will you have a volunteer bulletin board, or will volunteers receive copies of a staff newsletter? Will you have a volunteer newsletter? In print or electronic? Will you communicate primarily through face-to-face regular meetings or through volunteer e-mail accounts, Facebook, or Twitter? Does the library have a staff intranet that offers you a place for a volunteer services section for policies, information, and news that volunteers can access? Will volunteer communications be regular, such as monthly meetings, or sporadic on a time-available basis?

When your time is taken up with setting up procedures, recruitment, or training, an individual volunteer may feel neglected, "out of the loop." For some people, a hands-off approach works out well because they enjoy being left alone to do their assigned tasks. Others, though, may feel isolated or unwanted and may eventually quit. It is important to decide how often you (or specified staff members) will communicate with the volunteers, on what issues, and in what formats. These are important considerations that should be taken into account as you set up your channels of volunteer communication or review them to see if they are working.

There are communication peaks and dips in all volunteer programs. During one period, a group of volunteers may enjoy monthly light lunches and share information; as transitions occur and new groups of volunteers gain prominence, it may be hard to get anyone to attend a meeting. Today, for many people across generations, e-mail is certainly a viable option for sharing volunteer program information.

Volunteers will have comments to share with you about their experiences. It is from such bottom-up communications that you gain firsthand knowledge of what is and is not working in your program from your volunteers' perspectives. Being open to these comments is a good thing, but it can be challenging when volunteer suggestions and comments do not take into account the larger library administrative procedures. The more you know about library operations, the easier it is to address volunteer comments.

Good communication between you, the staff, and the volunteers is essential. It takes some trial and error to determine what forms of communication work best in your library with the types of volunteers you have.

VOLUNTEER PERFORMANCE, EVALUATION, AND RECOGNITION

Initially, you may have only enough time to share a few brief comments informally with volunteers about their work performance. For some, this is all the feedback they want or expect. There will be instances, however, when a sincere but less than capable volunteer is not performing according to expectations. In these situations, you may wish you had a more formal evaluation process in place. The evaluation interview is a useful tool for eliciting comments from a volunteer on a personal as well as a program level and for you to discuss positive or negative issues with the volunteer.

Think about your program and picture volunteers working and enjoying their experience. Now ask yourself what you can do to give them recognition for their efforts. Can the library provide the funds necessary to award and recognize these individuals? Do you have to look elsewhere in the community for gift donations or funds? Is money available, for instance, to support a luncheon or tea or small gifts? Your recognition program does not have to be elaborate or expensive, but some form of recognition beyond a personal thank-you is important for a successful volunteer program.

EDUCATING THE LIBRARY STAFF ABOUT VOLUNTEERS

Library staff members are not always enthused about the presence of volunteers. Even those who began their careers as library volunteers may view your program as a threat to their positions. Others may assume that your volunteers will take all the fun projects and assignments.

Recognize that in financially strained libraries the presence of volunteers may create fears that the administration is planning to replace paid positions with volunteer positions. Even when libraries are not financially threatened, the existence of volunteers places strangers into closely knit staff relationships. Moreover, a staff member asked to supervise or oversee a volunteer's work may feel resentment because this "extra work" is not part of the job description. In such situations, even a hard-working volunteer may feel unwanted.

Your task is to find ways to create a team relationship between paid staff and volunteers. How will you explain to staff the introduction or expansion of your program of volunteers? Who will select (or appoint) the staff members to work with or supervise volunteers? What direct benefits do you envision for a staff employee who agrees to do this "extra" assignment? How will you present these benefits to the staff?

You will find this aspect of volunteer administration an ongoing, fluid process that takes a lot of your time and energy. Eventually you may be able to have the duty of supervising volunteers written into the job descriptions of appropriate paid staff. Incorporating this task is a way for library assistants, librarians, and other library staff members to acquire job-related supervisory skills. This process also helps to establish positive relationships between paid staff and volunteers. Can pictures on the volunteer services pages of the library website be posted in a way that recognizes both supervising staff members and volunteers? In the interim, expect to build your program slowly on individual successes, case by case.

VALUING VOLUNTEERS

Volunteers are not free. Put on an administrative hat and ask yourself if volunteers are financially worthwhile for your library. One way to answer this question is to assign a dollar value for the volunteer hours donated on a monthly basis. Without trying to inflate your values, assign the current minimum wage rate for your state for the lower-skilled tasks and a percentage (e.g., 75 percent) of the paid hourly rate for higher-skilled tasks. Thus, to illustrate, a volunteer working five hours of basic clerical work may be worth $36.25 (5 hr at $7.25/hr), while a volunteer doing five hours of customer computer training may be worth $63.75, assuming paid staff earn about $17 an hour (5 hr at 75% of $17/hr) for similar tasks. These can be totaled by month or by year and posted on the website or on bulletin boards to show the financial value of volunteers.

The program's direct costs, including your salary, paid benefits, volunteer supplies, forms, and awards, can be tracked to account for these costs. Indirect costs, such as staff and volunteer training, supervising time, time for redoing poor work, and meeting times, can only be estimated.

If you are setting up a new program (or reorganizing an existing one), you need to decide which data to collect and which reports will be most useful for you and for the administration. You will want to identify the best ways to share the success of your program with library administration. In citywide volunteer programs, you may be required to complete reports on volunteer hours and program costs on a regular basis. In small libraries there may be no required reports. In any case, tracking volunteer hours and costs can give you, the volunteers, and the administration a sense of satisfaction about the overall impact the volunteer program has on the library. This information also provides the library director with factual information that can be shared back into the community.

In the more subtle but equally important area of valuing volunteers, see what other kinds of data can be collected from conversations with customers, notes, letters, and e-mail from volunteers, staff comments, letters to editors in the local papers, and the like. These written comments also lend support to the value of library volunteers.

RESEARCHING VOLUNTEER INFORMATION

While setting up your program, you may need extra help or more information. There is a lot of published material on volunteer programs, but not all of it is directly applicable to libraries. Certainly this manual is a resource, as are other related publications (see bibliography).

On a practical level, the personal contacts you make within your library are important resources, especially with librarians who strongly support you and your program. Many professional librarians are on national library electronic discussion lists and share questions and information among themselves. A librarian who supports your program can look for shared information that relates to library volunteers and send it to you. This information may prove to be useful to your program or give you courage to add something new. The librarian may also be willing to ask a question on your behalf to other librarians on the electronic discussion list, and responses also can provide valuable information.

Finding out who does volunteer management at other local libraries can lead to a personal resource network and an opportunity to find out what is or is not working at other libraries. Establishing a personal resource network early in the process of setting up or restructuring a volunteer program can help you avoid some of the pitfalls that others have experienced in their programs.

A good personal resource network can also open up your range of program options. Discussing your program concerns with other volunteer services managers can give you and other network members an opportunity to share insights, experience, and materials. It is also likely that a problem or dilemma you currently face was already addressed by someone in your network. Members of your network can help you validate a new idea. Their volunteer successes can be part of your supporting data and lend credence to your new proposals. Often, library administrators want to know what other libraries are doing, and having examples of success at your fingertips is a good way to gain the support of your administration and demonstrate your competence in the area of library volunteerism. Finally, your resource network can serve as a source of personal support when you experience difficult days or program successes. It is a positive experience to share your joys and woes with others who really understand what you are facing.

SECTION 5 | RIGHTS AND DUTIES OF VOLUNTEERS

WHAT KEEPS VOLUNTEERS coming back? What makes the volunteer experience a positive one for the library as well as the individual? The answers are partly found in the planning process. It is important to take into account the rights, responsibilities, and duties of the volunteer as a contributing member of the paid and unpaid staff team and the reciprocal expectations on behalf of the library. These go hand in hand.

BASIC VOLUNTEER RIGHTS IN THE WORK SITUATION

The importance of understanding the rights, responsibilities, and duties of a volunteer cannot be overestimated. All community volunteers have a right to expect that their library duties represent work that

- Is meaningful (not "make-do work") to the functioning of library operations
- Is based on skills, interests, and backgrounds whenever possible
- Provides training time adequate for success
- Contributes to the library's overall management plan

- Can be completed within the agreed volunteer time commitment
- Has clearly defined job descriptions, whether short-term, project-specific, or ongoing
- Has supervising staff willing to provide clear instructions and performance feedback
- Is done in a physically safe work environment free of harassment and hostility
- Is recognized as a contribution of the volunteer's personal time and talent to the success of the job or project

Adding to positive volunteer motivation is an understanding of how assigned tasks fit into the larger context of library operations. Copying, collating, and stapling a six-page information booklet fifty times can seem to be nothing but dull repetition unless the volunteer understands how these booklets are important for an upcoming program and reflect the quality of the library in the community. Explanations do not have to be overly extensive to show how one task affects others, but volunteers want to know how their tasks relate to the larger library mission.

In addition to the above rights, volunteers have the right to a designated workspace. It may be a shared desk or a table in the reference area or just part of a backroom work table. Nothing alienates someone faster than starting a job only to find out on day one that there is no place to work. A volunteer scrambling to find an appropriate work area is not only uncomfortable but also counterproductive.

Finally, volunteers have the right to some limited control and input over their assigned tasks. This input contributes to volunteer buy-in of the project and fosters an atmosphere of participation within the library organization. Drawing upon the above example, there maybe half a dozen ways to print, collate, and staple booklets together. Let the individual evolve a personalized way to accomplish the end result. Using close supervision to tell the volunteer just what to do every step of the way is one way to drive off many good volunteers. There are library tasks that must be done in sequence and in precise ways, yet even paid staff evolve their own approaches. This happens with volunteers as well, who may find more efficient approaches than the one used by others.

PERSONAL RESPECT

Every community volunteer has the right to be respected as a unique individual who is contributing time and energy to the library. Respect can be shown in many ways, but the easiest is when paid staff acknowledge volunteers by name and treat them as coworkers. Using a nametag with the first name is one way of demonstrating respect for the individual volunteer.

ORIENTATION TO THE LIBRARY

Every library volunteer has the right to a general library orientation, a brief explanation of library volunteer policies and procedures and where to find them, and introductions to relevant staff. In large libraries, orientation training may be done on a particular weekly schedule for an hour. In small community libraries, orientation is often accomplished through a walk-around, a single page of user-friendly volunteer guidelines with discussion, and informal introductions to the library staff and other volunteers. The goal of new volunteer orientation is to help the volunteer transition from being an outsider to an insider. Feeling part of the team is one important element in creating a successful experience.

TRAINING

Every library volunteer has the right to receive adequate training based on the assigned tasks and personal skills and backgrounds. This includes training in safety procedures appropriate to the tasks. Additionally, volunteers have a right to expect ongoing training and educational opportunities when appropriate. These opportunities can be used to strengthen a resume, boost personal knowledge, or serve as encouragement to take on more difficult library assignments. If the cost of training volunteers would be prohibitive, sometimes a staff member with specialized knowledge can be assigned to provide the training. This is often the case for computer-literate volunteers who help customers with computer issues but receive specialized library training from reference or information technology staff.

GRIEVANCE PROCEDURES AND CONFLICT RESOLUTION

Every volunteer has a right to be treated fairly and to be able to air grievances during times of conflict. Conflicts can occur with other volunteers or with staff members. It is important to have a grievance procedure in place for volunteers. A volunteer who feels mistreated by the library staff will likely share the negative experiences with others in the community and possibly with those in influential community positions. Depending on circumstances, this angered volunteer can create a negative image in the community for you, the library, and the library director.

Most volunteer conflicts arise from minor misunderstandings that fester into strong feelings. If a particular conflict is faced early and quickly, it can often be resolved or at least mitigated. Your challenge as volunteer services manager is that you might not know about the conflict until it takes on its own life. In your position, you can set up a grievance and conflict resolution procedure that follows a traditional chain of command (staff supervisor to library director). You can use an open-door procedure in which you listen to the volunteer and the charges of unfairness. Then you can work toward a solution, subject to the library director's approval. If you follow such a resolution procedure, a volunteer who ultimately leaves is more likely to do so with a feeling that the conflict was heard fairly rather than with intense anger.

RECOGNITION

Volunteers have a right to expect some type of recognition for the work they perform. Recognition can take the form of a simple verbal thank-you from the supervisor, a written thank-you note from the volunteer services manager, or a formal luncheon or evening reception. Even a quick thank-you by e-mail is appreciated. The most important and enduring recognition is respect and consideration for a job well done.

RESPONSIBILITIES AND DUTIES OF VOLUNTEERS

Once accepted, library volunteers need to honor their responsibilities and duties in order to continue to serve as volunteers. Lists of responsibilities should be part of a volunteer policy manual and provided to volunteers as well as posted on bulletin boards and the library intranet. For many small libraries operating on informal relationships, the list of responsibilities shown below may seem excessive. In some large jurisdictions, however, specific responsibilities are required to be legally stated on the volunteer application form.

Not all of the following responsibilities and duties apply to all volunteer programs or to every type of volunteer. For example, volunteers providing homebound services, those working with children or vulnerable adults, and those in contact with customers outside library premises may be subject to criminal background checks, whereas those working in the public area within the library may not require such checks. As the volunteer services manager, you need to develop your own list of responsibilities, including those based on jurisdictional legal requirements or accepted conventions within your library.

Work Commitment Responsibilities

Perform assigned tasks following the job description in a proficient manner.

Perform duties to the best of one's abilities and be receptive to training.

Regard volunteering as a serious commitment.

Show up on time and follow the mutually agreed upon work schedule.

Notify supervisor as soon as possible if unable to work as scheduled.

Carry out assignments in good spirits and accept supervision.

Maintain an attitude of open-mindedness.

Follow through on any library work commitments made to others.

Seek the assistance of the supervisor or another staff person whenever a customer question occurs or a task project is completed.

Respect the duties of the library staff and contribute to maintaining smooth working relationships.

Follow the established library rules and policies regarding personal conduct.

Dress appropriately for the assigned tasks, including any special programs, events, and public meetings.

Stay informed about information posted on volunteer bulletin boards.

Read e-mail and pertinent announcements.

Stay informed about any ongoing changes that may impact the assigned work.

Commit to the mission, values, goals, and policies of the library.

Provide the supervisor with adequate notice before leaving and the reason, if possible.

Customer Service Responsibilities

> Maintain confidentiality of all information and records pertaining to library customers.
>
> Show respect to library customers by being friendly, courteous, and cooperative, and guide them to staff members when necessary.
>
> Remember that all volunteers work in a public setting as representatives of the library.

Employment Responsibilities

> Agree to criminal background checks on local and national databases.
>
> Agree to have references checked as listed on the volunteer application form.
>
> Agree to be fingerprinted and tested for substance abuse.
>
> Grant full permission to be identified by first name in photographs and other recordings for any publicity or promotional purposes including newspapers, television, and radio announcements or on the library website.
>
> Agree to carry car insurance when using one's own car while performing assigned tasks.
>
> Acknowledge that there is no salary or other compensation for performing volunteer work.
>
> Recognize that volunteering does not provide special advantage for any future full-time library position.
>
> Agree to the library's right to end the volunteer relationship for poor performance.

VOLUNTEERS AND LIBRARY FRIENDS GROUPS

AS A VOLUNTEER services manager, you may face issues related to the Friends of the Library and your role managing community volunteers. In small libraries, Library Friends quite often serve as the staffing backbone of the library. They are the informal group of committed individuals who operate and help raise funds for the library. They can literally keep the doors open. Sometimes the roles of Friends, library volunteers, and staff overlap so closely that a member of the Friends also may be assigned "volunteer hours" working in place of paid staff. For these people there is little, if any, difference between roles.

In your library, the Friends group may be chartered as a separate not-for-profit group organized under the federal tax code as a 501-(c) organization. Friends groups have identifiable officers and a membership list, pay dues, and may send out newsletters and other information. Alternatively, the Friends may be organized as a group under the umbrella of a 501-(c) not-for-profit library foundation. In both instances, the position of the president of the Friends group and your position as the volunteer services manager require getting people to donate their time to perform library services. Even though these are the same duties, you both "work" for separate organizations and should have distinct reporting relationships.

If your library recognizes that the Friends group activities are "external" to the library, for example, raising funds in the community, managing used book sales, sponsoring special events, or operating a library gift shop, you will probably have fewer conflicts. In this way, your volunteers are "internal" to the library operations even if they are physically delivering books to homebound readers. On the library website, there should be two separate links, one to the Friends group and one to your library volunteer services web page. By implementing a separate library community volunteer services program with its own policies and procedures, you can distinguish Friends group activities and members from your duties and your volunteers (see sample 6-1). In contrast, if your library treats both groups together, you may have an inclusive policy such as sample 6-2.

Conflicts can occur if you are coordinating an individual who is both a community volunteer and a longtime standing member of the Friends.

Community Volunteers and Friends Group Policies

Community volunteers may be invited, but not required, to become members of the Friends of the Library group.

The Friends meeting room is designated for Friends members use only and will not be used by staff, community volunteers, or the general public.

The volunteer services manager is responsible for reporting hours of volunteer service performed by community volunteers and court-directed volunteers. The president of the Friends group has the responsibility for tracking membership hours.

The annual library recognition day will recognize staff for outstanding achievements. Recognition for community volunteers will be held during National Library Week. The president of the Friends group is responsible for announcing the time and place of the Friends' recognition event.

The public library volunteer insurance covers only community volunteers working under the direction of the volunteer services manager or a designated library manager or staff person. Volunteer insurance does not cover the functions of the Friends group.

The volunteer services manager will maintain the volunteer applications and human resource forms of all community volunteers. It is the responsibility of the president of the Friends group to maintain the Friends' membership records.

Sample 6-1. **Policy Statements: Community Volunteers and Friends Group as Separate Programs**

Similarly, difficulties can occur if you are asked to take over the coordination of volunteer activities in areas traditionally handled by the Friends. To manage these and other potential conflicts effectively, consider working with the library administration to develop a set of library policies that define how these two areas of library volunteerism are addressed so that both can be successful in enriching the library with dedicated volunteers. The considerations reviewed in this chapter will help you write a policy.

DUES AND MEMBERSHIP REQUIREMENTS

Should library volunteers be required to be members of the Friends? No. There are volunteers who want to help the library without the obligations of

---

Community Volunteers/Friends Group Policies

Library volunteers include all individuals who voluntarily give their time and talents to help further the mission of the public library in providing materials and information to our community. Included here are trustees, Library Friends, docents, and community adult and youth volunteers.

Members of the Library Friends and local volunteers are equally important in enhancing the efforts of the public library's paid staff in providing outstanding library service.

Library community volunteers and Friends of the Library are considered by the public library as unpaid staff and are included in all library activities and share in all nonmonetary benefits and facility use that is open to all staff.

Library community volunteers and Friends are considered an integral part of the library staff and can use the lockers, break room, and kitchen facilities.

For administrative reporting, all community service volunteer hours, including the Friends group and court-directed volunteers, will be reported on a monthly basis.

Volunteer hours include any hours contributed for the betterment of the public library, whether on- or off-site, whether a community volunteer, Friends group member, or court-directed volunteer. Hours will be collected and reported to the library director on a monthly basis.

The public library's annual recognition event will award staff, community volunteers, and Friends of the Library.

Sample 6-2. **Policy Statements: Community Volunteers and Friends Group as a Single Program** attending meetings or paying dues. There are talented community volunteers who may want to work on a particular library project—for example, database management of volunteer statistics—but not be involved in the Friends' fundraising efforts.

Some public libraries, often the larger ones, establish a docent group whose members receive special training and serve the library in specialized functions. Docents are usually required to be paid members of the Friends group and may be managed separately from other library volunteers. Each of these library volunteer groups—community volunteers, Friends, and docents—serve libraries in slightly different ways. All can be valuable to the success of a library.

TASKS AND RESPONSIBILITIES

Who assigns volunteers to the library-related tasks that need to be done? Maintaining the community bulletin board or library displays may have been part of the Friends' efforts for many years in a smaller library. If these tasks suddenly come under your purview as part of library operations, it is important that the shift in task assignments be positively communicated to all concerned and formalized by job descriptions. The transfer of responsibilities may be smooth if the one or two Friends who handled these tasks were getting tired of doing them or were withdrawing from the Friends group. When this does not happen, a volunteer or a Friends member may be caught up in a conflict, trying to meet both the Friends group expectations and your expectations as the volunteer services manager. This situation seldom has a successful outcome.

DEVOLUNTEERING AND MEMBERSHIP

Not all individuals are suited to be library volunteers. For different reasons it may be necessary to "devolunteer" an individual—terminate that person's service. Although it is often difficult for a volunteer services manager to devolunteer a person, it is much easier when there is a clear distinction between a community volunteer expected to work according to specific job requirements and a member of the Friends group. Merely paying dues and attending meetings do not necessarily make for a useful or successful library volunteer. This type of transition quite often occurs when a library is growing and becoming more professional in operations and job expectations and moving away from grassroots Friends group control.

When an individual is both a community volunteer and a member of the Friends group, you must take the time to explain the distinction. Showing sensitivity to the volunteer's feelings is essential to keeping the devolunteering process from having a negative effect on the activities of the Friends group. You may find it useful to talk over the situation with the library director and the president of the Friends to see if there is another assignment the volunteer can be given within the Friends' scope of activities.

VOLUNTEER HOURS AND RULES

How will the hours of community volunteers and Friends group members be reported? Do the hours attending a Friends meeting count the same as the hours worked by a community volunteer doing the assigned tasks? Should the Friends group members count their time only for special events, such as the time spent preparing for and managing a book sale? Are both types of hours assigned a dollar valuation?

A community volunteer can be required to follow the rules in completing a time form or a sign-in sheet. On the other hand, there are dedicated, hard-working members of the Friends who feel they should not take credit for the many hours they contribute to the library. They refuse to complete time forms as a matter of principle. As a practical consequence, their hours of service are omitted or at best underestimated on any volunteer service reports.

RECOGNITION AND AWARDS

Will community volunteers and Friends group members receive the same kinds of awards and recognition? Will the two groups come together for recognition events? Consider that longevity for community volunteers is usually measured in months, whereas in some Friends groups longevity is often measured in years. Would recognition be given for "years of service" or "the level of accomplishment of a task" or both?

Some Friends groups use part of their dues to support special awards for their members. Some public libraries have no budget for volunteer recognition or awards. This discrepancy in funding can lead to difficulties trying to make a combined recognition event a positive experience for everyone. You may decide that separate functions held at different times of the year may work better.

The perceived status differences between long-standing library Friends and newer community volunteers can also cause some difficulties if not handled diplomatically. Giving the same type of honors (flowers, pins, plaques) or trying to select a "Volunteer of the Year" from members of both groups combined may create more problems than it solves.

RISK MANAGEMENT

Some public libraries carry special volunteer insurance as part of their general liability insurance program. There are insurance companies that provide stand-alone policies. Ask your administration about volunteer insurance. Few public libraries cover community volunteers by workers' compensation for on-the-job injuries. Some libraries specifically state on their volunteer application form that workers' compensation insurance is not provided. Most do not provide this coverage to a volunteer. This means that any accident that occurs while a volunteer working at the library has to be covered by the volunteer's own health insurance. This is the reason some libraries buy special volunteer insurance to cover medical costs. These insurance plans do not cover Friends members because Friends are usually a separate nonprofit organization.

These distinctions may seem like splitting hairs until a serious accident occurs and medical costs are incurred. It is important to clarify the liability insurance issues related to your particular program.

Additionally, as a volunteer services manager you can ask a volunteer to provide a motor vehicle record and proof of automobile insurance if the assigned duties require the use of a vehicle, such as for home delivery of library books. This would be prudent because the library insurance plan is not likely to provide automobile coverage for volunteers. Again, some libraries may also require a local police report or criminal background check. When a member of the Friends group is driving on behalf of the Friends in support of a library program, there is typically no such requirement.

LIBRARY SPACE

Does the library support separate Friends' meeting room, lockers, book storage, or display space within the library building? Can community volunteers use the room or lockers? Are your community volunteers treated more like paid staff or more like Friends members, or neither, when they store their personal effects, take breaks, or perform duties?

The degree of exclusivity and "control" over library space is a subtle issue that can affect the feelings of all those involved. In almost all libraries, especially small ones, space is at a premium. Often there is a subtle and informal negotiation process over this scarce commodity. The key point here is to find ways to reduce tensions over space issues. When library space becomes informally or formally allocated, you may have to negotiate space usage for your community volunteers.

In larger library systems, Friends groups may use a separate building for meetings and other activities, such as operating a used bookstore or a used clothing shop. When this occurs, Friends and community volunteers usually evolve into quite distinct entities and may have little contact with each other.

LIBRARY PERKS

As you view the two groups, do you see any perks or privileges given to members of the Friends group that are not given to community volunteers, or vice versa? Are the perks closer to those received by paid staff?

Perks for either group may include waivers on fines, opportunities to check out new bestsellers first, and the privilege of additional renewals. If community volunteers and Friends have been physically separated over time, the issue of differential perks is much less important to all parties.

LEGAL AND RISK MANAGEMENT ISSUES

THE LEGAL CONCERNS of a library volunteer program closely parallel those associated with the employment of paid staff. The legal and risk management issues surrounding the use of volunteers can seem overwhelming at first, but they are actually quite manageable when broken down into specific areas of concern.

Your first decision is how your library defines the term *volunteer*. If you adhere strictly to the set of library hiring guidelines by choice or by the legal requirements of your library, then volunteers are considered unpaid staff and their recruitment and "employment" must meet many of the required employment standards for paid employees. This seems to be a trend in public libraries over the past decade as concerns have increased over security and safety issues. Thus, for example, a volunteer program budget item for criminal background checks may be required when not that many years ago community members were allowed to volunteer without much bother.

In what seems to be a small number of libraries, the recruitment and "hiring" of volunteers have no legal rules, whereas the hiring of paid staff must meet specific employment standards. If you are newly taking over a volunteer program, or refreshing an established one, it is important to get clarification from your key administrators (e.g., library director, human resources, jurisdictional risk manager, library attorney) about how you should approach the "hiring" and "employment" of library volunteers.

VOLUNTEER RECRUITING AND DISCRIMINATION ISSUES

When recruiting volunteers, you are not legally required to advertise or post your positions to meet affirmative action standards. You may, however, be asked to follow the library hiring guidelines in posting or advertising volunteer opportunities. Numerous public libraries post volunteer positions on their websites, thus reaching a large number of diverse community members while meeting legal expectations.

Even if your library does not require strict hiring compliance, you want to be sensitive to the public relations problems if someone charges that your library has discriminated against certain types of volunteers (e.g., the disabled, specific racial or ethnic minorities). The burden of proof would be on you and the library administration to show that this was not the case.

There is a balancing act in employing volunteers. You definitely want to hold to the philosophy of recruiting the best volunteer from the available pool of applicants for every position. Yet you may have an obligation to honor the requests of departmental managers (your internal customers) who do not want particular types of volunteers in their specific areas of operation. For example, an obese individual may have good telephone skills and be available when needed to staff the information desk, but the information desk manager may feel that he does not present a professional library image. If the administration wants you to follow the library's legal employment guidelines, obesity is not a protected characteristic under the Federal Equal Employment Opportunity Commission laws or under most local employment laws. Nonetheless, it can come under the jurisdiction of the Americans with Disability Act, depending on the individual's medical circumstances.

In this circumstance, you have a willing and able volunteer who can do the assigned tasks. How would you handle this situation? First, make sure there is a well-prepared job description specifying the skills and competencies for the information desk position. This document gives you a basis for objective decision making in matching the individual's skills with the task requirements. It also serves as a basis for administrative review in the event a conflict resolution process is required. It may also allow the desk manager to see that this volunteer is capable of doing the defined job.

Second, recognize that the desk manager generally has the right to decide who works in her department or area of responsibility. The balancing act requires that you apply your talents in educating and persuading her that you have identified the best qualified volunteer for the position. Negotiate with her to set up a trial period with a specific end date to evaluate how the volunteer is working out in the position. At the same time, you may be able to offer the volunteer suggestions about other library volunteer opportunities that can use telephone skills or employ other skills he has within the library operations.

RECRUITING AND ADA PRACTICES

The Americans with Disabilities Act (ADA) does not address volunteers per se, although some library systems apply the same rules to volunteers as to paid staff. If volunteers come into the library as customers, they fall under the public accommodation section of the ADA. If they work in the library as volunteers, however, they are exempt from the act. Again, check with your administration on what rules apply.

Beyond the strict legal interpretations, you may have disabled volunteers apply for positions. Here again, your willingness to make "reasonable accommodations" in the workplace demonstrates a good faith effort on the part of the library to use the talents of disabled individuals from the community.

Disabled volunteers are often willing to help you adapt tasks to fit their requirements. In doing this, they are actually helping the library learn how to make reasonable accommodations, as required by law, in the event a staff member becomes disabled or a disabled individual is hired. The growth of virtual volunteering has enabled those who are disabled temporarily or permanently to use their computer skills from home on behalf of the library. Remember, the term *disability* covers a wide range of conditions, and many who are disabled have as many usable skills as others who are not disabled.

DEVELOPMENTALLY DISABLED VOLUNTEERS

The broad heading of disability includes young adults and adults who are developmentally disabled or have brain injuries. Some are enrolled in special "return to work" programs. A job coach from a private rehabilitation company may contact you to see if you are willing to work with a developmentally disabled individual in a nonpaid volunteer position. The rehabilitation facility is usually either paid by an insurance company or funded through a state or federal program to assist these individuals in finding gainful employment.

When the job coach calls you, set up an interview so that you can ensure that there are no hidden agendas (such as the expectation of a paying job, as noted below) and that the individual has the skills necessary to perform the available volunteer work. Do not be too quick to judge the types of tasks that the disabled person can or cannot do.

If the job coach's goal is to provide a volunteer opportunity for the disabled individual to gain skills, confidence, and experience in a work setting, or to enable that person to get out and be among people, you may be able to assist if the appropriate library tasks are available. If there is an expectation that the individual will move into a regular, paid position at some future date, it is important that this decision be coordinated with the human resources department and the library manager. Library employment guidelines and the authorization to fill a position may be outside your scope of authority as a volunteer services manager. If the individual transfers to either a part- or full-time position that is eventually downsized or eliminated, the library may face additional administrative and legal concerns.

Therefore, during your initial interview, talk with the job coach and the volunteer. Explain that, if a position opens up, the volunteer is welcome to apply, but all hiring is based on a pool of applicants and no special preference is given to volunteers. The hiring manager may review the volunteer's performance records as part of the hiring process, but this is only one factor among many that may be considered.

You may need to be sensitive to potential prejudices among the library staff and managers about having developmentally disabled individuals volunteering in the library. This prejudice should not limit your efforts to work with the disabled, because bringing these individuals into the library system supports staffing diversity policies and can benefit everyone. You may hear the negative comment that the library is not a social service agency. In recent years, the disability issues of returning military veterans from the Iraq and Afghanistan wars have increased public awareness and national discussions about physical disabilities so that more people are showing increased tolerance and acceptance. This may or may not be the case in your library.

Finally, it is important to know how much time the job coach will be on-site at your library and how much time will be committed to working directly with the disabled individual. The more time the job coach is willing to commit, the more likely the all-around success of the volunteer experience.

RECRUITMENT OF YOUTH

Youth (twelve to eighteen years old) may want to volunteer to complete high school graduation requirements or add service experience to their college applications. Other youth have local service requirements from organizations such as the Scouts. Still others may want to volunteer to gain library experience so that they can obtain part-time paid library positions such as a shelver when they reach the age requirement. Staff members will also ask you to find a volunteer position for a daughter or son.

There are two sets of quasi-legal issues when working with young people. There are state employment regulations governing the employment of youth and the hours they may work. As volunteers, these young people do not come directly under these statutes, but these regulations may serve as excellent guidelines for the times and hours you can use them. For example, if the state law does not allow a fifteen-year-old (or younger) to work after 7:00 p.m. on a school night, you can use this as a guide to determine appropriate hours for any volunteers under fifteen years of age.

A second quasi-legal area is the consent of a parent or legal guardian to work. If your library employs sixteen-year-olds in staff positions without requiring consent forms, you can use this as the basis for your own volunteer policy. Check with the human resources department on your library's legal age requirements.

If a consent form is required, it should include the following simple elements: tasks, safety or health issues, scheduled times, and the signature of the parent or legal guardian agreeing to let the young adult perform volunteer work at the library. If an accident happens, there is shared liability with the parents, although medical treatments are generally based on the parents' health care coverage.

Additionally, the consent form makes explicit that all volunteer positions carry task expectations. If the youth does not perform, you have a basis for notifying the parents or legal guardians that you will be devolunteering their young adult.

It is important to establish a minimum age limit for young volunteers. Sometimes young adolescents do not have the maturity to work in a structured environment without close supervision. If you decide to accept a young volunteer, make sure a parent or guardian will be close by to help supervise the child's activity. Consider the case of a nine-year-old who is caught throwing stones in the schoolyard and assigned to do two hours of community service by the principal. The parents ask you if their child can volunteer at the library to meet the principal's requirement. You might accept the offer as long as one of the parents stays in the library with the child.

YOUTH-AT-RISK VOLUNTEERS

Within the category of youth volunteers is the more specific area of youth at-risk. These young people often have serious problems at school, are in trouble with the law, or both. It takes a special approach and a lot of patience to work with them. Successfully using this type of volunteer in the library usually involves setting strict task expectations, giving positive reinforcement, providing appropriate and close supervision with some challenging tasks, and showing individualized interest. This takes a lot of your time. You may find a volunteer, possibly a former high school teacher, who has the skills and patience to manage this type of responsibility for you.

Keep in mind that if you or a staff person cannot give these young people the attention they require, you should think twice about hiring them as library volunteers.

VOLUNTEERISM AND COURT-DIRECTED VOLUNTEERS

Local court systems use community service as part of the restitution process for individuals convicted of relatively minor offenses. Court-directed individuals may be youth offenders or adults. The formal paperwork originates from the local court and stipulates the number of hours ordered for restitution; it often includes a secondary timesheet to record the actual hours and days worked as part of the judicial requirements.

In some library systems, a library manager or department head is responsible for court-directed community service volunteers, with the volunteer services manager responsible for only community volunteers. In others, the volunteer services manager coordinates both types of volunteers.

Not all library systems use court-directed community volunteers. If yours uses them, check with the court liaison to make sure these volunteers are covered by the city's or county's court medical insurance while working on library property. In most cases, the court coverage applies. You may also want to make sure they are covered after the date shown on the court form. For example, Jimmy is supposed to have all of his assigned restitution hours completed by the fifteenth of the month as shown on the form. He calls you with car problems two days earlier and promises to complete his hours on the sixteenth. If Jimmy has an accident at the library on the sixteenth, does the court insurance cover him? Find out before you agree to extend his completion date.

When you use court-directed volunteers, establish a firm policy on the types of offenses you will accept. Most libraries will take people convicted of Driving under the Influence (DUI), Driving while Intoxicated (DWI), and minor traffic infractions (e.g., no automobile insurance, speeding, excess parking tickets), truancy, and possession of a controlled substance. They will not accept individuals who commit crimes such as robbery, purse snatching, stealing, or similar offenses. You have a right to ask the nature of the offense and to accept or reject the individual, and you have an obligation to maintain confidentiality of this information.

You also have a right to enforce library standards of dress, behavior, and task expectations for these individuals. Some individuals think the library is an easy place to complete their community service, with the library obliged to meet their demands concerning times and tasks. This is not the case. If an individual is not performing his assigned tasks, does not show up on schedule, or leaves early, you have the right to terminate the relationship immediately.

CRIMINAL BACKGROUND AND REFERENCE CHECKS

The increasing use of criminal background checks on potential volunteers reflects a growing concern about personal safety and security in the library. Depending on the jurisdiction covering your library, background checks may be required or optional for library volunteers. Some larger library systems contract third-party commercial vendors that use public databases to do background checks either for the library directly or coordinated through a municipality or county department. Smaller libraries use local law enforcement or commercial agencies to do statewide checks, which are relatively inexpensive.

Criminal background checks vary greatly—from statewide checks to national checks. In a statewide check, only offenses showing up within your state appear in the databases. Find out what type of checks are performed so that you understand what is being check for and how extensively. Recognizing that background checks vary in depth and scope of information should keep you from getting a false sense of security about those you bring in to volunteer.

If your volunteers are going to represent the library off the premises, such as reading at nursing homes or working with youth or underserved populations, it is prudent to have a policy that requires a criminal background check. In highly transient urban or suburban areas, this procedure shows a good-faith effort on the part of the library to employ safe volunteers. Even small-town libraries are seeing changes in their demographics.

Your library may require both a criminal background check and reference checks before a volunteer can work. For some libraries, a volunteer can go through orientation training and any skills training but not be allowed to volunteer on a regular schedule until all background checks are completed. You need to find out which approach your library administration desires. Here too, consistency of practice is legally useful. You should not tell one volunteer to start right away and another to wait until the background check comes back.

Contacting the people listed as references by a potential volunteer is useful for getting general character information and verifying certain information on the volunteer application form. If the reference is from another library staff member or from a small nonprofit agency, the individual contacted may be a good source for sharing information. Larger agencies and private employers, concerned about lawsuits, may not be as free to discuss information about the individual. Listed volunteer references are often personal friends, neighbors, or local religious leaders.

If you decide to check references, you must be consistent in checking for all positions, or at least for all those that require the volunteer to leave the library premises or work with youth. Again, consistency is important to prevent impressions or accusations of discriminatory behavior.

Before doing reference checks, prepare a set of questions focused on the specific volunteer job duties and expected job behaviors. If you need someone with good computer skills, you can ask about computer skills, although neighbors and friends may or may not know this information. Similarly, if the volunteer position requires someone highly organized, then you can ask questions about the person's organizational abilities. In these instances, it would be inappropriate to ask about the individual's public speaking skills, since these are not required for the job. One useful approach is to describe the volunteer tasks and ask the references if they think the volunteer candidate can do the tasks. Then ask why. In the answer, you will be listening for the characteristics you are looking for to fill the volunteer job. Remember to allow time for additional comments that may prove important in your decision.

It takes time to prepare appropriate questions. You might want to have these questions reviewed by a knowledgeable administrator to prevent problems. Doing telephone reference checks takes time; the questions can be mailed instead, but be sure to enclose a self-addressed envelope marked "personal." Some libraries are now using e-mail to send questions to references. Just remember that what you learn is confidential and should be treated as such.

Finally, recognize that the vast majority of people are honest and good. Those who want to volunteer in your library do so for decent reasons. If a potential volunteer asks about the reason for a criminal background check, explain that everyone wants to feel safe in the library.

DRIVING RECORDS AND AUTO INSURANCE

For any position that requires a volunteer to drive a personal vehicle, it is prudent to ask to see both a current motor vehicle record and proof of current automobile liability insurance. Make copies of each form and keep these in the volunteer's file. You might also have a tickler file to follow up on yearly updates.

If a review of the driving record shows a DUI conviction or too many traffic infractions, you have sufficient reason to disqualify the applicant from a position that requires driving on behalf of the library. If there is an accident while the volunteer is on library business, the library can become party to a lawsuit.

Do not assign a volunteer to drive a library-owned vehicle without first checking with the appropriate risk manager, key administrator, or library insurance broker. The volunteer is not paid staff, and the library's insurance may not cover anyone not employed by the library system. Always check first.

Once a year, review your records for volunteers assigned to driving positions. You may find volunteers who have shifted to positions that require driving and you have no driving or insurance records for them. Always keep updated copies of insurance and license information as part of your records. If you or the supervising staff member feels there is a potential problem, you can ask a volunteer to bring in a current motor vehicle record to see if there has been some deterioration. If there is, it is likely that the volunteer will quit before bringing in a new record. Needless to say, it would be reasonable to devolunteer any volunteer caught using drugs or alcohol on library premises immediately, so that no driving accidents can occur on library time. If the library has a drug screening program, check to see if volunteers come under the policy.

HIRING AND HEALTH AND SAFETY REGULATIONS

As public agencies, public libraries do not fall under the federal Occupational Safety and Health Act. Occupational safety advice may be provided by the safety department within a municipality or county or through experts employed by the library's liability insurance company. These experts can provide basic safety training (how to lift, back protection, etc.) and ergonomics and give advice on library safety practices.

The "Right to Know" regulations covering chemicals in the workplace are useful guidelines that let people, including volunteers, know what chemicals are present and give them access to material safety data sheets. Libraries have numerous cleaners, solvents, book mending glues, and so forth. For most individuals, these chemicals are not a problem. For a few chemically sensitive people, coming into contact with any of them may cause allergic reactions.

In your job descriptions, it is important to detail accurately any potential health and safety issues, especially if cleaning solvents, insecticides, or other problematic chemicals are involved in the tasks. Usually a safety administrator can help you interpret the information in a material safety data sheet and show you where these sheets should be located in the library.

GENERAL SAFETY TRAINING

It is important not to fall into the habit of assuming that volunteers will always use common sense in performing assigned tasks. A volunteer may prop a ladder against the wall next to a large window and reach toward the window to water hanging plants. This is an accident waiting to happen. Perhaps this is the way this volunteer waters plants at home. You also cannot assume that volunteers are aware of safety and liability issues as they affect the library. In addition, some volunteers will be working in branches that you do not visit often and may have been given a cursory overview of job expectations, with little or no attention paid to safety concerns. Safety is often seen as secondary to getting the volunteer started as quickly as possible. As the volunteer services manager, you have an obligation to be aware of any health and safety issues as well as the emergency procedures associated with all assigned tasks. You or a staff member can orient volunteers about safety concerns, including the proper use of equipment.

WORKERS' COMPENSATION

Extremely few public libraries cover volunteers under a workers' compensation program. Some libraries formally state on their application forms that volunteers are not covered. The great majority of libraries do not provide medical coverage for volunteers who have on-the-job accidents or illnesses.

Although a volunteer cannot file a workers' compensation claim for on-the-job injury or illness (only paid staff can do this), the library's medical portion of the general liability insurance will probably be the source of funds if a claim is made against the library by an injured volunteer. This is one reason some libraries purchase additional special volunteer insurance coverage.

Consider this example: Volunteer Judy is carrying a box of books to the donation area for sorting. On the way, she trips and hits her head against the steel shelving, and the wound bleeds profusely. There are several possible scenarios that the staff can follow after this type of incident. Someone can go through Judy's purse for her medical card and call her health carrier for instructions, call a relative to take her to a clinic or doctor, or call 911 and let them make the decision. If you take her to the library's designated workers' compensation clinic, her health insurance carrier may not cover the claim, since the doctor is not part of its network. In this case, you would probably want to file the claim with your general liability insurance carrier under the medical portion of the plan and hope the carrier pays.

This kind of situation underscores the importance of having a written policy on emergencies involving volunteers. You can work with the safety administrator to design guidelines so that all staff understand what to do in the event of an accident involving a volunteer. If there is no safety administrator at the library, you might get assistance and advice from the safety administrator of your local school district. Safety professionals are useful resources to have at your fingertips.

Preventing volunteer accidents is critical. This is where your ability as a manager comes into play. You need to learn how to monitor what the volunteers are doing and how they are performing their tasks.

CUSTOMER CONFIDENTIALITY

The library rules governing customer confidentiality should be part of any volunteer training, especially the training of those working at or near the circulation desk or accessing the computer records of library customers.

A volunteer may overhear a staff member make inappropriate comments about someone's reading habits. It is important to instruct the volunteer that this information is confidential and cannot be divulged to anyone, including family members. The extra few minutes you take to explain this policy may pay off later.

SEPARATION INTERVIEW

A volunteer may leave with or without notice. If notice is given, you may want to schedule a separation interview. This technique is usually a good way to learn about your program from the bottom up and find ways to improve it. When volunteers leave on friendly terms, they are often willing to share their ideas on how to make the library a better volunteer experience.

DEVOLUNTEERING

In a formal devolunteering, it is important to review the situation with a trusted administrator. Are there other options to consider? For example, a volunteer is slow in completing the assigned tasks. Is there another type of work that might be more appropriate? If a volunteer is not getting along with a particular staff member or another volunteer, is there another time or part of the building he can work? Are your facts accurate? Can you counsel the volunteer about other agencies or explore an individual's interest that allows him to leave you and the library on good terms? Has the individual just been through a major life crisis that affects his work or staff relationships? Does the volunteer need some time away from the library? A decision to devolunteer requires careful preparation, including consideration of any possible legal ramifications based on the circumstances.

GOOD SAMARITAN LAWS AND VOLUNTEERS

The federal Volunteer Protection Act of 1997 grants immunity from personal liability to volunteers in nonprofit and government organizations who are acting within the scope of their duties. This law covers volunteers in a public library as a government organization and the Friends of the Library as a nonprofit, 501-(c) organization. In addition to this federal law, all fifty states have laws that limit the personal liability of volunteers.

Under a typical good samaritan law, volunteers are protected from personal liability when they act in good faith or make honest mistakes. For example, a volunteer reading in the children's section gives medical assistance during a medical emergency. For some reason, the parents decide to sue the library and the volunteer. The library and the volunteer will find legal relief under a good samaritan act. Volunteers are not protected for willful misconduct, crimes of violence, committing a sexual offense, or violating someone's civil liberties.

Check with your library attorney on the applicable state or local laws and the federal Volunteer Protection Act as they affect your program.

VOLUNTEER INSURANCE

A library system can purchase inexpensive volunteer insurance to provide additional coverage for volunteers in the areas of accident, individual liability, and automobile liability. For example, if a volunteer is involved in an auto accident while driving to a customer's home to deliver books, the additional automobile coverage can provide added protection to the library in the event of a claim or if the liability limits are reached on the volunteer's automobile insurance. Ask your library administration if such insurance is in place. If it is not, ask the library insurance broker if purchasing this coverage would be worthwhile for your library.

| # VOLUNTEER PROGRAM COMMUNICATION

THERE ARE SEVERAL channels of communication within the library organization and to and from the local community. To develop a successful volunteer program, it is important for the volunteer services manager to learn to use these channels effectively.

THE FLOW OF INFORMATION AND INFORMATION NETWORKS

Every library has an internal communications environment that silently defines the dominant directions and patterns of the flow of information. In some libraries, staff can directly e-mail the library director without providing a copy to their supervisor. In others, formal announcements come from the top down and only supervisors can send written correspondence to higher levels of management. In still others, communication can be sent and received diagonally throughout the organization, thus tying together staff and managers in different departments, locations, and authority levels. At one end of the spectrum are libraries where the flow of communication is open and easy in both written and face-to-face forms; at the other, communications are guarded, restrained, and restricted.

New volunteer services managers might not understand the existing communication networks and therefore hesitate to use them. If you are in a split position with the management of volunteers as only one part of your workload, you will have to step back and assess the networks from your two positions. In one position, for example, as a reference librarian, all communications may have to follow the chain of command through your immediate supervisor, but in your position as volunteer services manager a variety of internal and external networks may be available to you.

To assess your library's communication environment, review the e-mail and attachments you have received. Is there a distinct sequence or ordering of names on the internal correspondence? Is there a standard listing of people in the library who receive e-mail related to your position? You will be more successful if you follow the established networks. On the other hand, if there is ambiguity or you are in a loosely structured organization, this situation can work to your advantage if you take the initiative to establish new networks that are useful to you in your role as volunteer services manager. For example, establishing a resource network of staff and managers you can contact, regardless of their formal positions, is advantageous in helping you discover new jobs for volunteers. There are also individuals in the library and groups in the community who can help you recruit volunteers.

EFFECTIVE COMMUNICATION CHANNELS

Communication channels can be separated into written and verbal formats. Written communication includes general or confidential e-mail, formal letters to managers or library board members, volunteer forms, form letters, newsletters, position announcements, handbooks, directives, certificates, spreadsheets, budget request forms, Facebook postings, graphics, notes on whiteboards, comments in the margins of letters or e-mail, flipcharts, PowerPoint presentations, text messages, and web page postings. These are all ways you can send and receive written information to individuals or groups through the formal or informal networks within your library. In some libraries, formal written materials have specific style and format requirements and require approval to post or send out.

Few people communicate effectively in all of these mediums. Poorly written or inappropriate communication can lead to problems. The cryptic note in the margin of a printed e-mail can do more immediate communication damage than a poorly written volunteer form. A difficult-to-read note scribbled on the volunteer information board can lead to minor misunderstanding, and a widely circulated e-mail message written in anger can have ramifications for weeks. A formal style of communication, though appropriate for staff, can be viewed as cold and uncaring when sent to a sensitive volunteer.

Oral communications include day-to-day conversations with volunteers, community members, staff, and managers in either an individual or group setting. They also include pleasantries and acknowledgments, grapevine chats, task instructions, telephone conversations, voicemail, and video presentations. All of these forms involve the "reading" of nonverbal messages. The subtleties of verbal communication can be distorted, as when you accidentally fail to acknowledge a volunteer just starting a shift or your voice on the telephone is wrongly interpreted as one of anger.

Books and instructional guides on written and oral forms of communication covering appropriate techniques, styles, limitations, and etiquette are available. Your library probably has some of these books, and there are numerous online sources. You can build the necessary skill sets to become a competent communicator with practice, patience, and some trial and error. At the beginning, identify the staff you think are effective communicators and pattern your style after theirs until you gain the confidence to develop your own style.

COMMUNICATION WITH VOLUNTEERS

The individual community member's first contact with you may be through a letter or e-mail in response to a volunteer job posting on the library website. At this point there is no face-to-face contact, yet there is communication of information. In another situation, a potential volunteer may have picked up an application form and sent it to you or left you a message on your telephone. Although you have had no personal contact with the individual, information is being communicated to you in all of these situations. Impressions are formed during this initial phase on the basis of these communications and, of course, your written or oral communications back to the potential volunteer.

Once your first oral conversation with a potential applicant begins, most impressions and judgments (correct or incorrect) are made during the first two to three minutes. You are deciding whether this individual may make a good volunteer, and the candidate is deciding whether to work with you. In an important way, you are in a community relations role as a representative of the library. Even if the conversation goes no farther than the initial meeting, your communication style will leave an impression and reflect on the library.

In the formal interview phase of recruitment, oral communication requires the skills of active listening to what is and is not said. The use of a written job description can help clarify the points you make about the job. Your openness in sharing the positive and negative aspects of the position and your ability to interpret nonverbal communications are all part of the mutual clarification process.

It is important that the staff person assigned to supervise the volunteer have good oral skills to explain accurately what is required and the patience to review the job task list. As the volunteer continues to work, the supervisor must have the verbal skills to provide feedback and give positive reinforcement for a job well done, nurturing the volunteer's ego and loyalty. Along the same lines, day-to-day pleasantries and acknowledgment by name provide additional reinforcements.

Effective communication with the volunteer staff is in part determined by the size of your volunteer pool and in part by your own communication style. A small number of volunteers can be informed of policy changes, special events, and training opportunities through informal meetings, special notices on bulletin boards, e-mail, or personal telephone calls. As the number of volunteers increases, a monthly or quarterly newsletter or meeting can augment these forms of communication. Throughout the year, a periodic personal meeting with each volunteer lets you know how the program is working and what each person feels about the volunteer experience.

COMMUNICATION FEEDBACK

Managers sometimes assume that, if they talk to a staff person or e-mail a message, the communication will be understood and acted on according to their intent. It is easy to fall into this trap as a volunteer services manager. But receiving a communication does not mean understanding the message. Further, understanding a message does not mean agreeing with it. And agreeing with the message does not mean responding to it as was intended.

Volunteers can experience additional difficulties because they are approaching your oral and written messages from widely different communication contexts. Telling a volunteer that the job will be cleaning books may easily create the image of a large pail of soapy water. Asking a volunteer to put the books in order on a cart may be interpreted as ordering them by size or color and not by the Dewey Decimal system. Most of the messaging done within a library organization is based on implicit understandings that in turn are based on the contextual knowledge of the way things get done in the library.

A major component in communication is completing the information loop, which is accomplished by getting feedback on the messages you send. In the simplest case, you can ask a volunteer to repeat and explain what she heard. For example, if you say, "Explain to me how you would go about two-sided copying and collating this twenty-page handout," you can listen to the explanation to determine if the volunteer understands how to operate the copier and do two-sided copying.

During a volunteer meeting, you may see heads nodding as part of the nonverbal behavior of participants, but this does not mean that you are getting agreement on a set of actions. You can get feedback by asking questions and getting the volunteers' opinions and commitments on who will undertake which actions and when. You can also follow up with individuals after a meeting either in person or by telephone and encourage them to ask questions about topics or concerns they are still not sure about. Here, too, silence does not necessarily mean understanding, agreement, or action.

Communications need to be clarified. For example, a volunteer e-mails you on a possible community service project. Before meeting with the individual, you can clarify by e-mailing specific questions back: "How many hours will this take?" "Do you know anyone else who is interested?" "Is there a financial cost to the library?" This shows your interest and allows the individual time to provide clarification of the proposed project so that your meeting time becomes more effective. Even if the project does not materialize, the volunteer can feel you were interested and understood what the proposal was all about.

Another way to get feedback is to establish action dates on your calendar and then check back to see if the activities that were to be accomplished were actually done. Hearing the words "Everything is fine" does not necessarily mean that everything is fine.

Exit interviews and exit surveys are ways to acquire feedback about the volunteer program and the individual volunteer experience. A volunteer moving out of state or returning to full-time employment is likely to share honest opinions about the program. This is important feedback.

If your library allows volunteers to have e-mail accounts on the library computer system, you can request and give communication feedback. Let your volunteers know that information sent through electronic methods such as e-mail and voicemail is not confidential.

Communications technology is changing rapidly. With the ubiquitous use of cell phones and smartphones, will you be tweeting volunteers in the future? Will your library set up Skype software on your computer so virtual volunteers can call you over the Internet? Will you have a separate volunteer services Facebook site that you use to communicate with volunteers? Will you be setting up a volunteer services blog to communicate with volunteers? As communications technology continues to change, quite likely the modes of your volunteer communications will change as well.

Ultimately, good communication relies on your ability to keep the informal and formal networks open and your willingness to accept and hear positive and negative comments no matter what the format.

| # VOLUNTEER PROGRAM EVALUATION

SUCCESSFUL VOLUNTEER PROGRAMS require some level of evaluation, even if you conduct the evaluation on an informal basis. As this section and the accompanying Volunteer Program Evaluation Checklist (sample 9-1) illustrate, evaluation means different things for the administration, library customers, the community, the library staff, the volunteers, and you, the volunteer services manager.

ADMINISTRATIVE SUPPORT

Do you have administrative support for the volunteer services program at all levels of the library organization? What kind of information would key administrators like to have to feel comfortable with the program or to consider it successful? Without much hesitation, most would want the statistics generated from the time reports and financial worth of the donated time by volunteers. By incorporating these into regular reports, you can demonstrate one of the strengths of your program to the overall operation of the library.

Adding narratives about particular accomplishments of volunteers and project outcomes and how these affect specific library services helps drive home the success of your program. Discuss with your administrator alternative reporting options that highlight your program successes. Could video reports from volunteers be incorporated into library board presentations? Could a short questionnaire to volunteer supervising staff be summarized to demonstrate program importance?

COMMUNITY SATISFACTION

Informally, a successful program produces verbal comments of thanks and expressed feelings of satisfaction from recipients. Library customers who are part of "read aloud" programs, whether at retirement homes, nursing homes, or childcare facilities, are often appreciative of the efforts of library volunteers. You can use these comments to document your success and consider them part of your evaluation feedback. Make quick notes of these comments for your program evaluation file, noting the date, place, and person making the comments. These comments can also be used to document your personal performance evaluation at the end of the year.

In addition, letters of appreciation sent to the library director, letters to the editorial section of the local newspaper, and positive e-mail to your office over the course of a year are useful documents that demonstrate the qualitative level of satisfaction for specific programs. In some instances, you can solicit letters from the directors of community service facilities, such as senior centers, that show their support and appreciation for the library volunteers.

If the library sponsors a community-wide recognition event for volunteers, such as a reception or picnic, the number of people who attend can be an indicator of community support. Are community leaders such as the mayor or city manager present? Does your guest list include the press or commercial and community media and library customers? Do they get special invitations to attend?

Be careful, though, when interpreting community and customer indicators of support. Newspapers do not publish every letter to the editor they receive; some put additional letters on their websites that you may or may not have read. Conflicting schedules may prevent key community leaders from attending a volunteer function. Weather conditions and competing community events can also lower the attendance. Nevertheless, make informative notes in your file to assist with future planning guides and provide information for your volunteer services program evaluation.

Volunteer Program Evaluation Checklist

	Currently Happening	Possible in Future	Improbable
I. ADMINISTRATIVE SUPPORT			
1. Paid volunteer services manager position			
2. Volunteer services program line item in library budget			
3. Paid administrative staff support for program			
4. Office provided for volunteer services program			
5. Approval given for a volunteer services policy handbook			
6. Volunteer program brochures are available			
7. Volunteer services has listing on library web page			
8. Volunteer services has separate web pages			
9. Provision for volunteer paid staff supervisors			
10. In-service training provided for volunteer staff supervisors			
11. Training funds available for volunteer services manager			
12. Program recognized as part of community relations			
13. Centralized volunteer statistics are collected and reported			
14. Dollar value attached to a volunteer's time and reported			

Sample 9-1. **Volunteer Program Evaluation Checklist**

	Currently Happening	Possible in Future	Improbable
I. ADMINISTRATIVE SUPPORT			
15. Volunteers recognized as unpaid staff			
16. Budgeted funds available for volunteer recognition			
17. Library director and key managers attend recognition events			
18. Library director supports volunteer services program			
II. COMMUNITY AND CUSTOMER SUPPORT			
1. Verbal expression of thanks by customers			
2. Written letters of thanks by customers, e.g., homebound			
3. Outreach programs use volunteers			
4. Written letters to editor about library volunteers			
5. Library social networking site(s) include volunteers			
6. Library community events include library volunteers			
7. Other_____			
III. STAFF SUPPORT			
1. Staff willing to supervise volunteers			
2. Staff willing to be coworkers with volunteers			
3. Staff identifies projects that won't get done without volunteers			

Sample 9-1. **Volunteer Program Evaluation Checklist** *(continued)*

4. Staff willing to identify new volunteer jobs			
5. Staff can identify benefits of using volunteers			
6. IT department provides support to volunteer program			
7. Staff provides supplies and equipment for volunteers			
8. Staff provides verbal, positive feedback			
9. Staff are positive in giving constructive corrections			

IV. VOLUNTEER SUPPORT

1. Assigned tasks meet personal interest and skill needs			
2. Assignments are interesting and challenging			
3. Volunteers are given opportunity to learn new tasks/skills			
4. Volunteers feel orientation training is good			
5. Volunteers feel they have been adequately trained			
6. Volunteers feel they are contributing to the library			
7. Volunteers feel they are contributing to the local community			
8. Volunteers are asked for their opinions			
9. Volunteers are assigned a staff supervisor			
10. Volunteers are introduced to staff and other volunteers			
11. Volunteers are given a tour of the facility			

	Currently Happening	Possible in Future	Improbable
IV. VOLUNTEER SUPPORT			
12. Volunteers feel they are part of a group or team			
13. Volunteers have a workspace to perform assigned tasks			
14. Volunteers have a place to store personal items			
15. Volunteers are willing to train new volunteers			
16. Formal volunteer recognition events are well attended			
17. Volunteers encourage others to become library volunteers			
18. Volunteer program diversity goals are being met			
19. Volunteers can appeal negative decisions			
20. Volunteers leave with positive feelings of accomplishment			
V. VOLUNTEER MANAGER SUPPORT			
1. Top administrators provide continued positive support			
2. Immediate manager provides continued positive support			
3. Peer managers provide positive support			
4. Volunteer program information shared in administrative meetings			
5. Growth in number of departments using volunteers			

Sample 9-1. **Volunteer Program Evaluation Checklist** *(continued)*

6. Growth in number of community volunteers			
7. Increase in number of paid staff willing to supervise volunteers			
8. Fewer number of program failures			

STAFF SATISFACTION

How does the staff evaluate your volunteer services program? Some staff members may see volunteers as a necessary evil. You may hear, "Yes, some volunteers are useful and know what they are doing, but in general volunteers get in our way, mess up our procedures, and take time supervising. Maybe the administration is trying to replace us."

A key factor in the success of the volunteer program is neutralizing such negative comments or, even better, making supporters of the staff. To have an individual express negative comments about volunteers and then turn around a year later and become a strong supporter is an excellent indicator of the growing acceptance of your program. Other indicators include the number of staff who willingly offer to supervise or just work with volunteers. If a workshop on supervising volunteers is offered, the number of staff members who sign up to attend would be indicative of staff support. These examples and numbers can be collected and used as part of the evaluation of the program. In the early stages, sometimes the percentage of supporters is not large, but quite often there does become a tipping point where the momentum of support grows.

VOLUNTEER SATISFACTION

Volunteers who are satisfied with their library experience will talk to you, the staff, and their friends. They sell your program. Satisfied volunteers often express a positive feeling of being part of the library team, offer to train other volunteers, and take on tasks that others do not want. Some volunteers will take time to write thank-you notes and comments about how much they enjoy volunteering at the library. Save these notes. In addition, take informal notes about the positive and negative verbal comments you receive. These can be added to your program evaluation file.

Volunteer Program Evaluation

Volunteer Name (optional): _____

Job Description: _____ Department _____

	Poor	Fair	Good	Excellent
To what extent did the description of your job represent what needed to be done?				
To what extent do you feel your job utilizes your talents and satisfies your reasons for becoming a library volunteer?				
To what extent do you feel you are receiving support from your supervisor?				
Rate your relationships with team members:				
To what extent do you feel that the paid staff in this organization have acknowledged and appreciated your volunteer contribution?				

Things I have particularly enjoyed about being a library volunteer:
_____
_____
_____

Suggestions for enhancing the program:
_____
_____
_____

Additional Comments:
_____
_____
_____

Sample 9-2. **Volunteer Evaluation of the Program**

Volunteers who have a mildly positive experience are not likely to discuss their feelings. They may be generally satisfied with their assignment because they feel their skills are being used to serve their community. To get a response from one of these individuals, you may need to conduct personal interviews or send out a short survey to capture their comments. Monitoring volunteer satisfaction on a regular basis is always a good way to maintain the quality of your program. You can use or modify sample 9-2 to obtain feedback from volunteers for your program.

When a program seems disorganized with no volunteer orientation, limited staff support, little or no training, vague task expectations, negative staff comments, no assigned workspace, or no place for personal items, negative feelings often translate into increased absenteeism and the loss of volunteers. This too can be a basis for evaluating your program. Attempt to talk to these volunteers. They may provide you with information for reevaluating your policies, procedures, communications, and staff/volunteer relationships. In the end, you may find that overall you have a highly satisfied group with the exception of one department, or one task area, or one or two troublesome individuals. Although small in number, the negative individuals may complain to anyone who will listen rather than find other volunteer opportunities in the community.

INDIVIDUAL PROGRAM SATISFACTION

Keeping statistics and writing up successful volunteer projects gives your program additional validity. You can keep track of the number of volunteers, types of volunteers, their hours, and specific project statistics. At the end of a major project, you can celebrate by giving the volunteers special recognition such as a small party or computer-generated bookmarks with the title of the project. By targeting these individuals, you give them additional encouragement and satisfaction to continue on.

VOLUNTEER SERVICES MANAGER SATISFACTION

Establishing multiple evaluation criteria, such as those in the Volunteer Program Evaluation Checklist (sample 9-1), is one way to keep a balanced perspective on your program. By shifting away from one criterion (e.g., only counting the number of volunteers or the number of volunteer hours), you can help yourself and others appreciate and evaluate the impact of your program throughout the entire library organization.

PART 2 | # **VOLUNTEER RECRUITMENT**

| # VOLUNTEER MOTIVATION

THERE IS A tricky relationship between the personal benefits felt by volunteers (see section 3) or seen from the viewpoint of the volunteer program and the underlying motivations of the desire to volunteer in a public library. Almost all of our personal actions subsume multiple motivations—some articulated and others hidden, even to us. We also reinterpret our motivations in terms of positive and negative life events and later reassign different motivations to our earlier actions. This is just part of our everyday lives.

Motivational experts have long distinguished between intrinsic motivations, such as the internal sense of satisfaction we derive from doing something we enjoy, and the extrinsic motivations derived from external sources, such as getting a service reward. In your position as volunteer services manager, you spend a lot of time interviewing new volunteers, conversing with established ones, and listening to those who have life challenges. In these discussions, if you listen closely, you will discover just how fluid personal motivations are and how these are used to interpret and reinterpret the reasons for volunteering at the library.

For instance, during the initial interview a volunteer might state that in the spirit of giving back to the community he wants to volunteer and does not expect or want any rewards. All the same, if by accident you omit him from the annual volunteer recognition luncheon or the list of volunteers who receive formal thank-you letters from the library director, you will likely have an upset volunteer on your hands. You may not even hear this directly from him, but indirectly from a staff member or another volunteer.

Then there is the volunteer who sees the library as a "fun place to volunteer" and later finds that her personal organizational abilities are put to good use, and this intrinsic satisfaction keeps her motivated to come back month after month.

The unwritten, yet important agreements between the volunteer and you and the library about what each expects to give and receive are referred to as a psychological contract. When your expectations about what the volunteer will bring to the library—a certain level of commitment, performance, pleasantness—and the volunteer's expectations about what the library experience will provide are both met, then there is a good chance for a successful relationship. When a software-literate volunteer expecting and motivated to build up a resume during a layoff is assigned by the supervising staff the duty of unloading the book and video drops, he may well feel that the psychological contract with you and library has been broken. That same person reassigned to work with the library webmaster on new volunteer services web pages would likely feel that the psychological agreement was being upheld.

Life situations change motivations of volunteers, and changing motivations change life situations. As the volunteer services manager, you have to accept the fact that you are at the crossroads of many peoples' lives, and some of their motivations for staying or leaving are outside your grasp.

When the explicit reasoning for being a volunteer is not an obligation to a school or service group, a great variety of reasons are given by potential new volunteers: opportunities to serve the community in a leadership capacity; giving back to the community by helping others; enriching family life; time away from the demands of home and work; acquiring or enhancing job skills; personal enrichment; seeking a career in libraries. For most people you can accept these statements at face value, not knowing if these are the "real" motivations for desiring to volunteer at the library, for most of the stated reasons can also apply to many other community service organizations. Some volunteers talk about their "love of books" or "desire to share the love of reading with others." Others describe an idyllic sense of the libraries of their past as quiet settings, not fully comprehending the high level of activity required to operate today's public libraries.

Successful volunteer recruiting and placement require that you respect the wide range of reasons people give for volunteering and accept that everyone interviewed has a set of mixed motivations, some of which you may never be privy to.

COMMUNITY LEADERSHIP

Individuals who feel the need to become active in government and make changes in the community and political system can feel comfortable in a library setting. Their need to influence change can be satisfied if they work as a library trustee or board member. These individuals also may be adept at fundraising or working as a liaison in the community to help sway the electorate in future decisions involving the library. They feel comfortable working with the library director and other library trustees. You may be able to steer these types of volunteers to high-level administrative and public positions.

Others with similar political and persuasive talents may be at a time in their lives when they just want to be a regular volunteer in your program. Recognize that they probably still have excellent managerial skills, often accompanied by talents in diplomacy—and this may be just the type of person you need to supervise larger volunteer projects. They may also serve you as a "sounding board," to brainstorm and draw upon their often extensive experience.

HELPING OTHERS

The desire to help others and to give back to the community are often the stated reasons people volunteer. These reasons are backed by strong social motivations. For some volunteers, this means working one-on-one with an individual, as in a literacy program; for others, it is working with a fun group that allows free-flowing conversations during assigned tasks. Some of these volunteers might be described as warm and caring, others as enthusiastic and gregarious. Translate these personalities into volunteering at the library: an enthusiastic and outgoing volunteer assigned to a young adult department can be a good match; a volunteer who likes small groups can read stories at skilled nursing facilities while representing the library.

ENRICHING FAMILY LIFE

The library can be a good place for families to volunteer. Job opportunities for them include the delivery of books to retirement communities, working together to present a storytime, shelving books, or "adopting a shelf" in a favorite subject area. Children learn by example. Providing children the opportunity to help the library with their family as a way of helping their community also encourages a positive self-image of serving and assisting others in a learning environment.

Volunteering in the library can also give children a love of books, a desire for lifelong learning, and a respect for libraries. Providing these kinds of opportunities for families is good community relations and helps build a strong customer base for the future.

TIME AWAY FROM HOME AND WORK

A young parent can find some time away from her children and other responsibilities by volunteering at the library nights or weekends when childcare is available. Similarly, a caregiver for an elderly parent or someone who works full-time can use library volunteer time as a necessary respite from daily routines. Many of these volunteers often want a stable and consistent set of duties that are important to the library but routine in nature, giving them a mental break from the demands of their everyday lives.

Sorting and shelving books and magazines and cleaning DVDs are the types of tasks that bring people in contact with others and do not require extensive training or time commitments. These are important considerations for individuals who want to volunteer but have family or work obligations.

ACQUIRING OR ENHANCING JOB-RELATED SKILLS

For individuals who are computer literate and conscientious, there are increasing opportunities to use their skills. Volunteers can help with computer training and assist with catalog and other online searches, thereby supplementing the work of library staff in providing personalized assistance to customers. These are well-established jobs for volunteers. Further, volunteers can hone their computer skills by working with word processing, spreadsheet, or database management packages. Thanks to advances in wireless and high-speed connectivity, such volunteers may be able to work from anywhere in the library building, from the local coffee shop, or in the comfort of their home. They can identify books for the homebound, beta check new flash videos, and identify broken links on the library website, to name a few possibilities.

Volunteers can also gain marketable job skills not directly related to computer technology. A volunteer who is thinking about starting a home business can accompany and assist a knowledgeable library marketing staff member and learn about presentation techniques that work in the community. She can also learn what works with various targeted populations. In some instances, she might be able to do a small part of the presentation about the library and could gain additional confidence about being in front of various groups.

PERSONAL ENRICHMENT

There are periods in life when people feel their discretionary time and activities are not providing a sense of personal fulfillment, challenge, or new experience. Some may say they just need to "get out of the house," and for these people library volunteering affords a wide range of new types of tasks and duties. Even the more mundane tasks, such as preparing downloaded clip art for children's storytimes or sorting used books, can be beneficial for someone wanting something different to do.

SEEKING A CAREER IN LIBRARIES

For many library staff members, their work in a library organization is their second or third career. This diversity of prior work experience enriches the library environment. Some staff career histories point to prior library volunteering as young adults or adults. Thus, there are community members who want to do library volunteer work to either seek a professional or paraprofessional library career or determine if they should choose such a career.

STAFF EXPECTATIONS

Missing from this section on volunteers' motivations are the numerous and diverse expectations of staff members. Briefly, staff expectations toward volunteers range from being negative and mildly hostile, to some level of toleration and acceptance, and finally to positive and enthusiastic. We address these expectations in section 3.

| # VOLUNTEER NEEDS ASSESSMENT

BEFORE BEGINNING THE recruitment process, you as volunteer services manager must determine your library's need for volunteers. One way is simply to ask the staff through an interview/conversation process. Another way is to use a short needs assessment questionnaire tailored to your library. Alternatively, you can identify opportunities where others might not be looking by reviewing the list of tasks and duties volunteers currently do for other libraries. You can also ask your counterparts at other library systems how they use volunteers.

The importance of a thorough volunteer needs assessment cannot be overlooked. It saves you time, improves the quality of your program, encourages staff participation, and fosters volunteer retention.

NEEDS ASSESSMENT QUESTIONNAIRE

Determining a need for volunteers is not as straightforward as it sounds. Staff members who are overtly or covertly negative to volunteers generally see them as unnecessary to the operation of their departments. They point out, with good reason, that one or more of the staff members would have to take time away from their job to train them and additional time to supervise and monitor their performance, and if errors occur they have to redo the volunteers' work. These staff members are unlikely to complete a needs assessment questionnaire because they see no reason to do so. Sharing a few case examples of similar-size libraries using volunteers successfully in the same type of department might help to loosen up their thinking, but it will not likely change their opinions at this stage.

Staff members who are neutral or have not given the topic much thought, and those who are positive toward volunteers, will likely be willing to talk with you or complete your needs assessment questionnaire.

In larger libraries, the needs assessment is determined at the department, branch, or system level. The larger the library, the more formal the needs assessment must be to prevent misunderstandings in your volunteer recruitment, selection, and placement efforts.

A short questionnaire can be designed to determine the need for volunteers, as in sample 11-1. It can be e-mailed to all department and branch managers to determine what they see as their current volunteer requirements. There may be some resistance to completing the form. Some managers may feel that by answering these questions they are pointing out personal or departmental deficiencies or limiting their ability to get additional paid staff positions. For these and other reasons, it may be wise to follow up with a telephone call to discuss their concerns.

Needs Assessment

Department: _____ **Date:** _____

1. What kinds of responsibilities do you have that can be delegated to volunteers to free yourself for higher-priority tasks?
2. What library services would you like to provide the community that you cannot because of time commitments?
3. What library services would you like to provide to the community that you cannot because of the lack of individuals with specific skills or training?
4. What concerns or questions do you have about involving volunteers in your department?
5. What information would you need from the library administration before you felt comfortable using volunteers?
6. What information would you need from the volunteer services manager before you felt comfortable using volunteers?
7. In what other areas or departments of the library do you think volunteers would be most effective? Why?
8. Any other comments?

Sample 11-1. **Needs Assessment Questionnaire**

NEEDS ASSESSMENT INTERVIEWS

The process for assessing the need for volunteers can be introduced at administrative and staff meetings, where you can answer general questions and suggestions can be exchanged. These meetings can be followed with small, informal interviews to acquire specific information about possible volunteer positions.

A variation to this approach is to have the unit head invite key staff members to participate in the interview process. Managers and staff working together to determine the need for volunteers in the department allows everyone to buy into your program.

As you meet with each department, be sure that during this initial phase your questions are specific and directed toward the volunteer tasks. For example, find out how many volunteers are needed and if there is a workplace for each one. Also, is there a time of day that is better for training volunteers (e.g., the hour before the library opens). How many volunteers can be trained at one time? What is the minimum number of hours needed per day, week, or month, and how many shifts? Do supervising staff need to be present while the volunteers are working? What are the physical, educational, and training requirements for each job? Do the jobs require strong attention to detail when interruptions can lead to errors? Which jobs have completion dates, and which ones are continuous or sporadic? These are important questions that need answers. You may have to do some follow-up after the initial department meeting. Your challenge at this point is to design workable volunteer positions with clear reporting relationships from the suggested list.

Review your list in terms of volunteer time requirements. Most volunteer shifts are in two-hour increments (e.g., two hours or four hours) or the length of time needed for a special event. Ongoing tasks can usually accommodate different blocks of time, because one volunteer can pick up where another has left off. Some project tasks may reoccur every few months, such as a quarterly reading program for children, and other jobs can be once-a-year events such as weeding the collection. A two-hour shift might be restricted to a couple of closely related tasks; a four-hour shift could entail diverse tasks to give the volunteer a variety of duties.

The more information you have during the needs assessment period, the easier your recruitment, selection, and placement process will be. Be flexible in your approach to each volunteer position. A manager may want a project done next week, but unless you have a volunteer already in mind it may take you a week or longer to find the right person. During your discussions with the manager, you may want to negotiate volunteer work schedules and completion dates to give yourself enough leeway to recruit appropriate volunteers.

Once you have written your notes or collated the needs assessment information into preliminary job descriptions or task lists, send a copy to the managers before you begin to recruit to make sure the information is correct and to clarify any gray areas.

VOLUNTEER JOB POSITIONS

Examples of volunteer positions currently being performed in public libraries are listed in box 11.1. In addition, box 11.2 lists specific positions filled by young adult volunteers. These lists are based on our review of library websites and are not intended to be exhaustive. You can use them as a framework for expanding your knowledge of what volunteers are doing and for assisting staff members who are skeptical about the use of volunteers. Box 11.1 also shows potential volunteer positions for the future, especially in the areas of outreach to underserved populations, literacy programs, and virtual volunteering.

One striking feature of our review is the great diversity and combination of tasks that fall under essentially the same volunteer positions. The old argument that small libraries need their volunteers to take on more library duties than the larger, professionally run libraries no longer holds. Properly trained volunteers take on many library jobs in both large and small libraries. In your position as the volunteer services manager, when you hear that volunteers cannot do a task it is not likely true.

The general headings shown in the tables may fall under library departments different from those in your library. Similar tasks may be duplicated within different departments. Duplicate job titles that overlap for the same volunteer position are shown in parentheses. Most of the listings are for volunteers to assist library staff with the identified duties.

Young Adult Jobs

Box 11.2 identifies specific volunteer positions and tasks accomplished by young adults in public libraries. Some libraries specify high school age only, others thirteen to eighteen years, and a few go down to eleven or twelve years. Junior volunteers start at age ten. Alternatively, in lieu of age categories, some libraries list school grades instead, or both.

Virtual Volunteering

Although computer skills are the foundation for a large number of virtual volunteer positions, it is somewhat surprising that our library website review

Adult Services Positions
Adult program assistant
AuthorSpeak assistant
Book discussion group leader
Book talk host
Citizenship teacher
Instructor of knitting class
Intercultural arts instructor
Language interpreter
Poetry contest party assistant
Program assistant
Resume building assistant
Scrapbooking leader
Special adult event volunteer

Administrative Services Positions/Tasks
Assist with editing, mailings, and statistical reports
Assist with data entry, web development
Assist with word processing, photocopying, writing
Office assistant
Receptionist

Advocacy
Advocacy speaker for libraries at public hearings and meetings
Campaigner writes letters, sends e-mail to elected officials, newspapers, letters to the editor, community online newsletters, television and radio stations

Book Store/Book Sales Positions
Book sale volunteers

Children Services Positions
Book cart organizer
Children's area organizer
Children's arts/craft instructor
Children's book maintenance
Children's desk assistant
Children's program assistant

Children's room study monitor
Children's tour leader
Cleanup volunteer
Craft preparations volunteer
Crafty creations instructor
Face painter
Gift processing volunteer
Preschool storyteller
Program and craft assistant
Puppet repair volunteer
Read Aloud/storytime volunteer
Researcher—children's stories
Researcher—media materials
Shelf reader of children's picture books
Shelf reader of juvenile nonfiction
Story program volunteer
Storytime assistant
Summer reading program assistant
Summer reading program volunteer

Circulation Services Positions and Tasks
Adopt-a-Shelf as a family
Branch assistant
Checks books/materials in on computer
Circulation desk assistant
Circulation volunteer assistant
Displaying materials
Donations sorter
Filing old magazine copies in storage boxes
Notifying customers who have books on hold
Pick items from "holds lists"
Pick up books from reading areas
Place security strips in new magazines
Processing materials for checkout
Processing paperbacks
Pull books reserved by patrons online
Pull expired hold items
Search for items on trace status
Search for lost books
Separate magazines

Box 11.1. **Current Volunteer Positions in Public Libraries**

Shelf dusting and cleaning volunteer
Shelf maintenance volunteer
Shelf shifting
Shelver (Page)—books
Shelver (Page)—media—DVDs and
   CDs
Sort returned materials
Staff volunteer assistant
Weed magazines

Computers Assistance Positions–One-on-One
Roving technical assistants
Techno host
Technology aide (coach) (tutor)

Computer Training Lab Positions–Classes
Computer assistant (aide)
Cyber seniors' assistant
Cyber seniors' trainer
Trainer (teacher, facilitator, instructor)

Facilities and Maintenance Positions
Handyman
Inside plant care (green thumb)
   volunteer
Maintenance assistant—washes
   tables, chairs, glass doors
Recycling volunteer
Yard and gardens assistant

Information Desk and Display Positions
Art, exhibit, display assistant
Display coordinator
Display designer
Organizer of community information
Public tour leader
Self-checkout assistant
Telephone receptionist
Welcome desk greeter

Government Documents Positions
Government documents assistant

Literacy Services Positions
Bilingual learning center volunteer
Homeschooled children Spanish
   teacher
Language instructor
Literacy tutors—English as a second
   language
Literacy tutors—English as primary,
   but reading below 9th grade level
Literacy—family reading programs
   volunteer
Reading aloud to children (English)
   volunteer
Reading aloud to children (foreign
   language) volunteer
Spanish language tutor
Spanish/bilingual teacher
"Talk time" facilitator (teacher's aide)
   English conversation groups

Local History/Genealogy Services Positions
Archivist assistant—compiles obituary
   data, catalogs photographs,
   creates photograph lists, reshelves
   materials
Genealogy assistant
Local history assistant
Office assistant—scans materials,
   photocopying, data entry
Oral history transcriber

Marketing Services Positions
Ambassador (community outreach/
   event representative)
Fundraising volunteer
Grant analyst assistant
Grant writer
Graphic art specialist
Library mascot
Marketing assistant

Office assistant—maintains media logs and clippings, writes and gathers information for press releases, edits
Photographer
Promotional publications assistant
Publicity assistant
Special events volunteer
Videographer

Media/AV Services/ Technology Positions

AV equipment assistant
Special collections equipment assistant

Outreach Services Positions

Assistant project director—virtual library, senior center
Audiobook reader
Books-while-you-wait delivery volunteer—provides children's books in waiting rooms
Computer aid—virtual library, senior center
Homebound delivery volunteer
Prison library volunteer
Read-Aloud to children and moms in women's shelters
Reader-Aloud to seniors volunteer
Senior programs volunteer
Technology for teens in transitions volunteer—Internet training for incarcerated juveniles
Wagging tails volunteer—provides service dogs for children to read to

Reference Services Positions

Bibliography compilation assistant
Language interpreter
Newspaper indexer
Reference assistant

Reference patrol volunteer
Subject bookmarks assistant

Technical Services Positions and Tasks

Add/remove stickers from books
Bar coder
Book detailer
Cleaner—DVDs, music CDs, and books
Comparing reports to materials on shelves
Creates databases
Materials processing assistant
Mender
Place sensitive materials in plastic covers
Repairing/replacing DVD cases
RFI project assistant
Sorter—boxes donated materials for book sale
Technical services assistant
Unpacking new books

Virtual Volunteers (Cyber-Volunteers) Positions

Beta tester—test new technologies for library
Promoter—group tours

Volunteer Services Positions

Administrative assistant—data entry, spreadsheet, databases
Program assistant
Special project assistant
Volunteer online newsletter assistant

Youth (Teen Services) Positions

Homework helper—teen lounge
Movie host
Youth bulletin board volunteer
Youth outreach assistant

Box 11.1. **Current Volunteer Positions in Public Libraries *(continued)*** identified only two public libraries that listed virtual or cyber volunteer opportunities. One library offered a virtual position to promote group tours, the other was for beta testing new library online software products.

Specialty libraries also take advantage of virtual volunteers. The Indiana State Library uses them for genealogy research and for reviewing the accuracy of talking book recordings. Victim Assistance Online (www.vaonline.org/rvolunteers.html) uses academically qualified virtual research volunteers to search in specific subject areas for online articles and bring them to the attention of staff members; its website describes the benefits of volunteering and provides a research volunteer job description and application procedure. The Senior Net Virtual Volunteering Prison Library Project collects and distributes books to prison librarians (www.seniornet.org, see "Book Donation Initiative").

Virtual volunteering is not a new concept, but the use of this type of volunteering in public libraries has not evolved, so the potential lies in the future; *The Virtual Volunteering Guidebook,* by Susan J. Ellis and Jayne Cravens, is one useful source. The guidebook and associated website offer useful suggestions on types of virtual volunteers and relevant content information about virtual volunteer programs. It has no library examples, but many of the virtual volunteer positions are related to libraries.

Rapid, widespread use of high-speed Internet connections and wireless networks has set the stage for the expansion of virtual volunteers. WiFi and 3G networks for smartphones allow people to stay connected almost everywhere they go. At the same time, libraries have been incorporating into their website upgrades software that provides fast uploads of graphics, text, video, and audio. For those age forty and under, carrying a laptop or smartphone is all they need to be "at their office" and connected to the world, whether working at home, at a coffee shop, in an airport terminal waiting for a flight, or at their local library. Similar to telecommuting by corporate employees, virtual volunteers can fill useful functions for libraries.

Libraries now encourage customers to use online library resources for research, placing holds, requesting interlibrary loans, or checking their accounts. Colleges and universities have developed online academic programs. Both of these sectors have increased the number of people who are computer literate.

Virtual library volunteering can use the talents of many different individuals. These are just a few categories:

- Disabled with mobility problems yet able to volunteer out of their homes
- Family caregivers required to stay close to home

- Computer-literate, semiretired seniors
- Busy people who want to use computer knowledge but not travel to the library
- Individuals who operate web-based home businesses and have blocks of time available to help out
- People who are temporarily homebound due to medical conditions

Volunteer positions can be blended between on-site time and virtual time. For example, a volunteer who works for the department that delivers books to the homebound can select books as a virtual function and then pull the books from the shelves, check them out, and deliver. Marketing volunteer assistants can work on small program pieces, share these online for staff input, and attend an on-site meeting to finalize the project. A blended volunteer can be on-site to videotape a children's puppet show, edit and transmit the video from home to the library, and finally upload it to the children's services web page. This is an exciting service for children who have extended illnesses or disabilities and cannot get to the library. In a similar manner, a volunteer can create a podcast or video podcast to upload to the library website.

Adding to these few library examples, box 11.3 suggests a list of virtual opportunities for libraries in the future. Each task can be a distinct virtual position or be combined into a larger job position. Job description requirements would include keeping the supervising staff person updated on a regular basis.

Virtual volunteer recognition can be simulcast at volunteer recognition events as streamed video by a webcam through a library computer network or through a local service provider on the Internet. Pictures of virtual volunteers, backgrounds, acknowledgments, and awards can be handled just as they are for on-site volunteers.

This is an exciting new area for library volunteer services, but there are cautions to be taken. Experts on virtual volunteering warn against starting a stand-alone virtual volunteer program. You should have a well-running on-site program with administrative policies in place before initiating jobs for virtual volunteering. Exploring these new kinds of opportunities with staff members may initially produce negative reactions, but focusing on one or two virtual positions and getting some willingness to try for a period of time are a good way to identify and work out any key differences between on-site and virtual volunteer staffing issues. Virtual volunteers, including some who may be existing volunteers, do not take away from paid staff positions. They supplement and expand staff capabilities to serve the community. Furthermore, virtual volunteers do not compete for tight library workspace.

Two decades ago, many managers in the corporate world had a difficult time allowing employees to work away from the office. In their mind, daily

Youth (Teen) Advisory Board (Committee) (Council)

Assist editing a literacy magazine for teens

Assist with website content on youth and children's pages

Box donated books

Create and perform in videos (e.g., a library's YouTube video)

Label donated paperback books

Perform clerical tasks

Prepare teen book reviews for display or posting on library teen web page

Program participation

Provide program suggestions to teen services librarian

Teen book critic

Teen outreach

Write and read book reviews or public service announcements for radio, podcasts, and cable television

Children's Department (Young Adult)

Answer the phone

Assist in creating craft projects

Assist teens and families signing up for summer reading program

Assist with bulletin boards

Assist with programs

Clean board books

Clean up craft stations

Create displays

Cut storytime shapes—Ellison die cuts

Distribute prizes to children

Greet children

Homework helper for children in grades 2–5

Keep statistics

Make flannel board pieces or puppets

Mentor a child during read-aloud sessions

Prepare crafts for children's events

Program assistant

Provide computer assistance to elementary students

Provide computer assistance to middle school students

Read to small groups of children

Reading buddy (read and listen to children read)

Record the time children spend reading

Register children for summer reading program

Review materials

Sort and organize materials

Sort supplies

Summer reading program assistant

General Library Services (Young Adults)

Assist with special projects

Clean DVDs and CDs

Clean materials

Clerical support

Help customers locate materials

Make fun slideshows for teen center

Mend books

Process new books

Repair minor spine damage

Replace spine labels

Shelf reading

Shelve holds

Shelve videos

Update online subject lists

Wash and replace book jackets

Box 11.2. **Current Young Adult Volunteer Positions and Tasks**

face time was equivalent to productive time. That is not the case today. There are also library managers who believe that, if the volunteers are not on-site, they are not being useful. However, as these volunteers produce the required results and maintain contact with their supervisors on a regular basis, there

Reference Services

Check for broken links on library web
pages
Conduct focused online searching
Research current awareness articles
Review and update community
organization links and information
Review timeliness of library website
information
Translate documents

Marketing

Design and edit marketing pieces and
brochures
Develop fundraising contacts
Develop multimedia presentations
Set up school and community group
tours
Write and review grant proposals

Advocacy

Post information on local and
legislative issues
Prepare e-mail alerts
Track legislation

Volunteer Services Administration

Collect and post digital pictures of
volunteers

Edit brochures
Edit volunteer newsletter
Organize online meetings
Post volunteer opportunities online
Prepare online orientation and special
training tutorials
Provide online mentoring of new
virtual volunteers
Visit homebound electronically

Adult Services

Facilitate online book clubs

Youth Services

Post online book reviews by teens on
website

Computer Web Assistance

Beta test new library web software
Design streaming videos
Library web page consumer
reviewers—reviews for errors, user
friendliness, etc.
Test the library website for
accessibility for those with
disabilities

Box 11.3.   **Potential Virtual Library Volunteer Positions**

will be less hesitation to use volunteers virtually. You may also discover that staff members who do not like being put in charge of on-site volunteers may be the ones most receptive to virtual volunteers, because most communication will be electronic.

There may be volunteer services managers in local community organizations who are using virtual volunteers and can give you tips and case examples on how to make your efforts successful. Additionally, websites such as VolunteerMatch (www.volunteermatch.org) can identify local organizations that use virtual volunteers. The convergence of libraries, technology, and communication mobility will make this a growth area for library volunteering.

| # JOB DESIGN

JOB DESIGN IS an organizational process that combines a set of tasks and requirements into a job package that you can use to recruit, evaluate, and supervise volunteers. It includes the formal job description, the skills and characteristics required for the job, and the advertising recruitment announcement and evaluation criteria. Whether you plan a formal and detailed job design or something informal, take time to think about each volunteer job and time requirements before spending time writing it up.

In this early phase, work for volunteers is usually instigated by one of three sources: staff members who have a project or task, potential volunteers who have a specialized skill you can use, or work that needs doing badly enough to become obvious to even the casual customer.

Solid advanced planning and organization are the cornerstones of a good volunteer program. Staff should understand that they cannot get volunteer help immediately on demand. A staff request for volunteer help with little or no notice may go unfilled; unless you happen to have a "general purpose" volunteer with available time, you obviously cannot meet such requests. To avoid this problem, work with the staff to organize potential projects or tasks ahead of time.

In this section we review the key points to consider as you begin the process of designing jobs for your volunteer program.

TASK COMPLEXITY AND COORDINATION

Tasks can range from the very simple and routine to the highly involved and complex. A single task such as clipping articles for a pamphlet file can involve hidden complexities in judgment and decision making. Merely handing a pair of scissors to a volunteer and instructing her to cut out articles in the newspapers that relate to local schools involves some judgment on her part. Should she cut out a small article buried in the sports section on the high school wrestling meet? Should she read and mark appropriate articles first so that an another article expected to be preserved on the reverse side of the page is not destroyed?

Even the overtly simple task of shelf maintenance can involve some judgment on the part of a volunteer. Questions such as where to shift books when the shelf is full or how to place large books need to be addressed by staff before the volunteer actually begins to work.

A volunteer position that has many different tasks to complete may be complex but still considered one "job" because each task is related to the same specific goal. A good example is setting up a meeting room that includes microphones, amplifiers, and a computer with a data projector for a PowerPoint presentation. The job requires knowledge of electrical equipment, including computers, and the physical ability to move and set up furniture according to a designated layout. Few new volunteers would have all the experience required in this one example.

Conversely, if a library manager wants to supervise only one "multipurpose" volunteer, this leads to a different type of complexity. This individual may be expected to work on a data entry project, dust the bookshelves, and reshelve the magazines. The skill sets, interests, and primary responsibilities are too diverse for a single volunteer. If you did have someone interested in all three tasks, he would probably prefer one task (e.g., data entry) over others (e.g., dusting stacks), and less desired work might be ignored or sloppily performed. If you pressed such a volunteer about doing all three assigned duties, he might well quit.

Task coordination is an important element in job design. Does the job require working with another volunteer or closely with staff, or is it a relatively isolated function independent of others. A volunteer delivering books to a community center is usually dependent on a staff member to pull and check out the books to be delivered. Thus, two people have to coordinate their efforts to make the outreach program work. A volunteer who distributes program fliers at local schools is free to set her schedule as long as the fliers are handed out by a particular date. She does not need to coordinate with anyone to get her task done.

As you review the subtleties of the tasks and coordination requirements, especially for new positions, be sure to write down any areas that are not clear and review these with the assigned supervising staff member. The information and notes you take become the basis for writing the job description and recruitment announcements.

SKILL SET REQUIREMENTS

It is not uncommon for a highly experienced staff member to flippantly say, "Any dummy can do this job." Years of experience hide the skills necessary to do a task. We all tend to forget what it takes to first learn a task that we now do by rote. A volunteer who has worked in a bookstore may still have to learn a lot to run a no-budget book sale for the library, and an experienced administrative assistant may take a while to learn a different version of software used by the library.

As you design the volunteer jobs, you need to determine the types of skills required for the volunteer to be successful. Tasks such as writing promotional materials or performing online searches each require a level of skill to be successful. Can the supervising staff member explain precisely what skills are required for a task? During your discussion, focus on the skill set and take notes. If you have the time, try to perform the tasks yourself to get a better understanding of the job expectations. It is important to see a total process, from designing a complete job description that can be used to recruit volunteers to final completion of hiring, where both the volunteer and staff member can feel good about the outcome. This is an important part of building a successful volunteer program.

At this stage, your notes on the complexity of the task and coordination requirements may be only a scratch list of the expected procedures to be followed and a list of skills needed. It is important to stay focused on the job's characteristics and avoid stereotyping personality characteristics and types associated with the position. By building on skill sets, you can be a better decision maker later when you have to make recommendations on the volunteers applying for the job.

TRAINING REQUIREMENTS

Training time depends on the complexity of the set of job tasks as defined by the expectations of the supervising staff member. Do not underestimate this time. For some individuals with previous experience, a few minutes of instruction and a quick demonstration are all that are necessary to get started. For example, an elementary school teacher volunteering to put up a bulletin board display for National Library Week will likely understand the directions and intent of the supervising staff member. In this instance, you recruited an individual who is bringing job-specific training to the library, since most elementary school teachers are familiar with designing displays and bulletin boards for their classrooms. However, most new volunteers will not have the level of focused experience that may be required to do what looks like a simple project.

With volunteers working different shifts throughout the days, evenings, and weekends, how will training be accomplished? It is not uncommon that when a new volunteer shows up, everyone is busy and training is left to a staff person or another volunteer who might be least qualified to show the new volunteer what to do. Such training may or may not demonstrate the correct way of doing the tasks. If the supervising staff member is not around, then who does the training?

An important aspect of designing a job is taking into consideration any physical demands such as reaching, bending, or picking up full boxes and the level of safety training required to accomplish the work. Examples include demonstrations on how to push a full cart of books from the technical services processing department to the shelving back room or how to lift and carry boxes of books. In addition to face-to-face demonstration, there are commercial videos and safety handouts that show how to lift, stoop, and so forth. Many of these can be downloaded from safety organizations' websites. It does not take long to provide safety tips and some examples, or to post them in the work area.

In addition to skills and safety training requirements, your notes need to identify the equipment, tools, and solvents related to the task, such as stepping stools, ladders, hammers, garden rakes, lifting equipment, sharp tools, or cleaning chemicals. Remember that most potential volunteers have limited knowledge of the jobs and activities that occur behind the scenes to make a library operate efficiently. Providing this type of information up front is a way to reduce mismatching volunteers with job assignments.

If you are in a multiple branch library system and are fortunate enough to have designated branch volunteer coordinators, you have the opportunity to bring them together for workshops. They can share the challenges they face when matching jobs with volunteers, volunteer training, and general volunteer management issues. You may find that what you thought was a "standard" volunteer job is performed differently at various branches, with some volunteer tasks eliminated ("staff-only duties") and others added.

TIME REQUIREMENTS

Is the job designed for a one-time project, short-term project, ongoing activity, or repeated seasonal event like a summer reading program? There are volunteers who want only a short-term commitment, and a one-time project fits their needs. Most community volunteer assignments are centered on routine, ongoing set of duties vital for everyday operations. In these cases, orientation, training, and job performance are tightly bound together. For people who want consistency in their lives, ongoing tasks may be the best fit.

One way to frustrate new volunteers is to assign tasks that cannot be done within the designed two- or four-hour shifts. Can two full carts of books be shelved within the two-hour shift? It is important to recognize that a new or less experienced volunteer takes longer to complete most tasks than a veteran. The supervising staff member must understand the need for a flexible training period for a new volunteer to become proficient, since this time varies from volunteer to volunteer. A new person may be diligent to do shelf grooming while reshelving materials; another volunteer may just get the books shelved as fast as possible.

In some instances, a short-term project is successful and the supervisor decides to continue it as part of ongoing operations. The volunteer recruited for the first project may have all the skills and interests, but not the commitment, for an ongoing project. The job design has to be modified to reflect this change, and a new volunteer must be found to fill the position.

PERSONAL CHARACTERISTICS

Up to this point in your development of volunteer jobs, identifying volunteer job tasks and duties is relatively objective. A material processing volunteer has to pick up and lift boxes weighing up to 20 pounds onto a worktable, use a sharp knife to open the boxes, stack new books and materials on the "new" book carts, and accurately check packing slips. A shelving volunteer must push 100 pounds of books on wheeled carts and must be able to stand, stretch, and bend to shelve books using Dewey Decimal order. The computer assistant will help the Wednesday morning senior group at the public terminals to search the library catalog, search other libraries' catalogs, place holds, and order interlibrary loan materials.

Assessing the personal characteristics of volunteers during recruitment is definitely more subjective, but nevertheless important for successful placement of volunteers. The material processing volunteer needs to be able to work away from others, work in a relatively small area in a backroom work environment (no office space), have stamina and physical strength every shift to perform the tasks, be open to getting dirty from shipped boxes, enjoy detailed clerical work, be organized to keep track of multiple shipments and lost boxes, and manage time well. At some libraries, this assistant also enters the information on received materials on a computer.

The computer assistant certainly needs computer skills but in addition must have great patience to assist seniors who are not computer adept, be supportive in the learning process, enjoy working with people who may take longer to learn basics, have a willingness to answer the same questions repeatedly, and still stay friendly. There are many computer-literate people who lack some of these personal characteristics and would not be good matches for this particular position.

Assessing personal characteristics in interviews is subjective, but having a staff member list the needed personal characteristics is a good start. This discussion can lead to an agreement on the type of person who can succeed. You can use some of the desired characteristics in your job postings, which allows applicants to self-select themselves out of the position and look for something else. In an interview setting, some people might say they have a lot of physical stamina, since they run or walk every morning, not understanding that opening box after box on their volunteer shift requires a different type of stamina. Others have only worked in office environments and might find volunteering in a backroom work area not to their liking.

ADMINISTRATIVE LEGAL REQUIREMENTS

Your library's policy may be that those who perform certain types of jobs, whether they are paid staff or volunteers, must meet certain administrative legal requirements. The legal component is related to the risk management and potential liability that goes with performing particular library functions. Individuals driving vehicles for the library must produce a valid driver's license, show proof of insurance, and submit a current driving record. In an accident situation, a volunteer's own vehicle insurance would cover the car and injuries, but the library can be held negligent for having a volunteer with a poor driving record perform library driving duties. You would be expected to eliminate volunteers who had too many driving infractions; although every volunteer situation is different, your library administration should specify how many is "too many" before you recruit for such positions. Similarly, volunteers working in the children's department, reading to groups of children off-site, or delivering books to homebound customers may have to agree to background checks to meet your library volunteer policy.

An important administrative legal issue to consider is the physical demands and equipment requirements for a volunteer position. Will the library make reasonable accommodations for a volunteer who has a physical disability? Although individual cases require individual decisions, it would be good to have a policy in your volunteer manual that covers these concerns before advertising your positions.

SECTION 13 | **JOB DESCRIPTIONS**

DO NOT REINVENT the book cart! Volunteers are brought into your library to "support," "enhance" "expand," and "assist" library staff capabilities to serve library customers better. In other words, volunteers perform many of the same tasks as some of the staff members. You can draw upon existing staff job descriptions to write your volunteer descriptions. Whether you are a volunteer services manager writing new position descriptions or refreshing an existing program, it is a good idea to be sure that the job descriptions are accurate for the current hiring conditions. Duties of the past may no longer be performed, and new duties may have been added to the positions over the years.

A volunteer job description is a single document that combines all the pertinent information needed to perform the job. A well-written job description is the basis for recruiting, interviewing, and selecting a volunteer for a particular position. It allows volunteers to decide if they have an interest in and willingness to do the listed tasks and expectations. A job description reduces any misunderstandings about a volunteer's duties and encourages staff acceptance of the volunteers and your program. Having a job description to post on the library website or hand to an applicant gives a sense of importance to the position and commitment by the volunteer.

COMPLEXITY OF JOB DESCRIPTIONS

In the library field, there is a spectrum of voluntary job descriptions, from exceedingly informal to exceedingly formal. The informal, easy-to-understand, plain-English description uses "you" to personalize the statements and employs short paragraphs or bullets to identify the key tasks and time expectations. Job postings in this informal style might use creative job titles to draw people's attention to the jobs. Lincoln (Nebraska) City Libraries use such job titles as "Nose for News" describing the job of organizing newspapers and magazines, "Exercise in the Stacks" is used for a shelving position, and "Early Bird Special" has volunteers searching for items in the stacks off computer lists. Another variation of titling jobs is to convert the library activities into nouns—Book Talker, Shelver, Story Reader, Research Assistant, Circulation Assistant, Computer Trainer, Homework Helper—which reduces the abstractness of the tasks by focusing attention on a volunteer performing the duties.

At the other extreme are the very formal and legalistic job descriptions that set out in precise administrative detail the duties, expectations, and requirements for the position. This style is closely patterned after those for paid staff. If you are part of a city or county library, there may be a requirement that your job descriptions be in the same writing style and format of those of paid staff. These are not reader-friendly descriptions, and they often contain much library jargon that most community volunteer applicants may not understand.

Between these extremes are administrative job descriptions that are written in a formal, business-like style yet are less legalistic. Samples of a whole range of job descriptions are provided at the end of this section.

STRUCTURE OF A JOB DESCRIPTION

A written job description organizes your job notes into a set of titled sections. Typical section headings include job title, supervisor (i.e., supervising staff member), job responsibilities or duties, time commitment per shift, length of time commitment, training, skill requirements, and qualifications. Additional sections can include working conditions, physical requirements, education, age (for youth jobs), language requirements such as bilingual skills, desired personal characteristics, special position requirements (driver license, background check), and location.

If you review the paid staffs' job descriptions, you will find many or most of these same headings. Whether your volunteer job descriptions need to be as complex or as extensive as the staff descriptions is a decision that should be approved by your library administration. Again, in some library city or county jurisdictions you have no choice because this decision is determined by jurisdictional policy.

If you have choice in writing and designing or redesigning job descriptions, you may want to experiment with different styles and get comments from volunteers to determine which design is the most readable and useful. Try to stay away from legal and library jargon as well as long, complicated sentences and abstract descriptions of functions. Keep it simple and to the point. The current trend is to design job descriptions that also can be used as recruitment tools posted on the volunteer services web pages, given as handouts to interested individuals, or placed in a display rack.

INTEGRATING STAFF AND VOLUNTEER JOB DESCRIPTIONS

The volunteer job description usually contains a section on departmental reporting relationship(s), that is, the title of the position to which the volunteer reports. Most of the time, the supervisor is not the volunteer services manager. Therefore, staff members who supervise volunteers should have this function written into their respective job descriptions, thereby reducing the possibility of complaints. This integration of the supervisory function requires cooperation from the library administration or the human resources department responsible for updating staff job descriptions. Here are a few examples from staff job descriptions that include volunteer supervision:

_____ (position title) supervises the duties of library volunteers in the department, including instruction, evaluation, and recommendation for awards and recognition.

_____ (position title) supervises department volunteers so that the library provides better service to the community.

In nonsupervising positions, a statement can be included in the staff job descriptions:

_____ (position title, e.g., Library Assistant I) works with department volunteers to enhance service to the community.

By incorporating such statements into staff position descriptions, you demonstrate the importance of integrating volunteers into the library system. Staff performance appraisals can reflect the degree of a person's success in directing and working with volunteers.

A staff member may ask, "Why should I work with volunteers. What is in it for me?" This is a legitimate question. One immediate benefit is a chance to gain supervisory experience (including additional training), which is often not available in many library positions. This skill can be documented and added to the individual's human resources file and rewarded during the yearly performance appraisal. In addition, supervising skills can be added to a resume. Working with volunteers from diverse backgrounds can also bring different perspectives to a person's job and a chance to meet and work with new people.

USES FOR JOB DESCRIPTIONS

One major use for a job description is to recruit volunteers from the community to your volunteer positions. You can use the job description to create a two- or three-sentence "blurb" that can be posted on your website to advertise volunteer positions. Rather than post the entire job description, which is an option, this shorter blurb allows volunteer applicants to read quickly what types of volunteer positions the library offers. The most user-friendly websites provide an active link from the blurb to the entire job description and then to the volunteer application form.

Another important use is to develop interview questions for each position. The specific requirements noted on the job description can be converted into questions related to applicants' skills, qualifications, time commitment, and so on. Working with the branch volunteer supervising staff, you can develop focused questions that get at the information needed to make a good decision. If you do all the interviewing and selecting of volunteers, then work with the human resources staff to ensure that you ask legally acceptable questions as well as questions that get at volunteer skills and position requirements. Every item on a job description can be used to develop a qualifying question. For example, the job description statement that requires "the ability to access and retrieve computerized information from spreadsheets" can be rephrased in an interview to ask, "What specific experiences have you had using spreadsheets?" If the job requires the volunteer to work independently, you can ask, "In which jobs or volunteer activities did you work without immediate supervision? The follow-up question would be "What were your job duties?"

Another important use of volunteer job descriptions is to help inform the paid staff that volunteers are not being used to take their jobs. Having a staff member review a volunteer job description helps get buy-in and explicitly distinguishes the staff member's position from the volunteer job. In fact, inviting comments and critiques may provide additional insights into the tasks' requirements that can be used to better inform the job description and refocus an interview question. When you have a supportive staff member, the information gained is invaluable for more success of your program. Professional staff members who are not supportive of community volunteers nevertheless are often detail oriented, since this is the nature of the their occupation. If you ask them to critique a written job description, they will likely give you detailed positive and negative comments that can be used for additional clarifying conversations. This is better than placing a volunteer in a setting only to have him "fail" because incomplete information was given about the task requirements. In such a situation, this "failure" is then used by the nonsupportive staff members to justify not using volunteers for the job.

Job descriptions also imply a level of performance expectation, and this can serve as the basis of your volunteer evaluations (see section 27). In most instances, young and adult community volunteers want to do the best jobs they can for you and the library and will work to meet the job expectations. A job description gives you or the supervising staff member a basis to acknowledge the good job volunteers are doing relative to the assigned job description duties. If there are performance problems, the job descriptions can be used as the objective basis for pointing out performance deficiencies, thereby keeping criticism constructive and focused on the performance and not on the volunteer. For example, if a computer aide becomes upset with a customer's inability to "get it," the supervising staff member can point out that the volunteer agreed to be supportive and have patience.

Job descriptions also allow volunteers to ask about and explore other volunteer positions. Once a volunteer becomes a regular and feels comfortable in the library work setting, he has the opportunity to explore other volunteer jobs. If he asks, "What else can I do in the library?" you can direct him to the volunteer services website or show him other position descriptions he might find interesting. Remember to tell the volunteers that, if there are openings, they are handled as part of the library selection process. Some volunteers falsely assume that they are next in line for any volunteer opening.

High School Volunteer, Children's Department

LOCATION: Kenton County Public Library, Erlanger Branch Children's Department

RESPONSIBLE TO: Children's Services Coordinator, or other Children's Department staff member as designated.

JOB RESPONSIBILITIES: The responsibilities for this position will vary from day to day. These tasks may include, but are not limited to, assisting with:

- Preparation, setup, and cleanup of special event programs held in the Children's Department
- Facilitating special event programs held in the Children's Department
- Assisting with special projects like nametag creation, craft preparation, cleaning of toys, removing magazines and books in poor condition, cleaning of books, etc.

TIME REQUIRED: The schedule for this position will vary based upon Department needs. Some weekend and evenings will be required. Minimum shift time is one to two hours, but may go as long as 4 hours.

LENGTH OF COMMITMENT: The amount of volunteer time is to be determined by department need and student's performance.

TRAINING PROVIDED: Discussion of child safety and appropriate behaviors with children who are patrons in the library. Other training as needed.

QUALIFICATIONS, SPECIAL SKILLS REQUIRED, AND RESTRICTIONS
- Students must be in grades 9, 10, 11, or 12.
- Ability to provide friendly, patient service to children aged 0–12 and their families.
- Ability to abide by the policies of the Kenton County Public Library.
- Ability to follow instructions.
- Fine motor coordination is required for some work.
- Ability to lift, bend, stoop, and carry is required for some work.

ACKNOWLEDGMENT
I have read this position description and fully understand the requirements set forth therein. I hereby accept the volunteer position of _____
and agree to perform the identified essential functions in a manner in accordance with Kenton County Public Library's established procedures.

    I understand that my assignment is an unpaid volunteer position and thereby understand that my assignment may be discontinued either by the organization or myself, and such discontinuation can be made with or without notice.

Volunteer's Name (please print)_____

Volunteer's Signature Date _____

Supervisor's Signature Date_____

Sample 13-1. **Position Description: High School Volunteer, Children's Department**

Homework Center Aide

LOCATION OF POSITION: Louisville Public Library
POSITION TITLE: Homework Center Aide, Volunteer
SUPERVISOR: Teen Services Coordinator

JOB RESPONSIBILITIES
- Help guide students in completion of homework assignments and ensure that Homework Center and Library policies are followed

QUALIFICATIONS
- Desire to work with middle- and high-school students
- Effective oral and written communication skills; ability to communicate with teens and adults
- Knowledge of basic math, reading, science, and grammar skills; higher level of skills helpful
- Training or experience as a teacher, tutor, parent or youth volunteer helpful

JOB SUMMARY
- Help students interpret assignments; if requested by a student, review completed assignment(s)
- Talk with students about an approach or method to solve problems related to assignments
- Refer students to appropriate reference materials or a Reference Librarian
- Report any problems to the Supervisor
- Other duties as assigned to provide Homework Center assistance

MATERIAL & EQUIPMENT USED
- Internet computers and Microsoft Office applications
- Library reference materials

WORK ENVIRONMENT & PHYSICAL ACTIVITIES
- Comfortable desk and computer workstation in the well-lit and spacious Homework Center
- Ability to sit for up to two hours and use a computer

TRAINING PROVIDED
- Work with a staff member for approximately two hours
- Informational handouts and written policies

MINIMUM TIME COMMITMENT
- Two hours, one day per week

BENEFITS
- Being part of a team at one of the top libraries in Colorado
- Annual volunteer luncheon or other recognition

If you are interested, please complete a City of Louisville Volunteer Application. These are available at information desks in the Library and on the website. You may return it to the Library in person, by mail, or fax.

Once your application is received, the supervisor will contact you to discuss the position and your qualifications and availability.

Branch Library Storyteller

RESPONSIBLE TO: Branch Supervisor

JOB RESPONSIBILITIES: Read stories, play games, and do simple craft projects for children attending story hours at branch libraries.

TIME REQUIRED: 1 hour per week (Plus setup time)

LENGTH OF COMMITMENT: 3–6 months

TRAINING PROVIDED: Orientation and instruction provided by Branch Staff (volunteer will read from preselected kits that include stories, finger plays, crafts, and filmstrips).

QUALIFICATIONS, SPECIAL SKILLS REQUIRED, and RESTRICTIONS: Ability to work with preschool children, good voice for reading to children. Flexible personality and creative traits desirable. Must be dependable. Ability to read 10-point type. Ability to tolerate dust, mold, etc., accumulated on books. Ability to lift up to 40 pounds. Knowledge of library policies and procedures.

Sample 13-3. **Position Description: Branch Library Storyteller**

Children's Center Volunteer

RESPONSIBLE TO: Center Head or Designated Center Staff

JOB RESPONSIBILITIES: Sort bookshelves and carts and shelves; check media for media materials; put CDs and DVDs in alphabetical order; straighten bookshelves; put chairs away; prepare crafts; stamp withdrawn books; straighten magazines; pick up books; sharpen pencils and replace paper at computer stations.

TIME REQUIRED: 3 hours per week

LENGTH OF COMMITMENT: Ongoing

TRAINING PROVIDED: Orientation and instruction provided by Center Staff.

QUALIFICATIONS, SPECIAL SKILLS REQUIRED, and RESTRICTIONS: Ability to work with preschool children, flexibility in schedule, attention to detail. Ability to sort materials in alphabetical and/or Dewey Decimal order. Ability to access, input, and retrieve information from a computer. Ability to bend to floor level and reach a height of 75 inches. Ability to push movable carts loaded to a maximum of 75 pounds. Ability to read 10-point type. Ability to tolerate dust, mold, etc., accumulated on books. Ability to lift up to 40 pounds. Knowledge of library policies and procedures.

Sample 13-4. **Position Description: Children's Center Volunteer**

Children's Center Summer Reading and Game Volunteer

RESPONSIBLE TO: Center Head or Designated Center Staff

JOB RESPONSIBILITIES: Understands the way the Summer Reading Program works and explains it simply to children. Aids children in moving across the "game" board and in understanding other special features regarding the game. Shelves returned books.

TIME REQUIRED: 2–4 hours per week

LENGTH OF COMMITMENT: 2 months in summer

TRAINING PROVIDED: Orientation and instructions provided by Center Staff.

QUALIFICATIONS, SPECIAL SKILLS REQUIRED, and RESTRICTIONS: Ability to work with preschool children; flexibility in schedule and attention to detail. Ability to sort materials in alphabetical and/or Dewey Decimal order. Ability to bend to floor level and reach a height of 75 inches. Ability to push movable carts loaded to a maximum of 100 pounds. Ability to read 10-point type. Ability to tolerate dust, mold, etc., accumulated on books. Ability to lift up to 40 pounds. Knowledge of library policies and procedures.

Sample 13-5. **Position Description: Children's Center Summer Reading and Game Volunteer**

Administrative Assistant Volunteer

RESPONSIBLE TO: Department Manager or Designated Center Staff

JOB RESPONSIBILITIES: Works with book orders. Alphabetizes and word processes special lists. Types and replaces labels and color coding tape as needed. Adds or updates computer records to department database. Assists in processing withdrawn materials. Photocopies, types, files, and does other clerical tasks as needed.

TIME REQUIRED: Minimum of 3 hours per week

LENGTH OF COMMITMENT: 3 months

TRAINING PROVIDED: Orientation and instructions provided by Center Staff.

QUALIFICATIONS, SPECIAL SKILLS REQUIRED, and RESTRICTIONS: Ability to sort and organize materials in alphabetical and/or Dewey Decimal order; word processing knowledge. Ability to bend to floor level and reach a height of 75 inches. Ability to read 10-point type. Ability to tolerate dust, mold, etc., accumulated on books and materials. Ability to lift up to 40 pounds. Skill in operation of office machines and equipment. Knowledge of library automation.

Sample 13-6. **Position Description: Administrative Assistant Volunteer**

Shelver

RESPONSIBLE TO: Circulation Department Supervisor or Designated Staff

JOB RESPONSIBILITIES: Sort, shelve, or file library materials such as books, magazines, newspapers, DVDs, CDs, AV materials, microform, or other media.

TIME REQUIRED: Minimum of 3 hours per week

LENGTH OF COMMITMENT: Minimum of 3 months or ongoing

TRAINING PROVIDED: Orientation by Volunteer Coordinator and instruction in appropriate system by designated Center Staff.

QUALIFICATIONS, SPECIAL SKILLS REQUIRED, and RESTRICTIONS: Ability to bend to floor level and reach a height of 75 inches. Ability to push movable carts loaded to a maximum of 100 pounds. Ability to read 10 point type. Ability to tolerate dust, mold, etc., accumulated on books and materials. Ability to lift up to 40 pounds. Skill in operation of office machines and equipment. Knowledge of library automation system.

Sample 13-7. **Position Description: Shelver**

Senior Read-Aloud Program Volunteer

RESPONSIBLE TO: Adult Services Manager or Designated Staff

JOB RESPONSIBILITIES: Read aloud to senior citizens housed in assisted living homes or care centers on a weekly basis. Select appropriate reading selections from library collection or if desired have the library staff make the selections. Record volunteer hours on the volunteer timesheet. Meet informally with staff supervisor or library manager on a regular basis to provide program feedback (at least once every three months).

TIME REQUIRED: Must be able to commit to one hour a week for a minimum of three months.

JOB REQUIREMENTS: Must be dependable and provide own, reliable transportation. Must have a love of reading, a clear loud reading voice, and a desire to share with seniors who are often no longer able to read on their own. Must meet the expectations of the seniors.

TRAINING REQUIREMENTS: Orientation training to the library. Orientation to senior's program and facility.

Sample 13-8. **Position Description: Senior Read-Aloud Program Volunteer**

Spanish Language Tutor

JOB RESPONSIBILITIES: PLCMC seeks volunteer for Spanish language programs. Volunteer will work with 1–5 adult patrons, with sessions lasting 1 hour. Volunteer will train English speakers in conversational Spanish. Lessons will be based upon volunteer expertise but will also depend upon the needs of the students. Subjects can encompass Spanish vocabulary for use in the workplace and commonly used terms for both professional and personal use. Volunteers will be required to dedicate a 90-minute to two-hour time block for setup and cleanup of class materials and for the classtime itself. The Public Library will provide space and will handle program signups. Volunteer will be required to attend an orientation. First program begins July 2009.

TIME REQUIRED: Hours: Flexible—room availability & patron needs will determine hours.

QUALIFICATIONS: This opportunity is available at Morrison, Matthews, and Main Library. Ability to teach and speak Spanish to small groups. Ability to work well independently.

KNOWLEDGE: Proficiency in Spanish and English and, most important, the volunteer must feel comfortable with teaching these skills to patrons. Give sufficient notice (at least one week) if unable to complete a program. Ability to get along well with others and communicate pleasantly and effectively with patrons and library staff.

TRAINING: Attend one-hour volunteer training session at designated branch.

BENEFITS: As Volunteers:

- free parking
- a chance to teach patrons valuable language skills
- gain recognized work experience
- expand your social horizons
- serve in your own community
- help, and be appreciated for it
- contribute to the success of your public library

Sample 13-9. **Position Description: Spanish Language Tutor**

| # REQUISITIONING VOLUNTEERS

VOLUNTEER REQUISITIONING IS the process a department follows to request a volunteer with specific skills and aptitudes from the volunteer office. The process can be initiated informally by a conversation between the department head and the volunteer services manager or formally with the completion of a volunteer requisition or request form.

It is not unusual for a staff member to call you at the last minute to request a volunteer to help with a special project. At times you may feel that staff members are expecting you to be like a temporary employment agency and have volunteers standing by their telephones just waiting for a call. Operating on this basis can lead to false expectations and mismatched volunteers. If you try to respond quickly with a volunteer who is not capable of meeting departmental expectations, you can create negative feelings about using volunteers.

Set up the requisition process as a separate and distinct part of volunteer recruitment. All parties need to accept that there is a period of time between requesting a volunteer and placing a volunteer in a position. There must be some lead time to get a volunteer; the aim is not to find any "warm body" but a community person with the specific kinds of skills and interests that meet the requirements of the job. Certainly, if the need is for a volunteer to fill a well-established position, such as a shelver to help out on weekends, the requisitioning process is relatively easy. In fact, there may be existing volunteers willing to expand their hours for a few months. Quite often a volunteer who has lost a spouse will accept extra volunteer hours.

In an informal requisition system, a library staff member may say to you, "Our afternoon volunteer at the information desk will be moving out of state in two weeks. We need to find a replacement." At this point, you would post a recruitment announcement on the website and on a bulletin board. In a formal system, the department in need of the replacement completes a volunteer requisition form and sends it to you to proceed with the recruitment process.

In either situation, the requisition process initiates the action to recruit a volunteer. This process can be more problematic when you are recruiting for a new volunteer position in a particular department or for an existing position that has been greatly changed. In each of these situations, the job expectations probably have to be renegotiated by you and the current supervising staff member. Before you meet, it is important to use a tentative job description or have the staff member list initial job duties to serve as a basis for discussion and agreement. Even if the new volunteer duties are subject to change, volunteer applicants should be told, honestly, about possible changing duties in this new position during the initial interview. This is important for the success of the volunteer experience. You do not want volunteers to feel that you told them one thing about the job and then they are asked to do something very different.

Perhaps a suburban library needs a volunteer to collate and staple a large supply of customer handouts. The workstation is in the copy room with a telephone that has six lines. One department manager thinks it would be useful for the volunteer to answer the telephone during the extended monthly afternoon meetings. She is willing to write a short script to help the volunteer correctly answer the busy incoming lines. In the requisitioning process for this position, a clear description of the mix of volunteer skills is important. Some people might enjoy putting booklets together but not have good telephone skills, or they may enjoy telephone work but lack the patience to assemble booklets neatly and accurately. If the job requirements are not clearly described, then getting the right person for the position is difficult. In this example, if the telephones are answered but the booklets do not get done, or the booklets get done but the telephone calls are poorly handled, the volunteer loses and this reflects on your skills as the volunteer services manager.

KEY CLARIFICATION QUESTIONS IN THE REQUISITION PROCESS

Experienced volunteer services managers develop key questions to ask a department manager or staff member who is requesting a volunteer. The purpose of the questions is to verify what the requestors want to happen (job description), when they want it to happen (time frame), where it will happen (location), and what type of volunteer they want to make it happen (qualifications). If this is an ongoing volunteer position, you may have set questions just to reaffirm mutual expectations. You may know that a volunteer who is leaving the library has worked on Thursday mornings for months, but you may not know that the supervisor has decided that having a volunteer on Friday afternoons would be more useful; if you recruit with your reasonable, but false, assumption that you need a volunteer to work on Thursday mornings, you end up with delays and internal stress between you and the department.

Whether or not you decide to use a requisition form, making a follow-up call to the staff person using focused questions can help you ensure the successful recruitment of the volunteer. The following questions for a short-term project, given with somewhat typical responses, exemplify how focused questions can be used to clarify job requirements:

1. How soon do you need the project completed?
   (*I would like it done by the end of next week, but it definitely has to be completed by the first of the month.*)

2. Where will the volunteer be working in the branch?
   (*I can put the volunteer in the branch workroom, but that gets a little crowded. Better yet, I can use Sally's desk because she is on a three-month maternity leave.*)

3. Can the volunteer flex hours or does the volunteer have to work when you are there?
   (*I need to be available to supervise the volunteer. I can do this only on Tuesday and Thursday afternoons, after 1:30.*)

4. What type of individual are you most comfortable working with for this job?
   (*I don't want high school students because they are often too busy to come in regularly. I need someone who can follow instructions. I can work with a young mother who wants some volunteer hours or a retired senior who isn't doing a lot of traveling right now.*)

5. When are you available to talk to the applicants?
   (*I can talk to them only when I'm off the desk on Tuesday and Thursday afternoons.*)

In this example, you need a volunteer who is willing to commit to completing the short-term project and able to work in a situation of close supervision on Tuesday and Thursday afternoons. You may find capable volunteers from varied backgrounds who meet these requirements. Using your word processing skills, do a quick cut-and-paste from other volunteer job descriptions and you have created a new job description that can be shown in the interview or posted on your web page.

PROCEDURES FOR REQUISITIONING A VOLUNTEER

You will want to establish volunteer request procedures. The following are suggestions:

1. A library manager or staff member will identify specific projects or volunteers for ongoing positions and submit a volunteer requisition form to the volunteer manager.

2. The volunteer services manager will clarify the specific skill requirements and expectations of the position and review any pending volunteer applicants.

3. The volunteer services manager is responsible for recruiting the appropriate volunteer.

4. The volunteer services manager will collect volunteer applications, make initial contact, conduct screening interviews (telephone or in person), and make recommendations to the requesting staff manager.

5. The supervising staff member can choose to make a final selection decision on a volunteer or allow the volunteer services manager to select and recommend a volunteer.

USES FOR THE REQUISITION FORMS

Requisition forms can be used as part of the administrative process to

- Identify the number of staff needing volunteers
- Define the volunteer skill mix used by the library
- Document trends in the use of volunteers throughout the system
- Track the number of successful placements
- Make needed changes and additions in the recruitment and selection process

Although volunteer hours are most often reported yearly to library administration, these numbers do not track how busy you are in your position. For example, in one year you have one hundred regular volunteers and need to replace only five of them; the following year, because of a major community event such as a factory plant closing, you lose thirty volunteers and are able to replace twenty-six. The total volunteer hours fluctuated only slightly from one year to the next, but your work load in the second year increased greatly. The number of requests for volunteers either in new positions or as replacements is an important way to track volunteer department activity. Furthermore, a review of requests may show high volunteer turnover in one branch or one department—something you need to investigate.

MARKETING THE VOLUNTEER SERVICES PROGRAM

MARKETING MEANS PROMOTING your volunteer services program to the community, that is, keeping your program before the public eye. It is letting people know what you are doing and what is available to them if they decide to volunteer their time. It is putting volunteer information on the website and going out to groups and speaking, or developing fliers and brochures and placing them in visible places to draw positive attention to who you are and what you are doing. This is different from recruitment (see section 16), which is directed toward getting community people interested in particular volunteer positions.

Marketing occurs in numerous ways. When you write articles or submit pictures of library volunteers to the local newspaper or a community online newsletter, this is marketing. Your library volunteer services web page can draw people to your program and to you through the contact information. This is like a funnel that draws readers from one general information source down to your specific program and to you.

Another form of marketing spotlights a volunteer of the month on the library website or on a Facebook site. Thank your volunteers by offering to write a letter of appreciation for their volunteer services to their employers. This not only increases awareness of the employers about your program but also shows employee involvement in their community. Display volunteer accomplishments in your library through pictures and plaques, which can also be photographed and uploaded to the volunteer services web page. This allows everyone who happens to view it online to become aware of the volunteer program. Satisfied volunteers will recruit their friends and talk positively about your program in the community—one of the best forms of marketing.

MARKETING THROUGH THE LIBRARY WEBSITE
A Review of Library Websites

Going online is now the primary approach to getting information for millions of people across diverse generations. Over the past decade and half, public libraries and schools have greatly contributed to this trend. Libraries now have large pools of computer-literate potential volunteers.

With this idea in mind, we used two perspectives to review library websites across the United States, ranging from small-town libraries to large, multiple branch metropolitan libraries. One perspective was that of a hypothetical new resident to the community who goes to the library website to consider volunteering. Does this person find links to volunteer services pages easy to find, that is, is the website user friendly for potential volunteers? Are the pages inviting, with pictures and information about volunteer positions, locations, and time commitments? Is there a procedure and a volunteer application form to apply online or a link for e-mailing the volunteer services manager for more information?

Our second approach was to view volunteer services pages from the perspective of professionals knowledgeable of library volunteer programs. Here the focus was on presentation, completeness, and structure of volunteer information, such as the divisions between adult and youth information. We discuss this approach in section 17.

As a volunteer services manager, you are not expected to be the web-savvy expert, but you should take a second look at your volunteer services pages as if you were a potential volunteer, either youth or adult; assume that you know little about library volunteering. Or ask one of your new volunteers to go over your website with you. The question is, is it currently easy to find out about your volunteer program?

In our review, we found few library websites with homepages that linked directly to a volunteer services page. A few had co-listings on the homepage such as "Donations and Volunteers," which took two steps to get the volunteer page. This means that the majority of people interested in volunteering have to search and navigate a variety of dropdown or sidebar menus with terms such as "About," "About the Library," "About Us," "Quick Links," "Frequently Asked Questions," or "Services." After enough persistence and three to six key strokes later, if lucky, eventually one can find the volunteer services page. There is no hint to suggest where to begin looking on the homepage for volunteer information. This kind of website design is representative of staff members thinking about library operations, departments, and the internal structure rather than thinking from a consumer perspective—and it is a good way to increase user frustration. We are long past the novelty of the Internet, and online customers expect to find what they are looking for quickly.

It seems, however, that many library websites are still designed by staff thinking more about internal operations than about how diverse end users search and actually use the library web pages. For some libraries it seems that, because volunteer services were far down the status chain in terms of library operations, the goal was to make them nearly invisible, or at least hard to find. On websites where an internal search of the site was required, the problem became one of word choice, such as "volunteer," "volunteering," or "volunteer services," which produced different search results within the website, including no listing when in fact with extra effort volunteer pages were found. At some library sites, after an extensive search, the conclusion was that there was no volunteer program, which may or may not have been true. For still others, we might find a volunteer page that did no more than tell you to "Check at your local branch library."

As a visual society, we tend to hold a "show us the picture" point of view, and the Internet is accommodating us by moving swiftly from text to graphic-based formats. We are now comfortable in the use of icons, pictures, and videos as navigational aids and as a basis for information. In fact, we expect websites to have these features. Today, people want to see the picture or the video with a click of a mouse and then draw their own conclusions.

In our website review, only one library had a volunteer graphic button on the homepage that directly linked to the volunteer services page. A few libraries had static pictures of volunteers on the volunteer pages. Many were formally staged group or individual shots, and a small subset showed "working" photographs of volunteers performing duties. Only one had a flash video of volunteers—but this should be a direction for volunteer services managers in the future. Adult learning approaches support demonstrations and use of videos as ways to improve adult understanding and more effective learning of topical matter. Technology is available to show flash video demonstrations of different types of volunteer jobs. If these were used, interested people could gain information and draw conclusions about whether these positions are right for them.

Improving the Library Website

What steps can you take to better market your volunteer services on the library website? The first and most crucial step is to have an active, direct link on the library homepage to your first volunteer services page. This can be done using the words "volunteer" or "volunteering" in the menu title or, better, with the use of a graphic button that is an active link to the volunteer services page, such depicted in figure 2. When interested library customers read a list of headings on the left sidebar and the word "Volunteering" appears, there should be only one click to your volunteer services information web page. The tendency is to put headings in alphabetical order, which tends to place your "Volunteering" link at the bottom of the page where it will rarely be seen. To avoid this, instead use a sidebar heading "Become a Volunteer" if your library alphabetizes the headings.

If your program shares a heading with other groups or library concerns, the common ones are "Friends and Volunteers," "Donations and Volunteers," and "Gifts, Donations, and Volunteers." The key point is that a click on the heading must be a link to a clearly written and attractive interactive page that plainly differentiates the options with clarity from a *customer's* point of view. Gifts can mean money, books, and other collection materials as well as signed works of art. Donations can mean the same, but here monetary donations can be to the library, the library foundation, or special programs, not to the volunteer program. Some libraries distinguish between monetary donations and donations of time, which still needs to distinguish between volunteers and the Friends group. This is where some libraries cause unnecessary customer frustration, because it may take

Figure 2. **Graphic website "button" for library volunteers. This graphic is freely available for use on library websites as shown or as modified to fit the library website requirements.**

two to three links to get to your first volunteer services page. It should take only one additional click from the information the page to your volunteer program page.

Another approach to library homepage layout from the view of volunteer services is the less user-friendly use of topbar or sidebar headings such as "Get Involved," "Support Your/Our/The Library," or "I want to . . ." The first of these is better, but in each case it is not obvious that the heading leads to information about library volunteering specifically. For example, the word "support" brings to mind monetary support rather than volunteering. The least user-friendly headings are terms such as "Services" and "Library Information." "Services" is a staff word used within the library system and not a term directly linked in the mind of a community member to volunteering. Under "Information" comes a highly diverse set of subheadings, often with volunteering subsumed under yet another subheading, such as "Donations and Volunteering." Again, this requires extra links to get to the volunteer pages. Remember, the goal is to think like a new member of the community who is on the library website but is not familiar with the way the staff compartmentalizes library information.

When the community member gets to your first volunteer services page, are there engaging photographs showing visually interesting volunteer activities? Does the page draw adult and young viewers to an introduction to the program and the types of jobs that might be common or unique? For example, a smiling face of an adult volunteer assisting a customer at a public terminal communicates a lot of volunteer satisfaction, technical skills, and working in a public setting. A picture of a volunteer engaged in reading a story to an enthused group of children provides a quick visual of what that job might be like. Similarly, a young adult shown as a homework helper to a middle school student indicates the one-on-one qualities of the job. Being able to click on the picture and view a short video of what the picture depicts is the wave of the future. In lieu of that, at least being able to click on the picture and a caption and go to the adult volunteering page, or to click on a youth picture or caption and go to the youth volunteer services page, would draw community members deeper into your program. At this point, you are in the recruitment arena to be covered in section 16.

Whether you want to include posed group volunteer recognition pictures on your initial volunteer page is a strategic decision. On one hand, you are certainly showing that volunteers are valued and supported by a formal recognition event, such as a luncheon. This is certainty good marketing. On the other hand, a picture may also illustrate a particular subset of your volunteers by age, race, or gender. If you are trying to increase diversity among your volunteers, this type of picture is not the best marketing approach.

Your first volunteer page should also address court-directed community volunteers, which can be shown through a picture without a recognizable face, and with a click these potential volunteers (if you use their services) can discover what policies and types of jobs apply to them.

MARKETING THROUGH SOCIAL NETWORKS

Our search for "library volunteers" on YouTube resulted in about eight videos that ranged from amateurish to youthfully creative and informative. These are first-generation productions. In a couple of the more serious videos, only one actually showed a volunteer working as a shelver; the rest were informational about the library. In just a few years, YouTube has crossed generations and is watched by a broad sweep of the general public. With the fluidity of this particular social networking site, you should at least take a look at current videos listed under library volunteers to see what has been done.

Marketing library volunteer services programs on Facebook and YouTube—the current dominant social network sites—is still in its infancy. Although some libraries have Facebook sites, we were unable to find a volunteer services department with its own site. Facebook can give information on the program; show flash videos, photographs of volunteers working, and other graphics; and link to the volunteer job listings on the website. As a way of testing this online marketing approach for your program, you can direct a volunteer who is digital video literate to create two videos, one showing a range of adult volunteer tasks being performed and a second showing young adults performing tasks. Both can have background commentary, music, and information directing viewers to your library website. If adults or youth talk about seeing the videos, then you are successfully marketing your program. At the same time, you can have an interactive link on your volunteer services pages that links back to these videos. This allows users of the website to see what some of your volunteers do at the library. This link is a way to liven up your volunteer services pages. A word of caution: Review your ideas with your library administration. You may need to get signed release forms for volunteers whose faces are shown and get library administration approval before posting on YouTube.

Recognize that posting videos to YouTube can go much farther than your library jurisdiction. Nevertheless, these videos can serve as a general market- ing tool for the benefits of library volunteering. As with all social networking sites, the strength of the site depends on initial viewers sending links to others to look at the videos.

Twitter is a highly focused form of communication suited for both recruitment and general marketing. Tweets—text messages sent via a Twitter account—can be linked to the library Facebook page.

Currently there are library blogs for library directors and for youth services, but there do not seem to be any volunteer services blogs. Blogs can provide information and insights into what is happening at the library from a volunteer services viewpoint and draw upon the accomplishments and comments from volunteers. From a community view, the blog can be used to draw comments from library customers about volunteer services. It can be written for volunteers only or for the community and can be linked to the volunteer services Facebook page.

What has rapidly changed over the past couple of years is the cross-connection of electronic information sources. In both marketing and recruiting, the networking of information sources may prove useful for volunteer programs. For example, you might send out a tweet to your contacts to advise them of a new volunteer project that needs one-day volunteers as shown on Facebook. Both sites can have an active link to the volunteer services web page that shows job requirements and a link to connect to the one-day volunteer application form. Reflect for a moment that both television news and newspapers now refer their customers to their respective websites for more information and pictures of events. Cross-communication between current electronic formats is the new way to think for volunteer services managers.

VOLUNTEER SERVICES AND THE INFORMATION TECHNOLOGY DEPARTMENT

You probably chose or accepted a volunteer services position because you are a "people person" and like to leave the technical issues such as the website and its links to the library webmaster, web committee, or information technology department. In some city and county library jurisdictions, the computer staff are housed outside the library, with only a technical liaison staff member within the library. In these settings, what listings and information go on the homepage and the "look and feel" of the page are often based on staff conceptions and information of what they think makes sense, and not from the customer's viewpoint.

You do not have to be a technical person or have knowledge of the underlying website software to make useful suggestions about the library homepage or volunteer services pages. Remember, the goal is not to make changes for your benefit but to improve communications between the community and volunteer services and hence, the library.

Working with technical staff members, "show and tell" generally works much better than trying to explain what you want to do. With this in mind, in section 17 we provide a list of library websites you can visit to get ideas on how to improve the volunteer listing on your library homepage and volunteer services pages. If nothing else, these sites can give you different ideas. Initially, you may hear "techno-talk" from your technical staff that something is not possible, but do not give up. Recognize that today's computer servers have greater capacity, compatible web-based software, and greater bandwidth in most library areas. If you get technical staff on your side and provide the challenge, most of them want to show off their technical knowledge and capability. This may be an incremental process of change, but communities are changing, demographics are changing, and so are library customers' expectations.

TRADITIONAL MARKETING APPROACHES

You have to keep the volunteering program before the public eye. One way to do this is with fliers or brochures. Two of the library websites we reviewed uploaded electronic versions of their volunteer brochures to their web pages. These items serve double duty. If you choose to do the same, be sure that the brochures are readable and do not detract from your other pages.

Displays in the library of volunteers, their accomplishments, and awards serve a twofold purpose. The public sees that you have an ongoing volunteer program; this a primary marketing tool. And satisfied volunteers are encouraged to recruit their friends and talk positively about the program in the community; this is a secondary component of marketing.

Another approach is to thank your volunteers by writing a letter to their employers, with the volunteers' permission. This shows their community spirit and highlights your program with local businesses.

Writing articles for the local newspaper paper (print or electronic) serves to market the program to the local community. These articles can be about the accomplishments of your volunteers, a particular volunteer, or the health benefits of volunteering—all the while tying back to your program.

You can market your program by giving presentations to local organizations. You may have one or more volunteers willing to talk about their work and what it is like to be a library volunteer. Of course, this can be done with adult organizations as well as high school or youth interest groups.

Do not forget the internal marketing of your program to the library staff. You have those who are strongly supportive, mildly supportive, and not enthusiastic at all about having community volunteers in the library, or at least in their departments. This is where an article in an internal newsletter or a staff intranet posting for general library information can be useful. Writing up a volunteer success case serves to reinforce the opinions of staff members who are favorable toward you and the program. By acknowledging the efforts of the supervising staff member, you may have a secondary marketing impact. The staff member may have respect among one or two staff members who are not favorable to your program and now face what psychologists call "cognitive dissonance" because they hold contradictory information in their heads. One way they balance this out is to think less negatively about your efforts and the volunteer program. If this happens, then your program gains a small increment of support.

A NOTE ON MARKETING

Marketing your program is always ongoing. Whether you talk informally about what you do at the library with a neighbor or formally give a presentation to a high school service club, you are marketing. Although a certain part of your marketing effort is repetitive, there is also a creative part in getting information about the program out to the community.

You have smart volunteers, informed staff members, and community experts who can help you develop various marketing approaches. This is not recruiting, although after a talk you may have people ask how they can get a volunteer application form. For example, marketing includes talking to young adults in spring about volunteering to assist in the summer reading program and how their involvement can help the library, the children, and their own goals. You do not have the positions now, but you are getting them thinking about volunteering. In this process, there will be times when you wonder if you are doing any good. Marketing efforts are always hard to measure, even among professionals. Radio ads are read and repeated, but no one knows for sure just how many sales can be chalked up to a particular ad campaign. In your case, the reward may come when a volunteer applicant tells you about applying because of meeting and hearing you talk at a meeting a year earlier. This is a point of satisfaction.

SECTION 16 | RECRUITMENT OF VOLUNTEERS

RECRUITMENT IS A focused set of steps designed to find people in the community who can fit the requirements of various volunteer positions. Recruitment is not marketing in a direct sense, although announcing and describing a volunteer position implicitly markets your program and the library. Recruitment is not selection or placement. Selection is a decision about a particular volunteer being acceptable for a position. Placement occurs when the new volunteer has passed the background check and other prerequisites and is accepted by the supervising staff member. Often the terms *selection* and *placement* are combined, but they are separate processes. You may feel you have been fortunate to recruit and select someone as a capable volunteer, but placement may not happen because the supervising staff member does not want that particular volunteer. Keep in mind that this is a three-step process that requires you to think simultaneously about all three steps as you go through recruitment. In other words, as you conduct an interview, you need to ask if this is a person you can place in a particular position.

Volunteer recruitment can be viewed in terms of general age and social categories such as youth, single adults, families, and seniors as well as generational categories such as Millennials, Generation Ys, and Baby Boomers. Recognize that these categories do not have precise definitions. Different sources assign a different range of birth years to Millennials. Baby Boomers are divided into the early baby boomers, born between 1946 and 1957, and later boomers, born between 1958 and 1964. The former are at retirement age, and the latter may still have youth living at home. Seniors are divided by some sources into "young old" and "old old," with the former still working, traveling, and participating in active recreation and leisure activities. It is also important to realize that a potential volunteer may be "in" a generation by birth year but not "of" the generation socially.

For recruitment, these categories are useful only to the extent that they lead you to think of new ways to recruit people and to think "generationally" about the volunteer services program. Gen Ys, for example, represent those who have grown up with computers and are nearing middle age. Many are comfortable carrying their laptops, iPods, and smartphones, multitasking wherever they go. They can readily adapt to virtual library volunteering as long as the work is one of a series of episodic projects. A routine, on-site volunteer position would generally have little appeal for them, unless it was a particular project with an end result. As a generality or maybe even a stereotype, many Gen Ys would recognize themselves in this statement, but in recruiting it is important to accept that not everyone who is in this generation fits this particular profile. Active, "on the go" Baby Boomers are also usually not looking for long-term volunteer commitments but rather favor short-term or one-time volunteer projects. Some will commit to a once-a-year library event, if their travel or work schedule allows. Family volunteering requires tasks that can be done with some or all family members present and assisting at the same time. This requires you to think what tasks, other than shelf maintenance, can fit a family's requirements.

There is some indication that more men and ethnic minorities are now volunteering at libraries. How do these changing demographics impact how you recruit for your volunteer services program?

When your aim is to recruit the best person for the job, library services are enhanced. However, the reverse is also true. If there is a poor match between a volunteer and the job, the outcome can be a deterioration of library services and staff/volunteer relationships.

AGE
Youth

The youngest volunteers range in age from about ten years old to twelve to thirteen. They can be part of a family that volunteers at the library or take on projects as a Scout or for a school project. These young volunteers can also be the child of a staff member. Usually the parent or guardian is expected to be present when the young volunteer is working to reduce supervising time. These volunteers are not recruited. As the volunteer services manager, you should have a set of relatively simple projects available for them.

Young Adults/Teens

Usually defined by the teen years or high school age, these volunteers often are meeting a high school graduation requirement or fulfilling civic or community service requirements for local service organizations such as Scouts, church groups, or school service programs. The library provides an opportunity for some young adults to apply their knowledge of computers or online searching skills or to serve on a youth committee. It offers others a safe environment in which to complete their service or graduation requirements while increasing their awareness of library programs. A small number may be thinking about a career as a librarian, and volunteering is a way to determine if this is what they want to do.

Youth Interns

A volunteer youth intern is a high school–age young adult who commits twelve to fifteen weeks at the library for a specified number of hours per week under an agreement with a supervising staff member. The assigned work can be project-specific or part of library routine operations. The staff member agrees to provide extra guidance in directing the youth. An internship can be accomplished for a specific school requirement or as part of a career interest in a library occupation.

Adults

Adult volunteers, usually eighteen years or older, can be recruited from local service and professional organizations as well as from companies that offer incentive programs for employees to volunteer in the community. Individuals with home-based businesses volunteer as a way to reduce their feelings of isolation, just as parents with school-age children often volunteer to get out of the house and meet other active adults. In addition, people who have been laid off from their jobs use volunteering to keep busy and to learn a new skill.

Semiretired or recently retired individuals volunteer to help their transition from one lifestyle to another. The library provides a weekly structure to their lives and a new sense of community involvement.

Adult Interns

A few libraries provide volunteer adult internships associated with those who are in library school. This provides additional real-life experiences related to their academic studies.

GENDER

More library volunteers are female than male because traditionally the field of library science has been female dominated. Furthermore, mothers are in the library with children more often than fathers and get to know the librarians and observe volunteers performing their duties. The work is, however, gender neutral (mending, reading to children, archival research, data entry, or data management).

INTERESTS

Recruiting special-interest volunteers requires a well-defined focus and perseverance. For example, one large urban library needed a volunteer to take care of its plants. A poster advertising the position was made for the library bulletin board, a public service announcement was placed in the local newspaper, and contacts were made with the garden clubs in the area. After three months there were still no prospects. Eventually, through word-of-mouth networking, a local resident who raised flowers in her private greenhouse volunteered. She not only took care of the plants but also donated some from her greenhouse. In this case perseverance paid off. Although not all green thumb people are members of garden clubs, if you have a similar need you can e-mail garden clubs and see if they have an interested volunteer or link your posting on the volunteer services web pages.

Your goal is to match the *demonstrated* interests of a volunteer with the job requirements. An individual may never have read to seniors in a nursing home but have the interest and desire to try. Before you send the volunteer out alone, you would want to assign him to work with an experienced volunteer already reading at nursing homes. This allows firsthand experience and a way for him to gain the confidence and to see if this is really the position he desired. It is important to distinguish between a general interest and the demonstrated talent or ability to do what is required in the position. It is at this point that your recruitment efforts and interviewing skills can help you identify an individual's demonstrated interests. This knowledge can be important to the success of your program.

SKILLS, TRAINING, AND EDUCATION

Recruiting for specific skills, training, or education is easier than recruiting for specific interests. For example, you must fill jobs that require knowledge of computer graphics or desktop publishing with people who have the right specialized skills and knowledge. By phrasing your recruitment postings to reflect these skills or level of education, you limit the number of individuals qualified for the job. As long as there is a pool of candidates, you can interview each of them, look at their portfolios, or ask for references to verify their skills and knowledge. This does not mean that the volunteer will automatically be successful in a library context, but at least you have laid the groundwork for future recruitment efforts. Of course, the challenge comes when there are too many limiting requirements for the position and you get no responses. At this point, you need to reassess your recruitment campaign.

SKILL-BASED VOLUNTEERS

This new category of volunteering draws upon people's professional and occupational expertise, often with time off from a corporation, to volunteer. For example, an accounting professional volunteers to assist a nonprofit group with accounting problems, and a marketing expert serves as a volunteer to use marketing skills to improve outreach efforts of a community group. The volunteer gets training on the operations of a nonprofit community organization. This type of community volunteering resource is new to libraries.

TIME

There are two meanings to volunteer time. One is the weekly commitment, either total hours worked or the number of assigned shifts, often defined as two- or four-hours blocks of time. Volunteer weekly timesheets can be designed in standardized blocks of shift times throughout the entire library day. In one library system a shift is equal to two hours, and in another a shift is four hours. In addition, particular positions can be assigned different hours per shift; a volunteer on a busy information desk may have two-hour shifts while a mender has four-hour shifts.

The second meaning of volunteer time is the duration of the volunteer job. At the short end of this spectrum is the one-day volunteer, the community member who enjoys and wants to help with a one-day event. This may be the annual library fundraising event, the annual celebration to honor the library staff, or a library-sponsored event for the community. One-day events fit the schedule of active community people while serving the library.

A short-term or episodic volunteer position is defined by the length of the project. There are beginning and end dates, so the volunteer knows from the start when the assignment will be over. The yearly or semiannual weekend book sale falls into this category, and so does a one-month special project in which staff and volunteers go into the high schools to increase the number of young adults with library cards. Short-term projects allow newcomers to the community or to volunteering to test the waters to see if they want to make a longer commitment to the library.

Seasonal volunteers can be returning community members or newly hired volunteers who work for the library over the course of a calendar season. A library grounds and gardening group of volunteers may start at the beginning of spring and continue until the first frost. These volunteers perform a variety of tasks on an as-needed basis without having precise beginning and end dates. There may be annual fall school tours of libraries that volunteers assist with or conduct.

Long-term volunteer positions are generally ongoing jobs done as part of routine library operations. Besides the circulation, reference, and technical services functions, there can be ongoing volunteer positions in local history collection, administrative departments, and the computer lab. Some volunteers want a regular commitment and can structure their lives around ongoing library activities. For these individuals, developing long-term friendships and having the regularity of a volunteer job are important intrinsic rewards.

TITLES

The number and type of volunteer positions a library needs depend on its size and structure. At one end of the spectrum you can find community volunteers performing routine assigned tasks, and at the other end are the trustees (often overlooked as volunteers) setting library policies and standards. As the library organization grows, additional volunteer positions may evolve in the form of docents and ambassadors. These volunteers are usually separately identified, trained, and assigned specific kinds of tasks such as providing specialized customer service assistance, computer instruction, or tours of the library. In addition, some libraries offer student and volunteer internships that require more extensive commitments of time as well as a strong commitment on the part of paid staff.

Additionally, there are dues-paying Library Friends groups whose members serve as a liaison to the community as well as helping the library through fundraising efforts, special events, and programs. The relationship between library volunteers and the Friends group needs to be clarified, especially if there are individuals who volunteer in both organizations (see section 6).

LEGAL DISTINCTIONS

There are two distinct groups of volunteers found working in many libraries: court-directed (also referred to as court-appointed, court-referred, or alternative service) and community volunteers. The latter category is the largest group and includes both young adults and adults. This discussion focuses on court-directed restitution volunteers.

Court-directed restitution is the legally mandated sentence to perform community service volunteer work in lieu of a jail term or fine for a youth or adult convicted of a minor offense. Most of these individuals are first-time offenders. Their misdemeanors may range from truancy or school fights to driving under the influence of drugs or alcohol, other driving infractions, excessive parking tickets, or possession of drugs.

As the volunteer services manager, you need to clarify with your administration the policies regarding which offenses preclude individuals from being court-directed volunteers in your library. Many libraries do not accept anyone who has committed a burglary, robbery, been charged with possession of a hidden weapon, committed sexual offenses, or demonstrated violent behavior. Others do not take individuals with drug offenses. You also need to clarify from which court jurisdictions you will accept volunteers. For some libraries, using court-directed volunteers is a way to serve community residents by providing opportunities for them to make restitution back to the community. Busy courts lead to many people looking for places to do their community service hours. If you make your library accessible to too many court jurisdictions, you may find yourself swamped with calls and e-mail from court-directed volunteers.

Remember these three points: (1) you are not required to accept anyone the court refers to your library; (2) many of these individuals are talented and skilled people who made a mistake and want to work through the incident; and (3) you can terminate an individual whenever you deem it appropriate.

School principals, rather than courts, have been known to assign community service hours to their students for minor infractions of the school rules. In one case, an elementary school principal assigned community service hours to a nine-year-old boy for throwing rocks at the building during recess. The child wanted to work at the library. The volunteer services manager agreed as long as the parent remained in the library while the boy completed the assigned duties (sorting newspapers). This arrangement made it possible for the parent to share responsibility for the child's supervision.

DISABILITY

The term *disability* covers a wide range of perceived limitations. A person with an artificial leg has a disability, but such a person can be more physically active and involved than uninjured people who play computer games all day. When the word *disability* is used, often the first visual image is of someone in a wheelchair, but in fact those in wheelchairs are a very small percentage of those with some type of disability.

Individuals with physical or learning disabilities can be excellent library volunteers. It is essential that the supervising staff be willing and positive about supervising these volunteers. It is important that the work be appropriate to the volunteer's skill and ability levels and that the library be willing to make a reasonable accommodation, if necessary—that is, make some slight modification in the workplace that addresses the physical needs of the volunteer to be successful in the job performance. Often "disabled" volunteers are quite capable of making the accommodation in a way you might not have thought possible, because they are used to doing it in other areas of life. If a disabled person is part of a formal rehabilitation program, be sure to ask about a work coach from the agency to supervise during the work period.

There are extra considerations required in this type of commitment. You are not obligated to find work for the disabled, but a good match can be rewarding. This is an area of volunteerism with the possibility of growth, thanks to expansion in the use of virtual volunteers.

UNPAID AND PAID

Almost all library volunteers are unpaid, and some volunteer application forms specifically state the unpaid nature of the volunteers' relationship to the library. On occasion, a library may use volunteers from AmeriCorps or other federal or state programs in which individuals are paid by the agency to volunteer.

A NOTE ON DIVERSITY

Diversity in the library is pursued by working toward having a representation of volunteers from a cross section of the population within your community. This means not only race, gender, and ethnic background but also age, physical and learning disabilities, beliefs, skill levels, and a wide array of educational levels (high school, college, graduate, and technical school). Review your volunteer pool and decide if it reflects your community. Are you reaching out to diverse populations through specialty newspapers? Are you e-mailing volunteer postings to identified diverse groups in the community? Are there staff members who can make specific suggestions to you on how to reach out to diverse community populations? Reaching out serves the larger interests of the library, and in addition you may find new sources of volunteers.

It is quite often a difficult challenge to match the diversity of the community with your pool of volunteers, yet as a goal it can serve as a reminder as you conduct recruitment campaigns. It is easy to overlook good sources of volunteers.

DEFINITIONS OF VOLUNTEERS

The following definitions of volunteers used by specific libraries can help clarify your recruiting efforts and are essential to written policy statements:

A library volunteer is anyone from the community who agrees to donate time, talent, and services.

A library volunteer is an unpaid staff member.

Library volunteers are diverse members of the community who share a common interest in helping the library.

Library trustees are people elected or appointed to specific terms on the library governance board and are expected to initiate and affirm policy decisions for the library.

Young adult volunteers are individuals who are at least sixteen years of age and can demonstrate maturity and reliability. They are capable of working with little or no supervision.

Library youth volunteers are between the ages of twelve and fifteen. Projects are assigned to individuals or groups (such as the Scouts) when appropriate adult supervision is available.

Library court-directed volunteers are young adults or adults who are working at the library as restitution for offenses committed in the community.

Friends of the Library are volunteers who hold dues-paying memberships in a community group designed to help the library through fundraising efforts and sponsoring or supporting special projects and events.

SECTION 17 | RECRUITMENT APPROACHES

DEVELOPING A RECRUITMENT campaign is more multifaceted than it was just a few years ago, when word-of-mouth, a physical posting in the library, or a notice in the community volunteer section of a local newspaper was adequate. Now some library websites have their standard volunteer jobs listed, which takes the place of physical postings. A library's Facebook page or a "tweet" can serve to announce a new position.

Although community economic fluctuations can bring in potential volunteers, it is a good idea to plan out a recruitment campaign. There will be times when your volunteer pool of applicants does not bring in people you can match to positions. There may be a new specialized library volunteer position that requires you to seek out community members with particular skills. There may be established positions in which the work times are unusual and hard to fill. By filling a difficult volunteer position with a qualified volunteer, you and the volunteer services program gain in stature and respect among paid staff and administrators.

The following are useful guidelines to increase your effectiveness as you set up a recruitment effort: (1) know the position you are recruiting for; (2) develop a list of resources of potential volunteers and direct your recruitment efforts at those resources; (3) use your understanding of why people volunteer; and (4) be flexible and open to surprises. Although it seems obvious, to "know the position you are recruiting for" means that recruitment should be based on a valid current job description or set of tasks and not just on a staff member's need for a volunteer tomorrow. Will the requested volunteer be a direct replacement for a previous volunteer performing the same tasks, or have these tasks changed, as might occur with a department change in staffing? Will the new volunteer be working under the same staff supervisor and at the same times and same days of the week? It is easy in busy library operations to make incorrect assumptions and then find out that your recruitment efforts do not meet the changed expectations.

If recruitment is for ongoing operations positions, such as shelving DVDs, you already have in your mind what capable volunteers "look like" and the usual recruitment approaches that have worked in the past. Currently many libraries have these positions posted on their volunteer services page. The advantage in this situation is that there is less stress doing what has been working. One disadvantage is that you are not developing new resources for applicants within the community, which is especially important when your usual approaches do not work. Further, you may not be adding any diversity to your program.

If it is a new volunteer position, then you have to brainstorm on how to find possible applicants. For example, the children's services manager needs a read-aloud volunteer on Saturday afternoons. The current weekday volunteer story readers are not available. The library wants to try this new storytime for six months and then evaluate it. The supervisor writes up a request for a volunteer. You verify that the duties on the existing job description for a read-aloud volunteer are current and accurately fit the new Saturday program. You ask if the staff supervisor is expecting any special personal characteristics or skills, such as bilingual capabilities. At this point you need to think about your recruitment approaches. Will this be a passive recruiting effort or an active one? What resources are the most effective to recruit the type of volunteer needed?

Volunteer programs go through cycles. There may be a couple of years when passive recruiting works fine because you have little turnover of volunteers. People stay and enjoy what they are doing. Then the program undergoes a change in volunteers, often for a variety of good reasons, such as moving away, a major illness or accidents, deaths, or new family or employment responsibilities. Then you go through a period of active recruiting. It is good to know how to use a range of recruiting approaches effectively so you can respond to your program changes over time.

PASSIVE RECRUITING

The most passive approach to recruitment is to wait for "walk-ins," people who inquire at the information, circulation, or reference desk about volunteer opportunities. Some libraries encourage citizen participation by having a special check-off box on their library card registration forms with the idea that they will follow up on volunteering.

Another passive approach is merely to post a statement on the volunteer services web page such as "Check at your local branch library for volunteer positions." This approach works on the assumption that an interested person first views it on the website and then visits the branch. Also, putting up a small sign at the circulation desk like "Ask about volunteering" or a general notice about volunteering on a bulletin board are examples of passive approaches.

These approaches often do work if there are few positions and no requirements for specific abilities. As your volunteer program grows, though, specific types of skills are often required to meet either the needs of library staff or an increased volume of library transactions. If you are lucky, the right volunteers will "walk in" at the appropriate times. If you are not lucky, you will probably have to recruit volunteers actively from the community.

ACTIVE RECRUITING: THE WEBSITE

Active recruitment means engaging potential volunteers through your efforts. In some cases it means that you are willing to try new sources to find the best volunteers for your positions, involving some level of creativity on your part.

If you are recruiting for volunteers under age forty, you will most likely find them through online sources. They are on their laptops and cell phones. They will find your program by way of a posting on an electronic community information bulletin board, a tweet sent by an acquaintance, by an e-mail or text message from a friend, a posting in the community section of an online local newspaper, or a comment in a local blog.

These people evaluate your volunteer services program first by the look and feel of the library website, second by the look of your volunteer services pages, and third by the ease with which you link them to key information about the program, positions, procedures, and the online application form. If your web pages are confusing, unattractive, fail to grab attention, or contain incomplete information, it takes only one click to eliminate your program from further consideration. Ten years from now, the age group that now has high expectations about easy and accurate online sources will reach age fifty. So now is the time to look at your volunteer pages from the perspective of active recruitment and not just post general information about library volunteering and hope people see it.

Linking to the Volunteer Services Web Pages

By no means do all public library websites have volunteer services pages, and even when they do locating them from the library homepage is not always easy (see section 15). If you do not have a visible volunteer link on your library's homepage, then your program does not exist for many people.

Once people find your volunteer page, they need to see an inviting and interactive page in order to want to volunteer. First, then, it is important that you take responsibility for the design or, as often stated nowadays, the "look and feel" of your volunteer services web pages. These pages are part of your volunteer services program, and the computer staff should not simply be delegated to post your existing printed information on the library website. Community customers today have higher expectations of websites than a decade ago. They want to link quickly to relevant information. Active links, pictures and other graphics, directional information, contact information, and current information are ways to engage the user and are now part of everyday online expectations. Making volunteer service pages engaging is one way of drawing community people to your program.

And don't forget that other pages of the library's website can be excellent places to attract prospective volunteers and link them to the volunteer services web pages. In sample 17-1, the library's public announcement of a new project includes a call for volunteers and the link they need to follow up.

Designing the Volunteer Services Web Pages

As a volunteer services manager, you know what your program offers to members of the community. Do not expect anyone in the community to know library terminology or which volunteer jobs are available. Even customers who come to the library regularly and know particular staff members would be surprised to learn what all those members do in their library positions.

The first volunteer services web page should include a short welcoming statement by you or the library director indicating the importance of volunteering. This lets potential volunteers know that this is an important service to the library and community. The key here is to let people know they are on the correct page, and then get them directed quickly to where they can find

RFID and Automated Material Handling
and Self-Check at the Denver Public Library

Want to help the Library with this project? Please visit the RFID Volunteer page for more information.

What is RFID?
RFID, or Radio Frequency Identification, is a long-established technology that libraries around the world are adopting to identify and circulate their collections. It is widely used in wholesale, retail, shipping, and a variety of other industries.

Why is the Denver Public Library adopting RFID?
RFID is a proven, reliable technology that should increase staff productivity and reduce repetitive motion injuries. It will also speed up turnaround time, so that our customers have better access to materials. RFID will improve security and inventory control. Research from other library systems shows that RFID usually pays for itself in 2–3 years, by keeping staff costs constant while circulation increases.

How is RFID being funded?
The Better Denver Bond Program, approved by voters in the November 2007 election, is the funding source for the project.

What is the Library purchasing with this money?

- *RFID Tags.* These are adhesive tags about 2 inches square that can be stuck to books, magazines, DVD cases, or any other library materials.
- *Self-Checks.* The new modular self-checks will read the information on the RFID tags and the bar code on library cards, allowing card holders to check out their own materials more quickly and easily.
- *Staff Workstations.* These plug-in PC peripherals will allow our staff to check out and return materials with RFID tags and write new information to RFID tags. And, handheld versions will be used to search for materials on the shelf.
- *Automated Handling Systems.* These are book returns attached to conveyor belts and sorting bins. They will accept, return, and sort incoming items according to preset criteria. They will be installed at the Central Library and several other branches.
- *Security Gates.* The current security gates at the Central Library will be replaced with new gates that will use RFID to determine if items have been properly checked out.

How long will the conversion to RFID take?
Because of the complexity of the project and the size of the Denver Public Library collection, one to two years will be needed to complete the project. However, our goal is to RFID tag 88% of our 2 million-item circulating collection by the end of 2009 and install most of the staff workstations and self-checks as well.

Sample 17-1. **Project Announcement for RFID Volunteers**

What about my privacy?
It is very unlikely that someone would be able to obtain information from the RFID tags in the materials checked out to you. More important, the only information stored on the tag is the item serial number, a code number identifying the item as belonging to the Denver Public Library, and a number indicating if the item is on the shelf or checked out. The serial number of the item is randomly generated and has no relation to the title or subject matter of that item. Only a Library staff member with authorization to use our circulation system can determine the title of the item attached to that serial number. The first line of the Denver Public Library Privacy Statement reads as follows:

> *Your records are strictly confidential.* At the Denver Public Library, we go the extra step to ensure that your records remain your business and no one else's.

With all this new automated equipment, will there still be staff available to assist me?
Yes, and it is one of the main objectives of the project to free up staff to provide more one-on-one service. Making better use of staff time through RFID and eliminating the inefficient and excessive materials handling that can lead to repetitive motion injuries will allow the Library to provide better customer service and dramatically improve your access to all the materials and services the Denver Public Library provides.

How can I find out more about this project or other Better Denver Bond Program projects underway at the Library?
Updated information about current bond projects may be found at http://denverlibrary.org/bond.

Want to help the Library with this project?

Please visit the RFID Volunteer page for more information.

> Denver Public Library Online ©
> Updated: May 08, 2009
> http://denverlibrary.org/news/dplnews/rfid_volunteer.html

Sample 17-1. **Project Announcement for RFID for Volunteers** *(continued)*

information that answers their questions. Do this by providing answers to the directional questions people would ask if they saw you in person. Direct people with the use of attractive photographs or other graphics to active links that identify "Family & Children Volunteers," "Young Adult or Teen Volunteers," "Adult Volunteers," "Court-Directed Community Service Volunteers," or any other volunteer categories you use including "Summer Reading Program Volunteers," "Special Event Volunteers," or "Friends Group." This page directs people quickly to a category of information. The majority of public library volunteer services pages do not do this.

Once a person is at a specific volunteer page, such as "Young Adult Volunteering" or Adult Volunteers," you can provide the focused information using photographs or other graphics that draw the person one more step into your program. Do you want to discuss benefits as a way of getting people interested? If so, can a photograph taken in the library capture one or more of these benefits? If time commitments or particular schedules are important, can a simple hourglass be used as a small graphic or an active link to time schedules? There are libraries that overwhelm interested volunteer applicants with volunteer handbook information, volunteer policies, and administrative information that is not directly related to answering early questions potential volunteers have and certainly does not provide an inviting, friendly introduction to volunteer services.

Court-directed community service volunteers want to know whether the library can accept them given their specific offenses, the requirements they must meet, including attendance at a training/orientation session, and application instructions. At this early stage, court-directed people are not interested in reading general information that a community volunteer might be interested in.

Some libraries have separate application forms for court-directed volunteers and, if they do, there should be an active link to this page. Photographs (without face shots) or drawings can illustrate the range or types of tasks that might be assigned. If the library does not accept court-directed volunteers, then a list or active links to organizations that do are a quick way of providing information and reduce the number of calls to your department. Some courts provide a list that you can post on the website with links or contact information.

Listing Volunteer Positions

Potential volunteers at an early stage of interest usually have these key questions: What types of volunteer positions are available in the library? What tasks are expected to be performed? Where are these volunteer jobs located?

Quite a few libraries merely list typical volunteer jobs or tasks without any active links to expanded job descriptions or more information. In the recent past this would have been adequate given the web technology available at the time, including slow downloads on dial-up lines and lower customer expectations of what the Internet can provide. This is not the case today. People expect to have much more information, visual and textual, quickly available with a couple of mouse clicks or taps on a touch pad.

A slight improvement over merely listing jobs is the addition of a short (two- or three-sentence) description of tasks or duties under each volunteer position listing. This approach is used by many libraries and when done well adds a lot of good information. If you cannot link to job descriptions, this is an intermediate step. Avoid the mistake made by libraries that use too much library jargon in describing volunteer jobs. Write your short job summaries in plain English and get them reviewed by your nonlibrary acquaintances to see if they are clear.

A much better approach for selling your program is to add links from each volunteer position listing to a more thorough overview of the job. These links can be to the job descriptions or to the plain English versions of the duties. In this format, more details about library locations and time commitments can be provided.

This is the point where volunteer services pages can take advantage of the latest technologies and more visual formats. The detail page can include a picture of a volunteer performing tasks or a flash video showing a volunteer carrying out multiple tasks. A link to either a Flickr page or YouTube video can show a volunteer performing the duties. This provides an interactive and engaging involvement between the potential volunteer and your program. Just remember that using a link to a site outside your library requires a volunteer to check periodically to ensure that the link is active.

One more feature on this detail page of a volunteer position that can draw the interested person farther into your program is a link to an online volunteer application form (see section 18) along with the instructions on how to submit the form. As an alternative, you can provide a link to a "Volunteer Packet" that includes the application form and procedures.

Including Volunteer Policy Information

How much policy and procedure information to put in your volunteer services pages is an important decision that in part hinges on the purposes of the pages, library philosophy about volunteers, and jurisdictional requirements. In most paid library staff positions, handbook information and procedures are provided at the time of the interviews and made available in electronic formats on the library intranet only to employed staff members. Should you or can you do the same for volunteers?

Considering the purposes of your volunteer pages is a useful first step. Are your pages designed, as for some libraries, as a way to redirect people away from library volunteering to other volunteer opportunities in the community? In other words, are they designed to dissuade people from applying to be a library volunteer? This may be legitimate, but not a positive way to represent your program. More important is the question of whether the policy information applies to all volunteers. Does a young adult interested in library volunteering have to read two pages of information on adult volunteering information, including information on security background checks, only to find in the final two paragraphs procedures for inquiring about youth volunteer opportunities? Do court-directed volunteers have to read through these same two pages before finding that the library does not use court-directed volunteers?

If the first volunteer services page separates different types of volunteering and if specific policy and procedure information is deemed important for the particular types of volunteers, then this information can be provided just to those volunteers as needed via links. A family volunteering web page should have a link to the relevant volunteer policies and procedures information. Similarly, a potential youth volunteer should be directed via a link to the policies and procedures relevant to youth volunteering. In this way, you quickly provide the important information required to answer questions of those with an interest in specific types of library volunteering opportunities. This is what people expect from a website today.

If you are part of a city, county, or other jurisdiction that has strict requirements about volunteers, then you probably have to post and list particular requirements on your library volunteer pages following established rules.

To make the volunteer policy and procedure information engaging and user friendly, ask yourself how the wording can be presented in a more appealing style than typical dry, formal format. Numerous web sources and books provide information and examples on how to write in a more engaging style, called "Plain English," that can help you here.

In addition to job titles and definitions, these website subheadings of information often fall under the category of volunteer policies and procedure:

Mission/purpose of volunteer program

Types or definitions of volunteers

Requirements of volunteering

Age (for youth)

Background checks

Rights

Responsibilities

Recognitions

Procedures for becoming a volunteer

Volunteer brochure

Volunteer newsletter

Contact information

As you consider or reconsider your volunteer services web pages, how much of this information is needed and for which volunteers? You can ask your neighbors as well as new volunteers to review and critique your pages from the view of a community member looking at library volunteering. Information that might be clear to you and other library staff might be confusing to the public. Getting this type of feedback can help improve this important communication link to the community.

Listing Volunteer Opportunities with Community Organizations

There are arguments for and against listing other local organizations that accept volunteers. At particular periods and transition times in people's lives they often have a desire to volunteer (a need to do something different). The motivations vary. As a volunteer services manager, you know that you cannot place everyone who has an interest in volunteering. Advertising other local volunteer opportunities allows some self-selection out of your program to other local organizations by those who do not find the list of library volunteer positions appealing. If you do not provide listings, you will likely be referring people to other agencies either via e-mail or in person. You can have a brochure of local volunteer opportunities, or this may be posted on a library community list. Not having a list of community organizations on your volunteer services pages can increase your workload, but it does require adding, deleting, and checking links.

What criteria should you use to select groups and organizations for listing? Do you list only government agencies and local groups and organizations? Do you list regional and national organizations that have local chapters, such as the American Red Cross? Do you link to federal volunteer program such as AmeriCorps? Do you link to religious or special interest organizations? The advantage of having a listing of local groups is that you can allow community members to see a broader range of volunteer opportunities and self-select out of your program. At the same time, you can refer people who may not be selected within your program to an organization more suitable to their interests and abilities.

Internet Alternatives to Volunteer Services Web Pages

A volunteer services manager in a department with minimum staff support may find it difficult to think about adding another online site to construct and update. As an alternative, public libraries are adding "company" Facebook accounts in increasing numbers. Not only can a separate volunteer services account on Facebook be used to connect the community with your program, it is also a way for volunteers to communicate with each other and with the volunteer services department. A Twitter account can be linked to your Facebook page as well as any blogs you choose to write. If you have a personal Facebook account, you know the advantages in staying in touch with friends and family or being a "fan" or "friend" of a business, group, or prominent individual.

If your library is on Facebook, which means a paid staff member is keeping it updated, you can consider a volunteer feature that provides an engaging way to inform people of new positions, especially unusual ones that require well-defined skills sets. Uploaded flash videos of volunteers performing tasks or having fun at volunteer functions can serve as both a recruitment and marketing tool by drawing viewers to your program—and remember to add a link to your program.

Currently, library volunteer blogs are found primarily on youth services web pages. Although blogs directed at adult library volunteers may exist, we found none. Blogs can be either accessible to the public or internal to library volunteers and staff (a good way to promote library-wide communication). As a recruitment tool, you can use the external blog to ask readers to forward information about volunteer positions to others who might be interested. In addition, this form of communication can be especially effective if virtual volunteers are part of your program.

Finding Technical Expertise

If you have web computer staff in house or available to you, this can be an opportunity to effect web page changes and create online access to social net-working sites. However, in large city and county libraries there may be many extra steps to get approval for changes to your volunteer services pages or links with social networking sites. There may be the technological capability but no allocated staff time or limited library administration support. These are hurdles, but with persistence, use of examples, and sound arguments you can make headway for proposed changes.

If you are in a small library system, getting a web-savvy volunteer can be useful. You may be able to utilize the skills of a local high school computer teacher or an information technology staff member of the local school district to provide volunteer assistance. From the volunteer perspective, library youth services departments have a greater number of MySpace, Facebook, blog, and Twitter links than volunteer services departments, so you may

There are no national or regional "Library Volunteer Services Program Awards" with a set of expert judges making decisions. With total acknowledgment of the subjectivity of our website selection process, we here set out our own awards. We are also keenly aware that an excellent website does not mean a well-run volunteer program, and vice versa. We understand that library websites change and thus that our listings may not hold up at a later date.

With all these caveats, our goal is to provide particular categories of current exemplars from which volunteer services managers can learn and create their own customer-friendly and engaging web pages. Through this process, we hope to assist improvements in this part of library operations and community involvement. In the extra blank line in each category you can add your own meritorious library and use these to inform your technical and administrative staff members about ways you want to improve your own web pages.

Category: Best Web Page Link to Library Volunteer Services Web Pages
  Multnomah County (Oregon) Library, www.multcolib.org
  Your Nomination: _____
Category: Best Library Volunteer Services Web Page
  Southeast Steuben County (New York) Library, www.stls.org/corning/
  Your Nomination: _____
Category: Best Use of Graphics on a Volunteer Services Web Page
  Metropolitan Library System (Oklahoma County, Oklahoma), www.mls.lib.ok.us
  Your Nomination: _____

Box 17-1. **Our Volunteer Services Website Awards**

have in-house experts on the library staff with the knowledge to help you. In your neighborhood there may be a tech-savvy person who can be of help. All of these people can assist you to conceptualize alternative designs that will engage and draw people to your volunteer services pages and into your program. With web experience, these people can also converse in "tech talk" to see if the library software and servers can do what you would like. You may be lucky to have a library web staff person who enjoys the challenge of improving web pages to help you in this process. The key point is that you do not have to do this alone.

Over the next few years, you may be part of the growth of volunteer services managers who are computer savvy. Thus, if you are savvy, you can, for example, design your own volunteer services Facebook page, publish a volunteer blog, or create digital videos for uploading to the web pages.

Remember that web users today expect to find what they are looking for quickly and follow the cues, especially visual ones, given to them. They do not like to read material that does not answer their questions or written text that does not pertain to them. If they have gotten to your first volunteer services page, they have some reason for being there. From a web design perspective, you want to direct them to the right information and at the same time make them feel they are welcomed on your volunteer pages. Right now, few libraries do both.

ACTIVE RECRUITING: TRADITIONAL APPROACHES
Word of Mouth

Individuals can be recruited through traditional word of mouth or its e-mail variation. For example, a volunteer who enjoys working at the library will talk about the experience with friends and family. The enthusiasm encourages others to explore similar opportunities with your library. You can encourage such conversations by asking volunteers (perhaps through personalized e-mail sent to them) to tell others about the library volunteer program and the opportunities it offers. You can also ask these volunteers for comments about their volunteer experiences and, with their permission, use these statements as testimonials about your program on your web pages. Of course, such comments can also be videotaped and posted. This will increase the web page visitations, which can be tracked.

Posters and Fliers

Many libraries either do not have volunteer services web pages or, if they do, they are not used to recruit volunteers. With this in mind, traditional multicolored poster boards to identify current volunteer jobs placed in the library can still work. When they are posted by the main entrance, you have a cost-effective way of attracting attention to available positions.

You can make posters to identify current volunteer jobs. The key here is to provide information on how to contact you in person or electronically. There is a level of skill needed to create an eye-catching poster. Children's librarians usually have experience creating attractive posters and can offer advice. You may have a graphic artist on staff or available to the library who can provide guidance. You may have an artistic volunteer who can contribute talent and ideas. The use of traditional posters recognizes that not everyone has or is on their smartphone or computer all the time.

Bulletin boards located throughout the community are good places to advertise your volunteer positions. This approach is another way to attract a diverse group of interested people, namely, those who may not be regular users of the library.

Fliers take time to design, reproduce, and distribute, but they are a good traditional approach to volunteer recruitment in particular communities. Fliers are versatile because they can be used inside or outside the library and can be distributed in a variety of ways or posted on bulletin boards (see sample 17-2).

Group Presentations

An invitation to speak to local groups can serve as a means to recruit volunteers and advertise your program. You can put a plug in for your program as part of your talk and invite people to visit you at the library or visit the volunteer services web pages. If you have business cards, you can hand them out or have them available at a table in the back of the room with library information. Remember: Your enthusiasm for volunteerism is more important than your formal public speaking skills.

Public Service Announcements, Newspapers, and Newsletters

Locally operated community radio stations and local-access community television often accept public service announcements, including volunteer openings at the library. It is important to work with a knowledgeable station representative to make sure you include all the appropriate information for this medium. Realize, too, that because of limited time and volume in this media your announcement may not always run.

Large metropolitan dailies and small suburban or community weekly newspapers usually run your announcements as a community service in their printed or electronic versions, especially if you have a big event and need volunteers; check to see if they already regularly list community and volunteer activities. If you contact the editor first for specific information on submitting announcements, you can save yourself a lot of time.

Your community may have small, local weekly newspapers, alternative papers, or specialty newspapers. These may help you recruit volunteers with diverse backgrounds or a special skill you need to complete a job. Imagine, for example, that a collector donates twenty-five years of local sports photographs to your library. These need to be identified and cataloged so they can be put online and made available to the public. You might require a

Open the door to customers needing library services . . .

Be A VOLUNTEER
To The HOMEBOUND!!!

*It's Fun * Important * Rewarding * Helping * Caring*
Volunteering to the homebound is easy and requires so little time.

Here is how it functions

The Volunteer Services Department matches the homebound resident and the volunteer, usually based on geographic location. No actual assignment is made until the volunteer has been advised of the distances involved. You are furnished with a complete packet of general instructions, along with identification badge and a special "homebound volunteer" library card. (You are *not* liable for late fees.)

About the time involved

After your initial visit (which should not exceed 30 minutes), your subsequent visits will be only as long and as frequent as you and the homebound person decide. Many volunteers gain additional benefits from the newly found relationships they develop. The number of homebound persons always exceeds the available number of volunteers. Your services are greatly needed. Please call the homebound information number to offer your services or secure additional information. Your registration also will be welcome at any branch library.

Be a Homebound Volunteer

Sample 17-2.   **Volunteer Recruitment Flier**

volunteer with an interest in sports to work on the project, such as a former sports writer for the local newspaper or a long-time high school coach. Your first task would be to research the local print media to see which newspapers write about community sports. Then write a job announcement emphasizing the need for a volunteer interested in a short-term project to identify and categorize photographs of past community sports events. Before you submit your volunteer job announcement, and maybe a short article, remember to take into consideration the newspaper publication schedule and size of articles acceptable. Although many newspapers have been reduced in size, often local papers still have sections about volunteers and local groups.

Many local organizations—school PTAs, homeowner associations, civic groups, and garden, hobby, and travel clubs—have print or electronic newsletters. The library reference staff and the local chamber of commerce can provide you with lists of names and key contacts. The process you use is similar to placing an announcement in the local newspaper, but be aware that, although the library has great support in the community, many of these organizations have specific rules governing what goes in their newsletters. Most groups want an electronic version and they may support what you are doing, but still their policies do not permit them to run your job announcement. Sometimes they accept a feature article, which is an indirect way of recruiting.

Numerous electronic community newsletters and bulletin boards also serve communities. Quite often they are willing to support the library through your volunteer postings. These reach community members who might not be tied into local organizations or not know much about the library. Certainly community leaders know about these newsletters, as does your reference librarian. These are all no-cost or low-cost ways to recruit in your community actively.

Volunteer Referral Organizations and Networks

Nonprofit referral groups such as VolunteerMatch are resources where you can post volunteer positions. If you are not listed with these referral sites, it would be useful to explore whether they might serve your recruitment needs for some of your volunteer positions.

Volunteer Fairs

Some communities organize volunteer fairs for nonprofit groups on an annual basis. It is certainly advantageous to attend one of these fairs and distribute literature about your program. If WiFi is available, you can bring a laptop and show your library services pages plus web features offered by the library. Quite often you will meet someone at any fair who can provide additional tips on recruiting and share stories of success or failure. Both are useful. Getting a couple of people who are interested is a success, plus it is good publicity for you and the library.

BEING FLEXIBLE AND OPEN TO SURPRISES IN YOUR RECRUITMENT CAMPAIGN

It is nice to think that your first efforts in recruiting will pay off. When they do, you have a great feeling of satisfaction that what you did worked. Being knowledgeable and astute about recruitment increases your success. There will be times, though, when your first efforts prove unfruitful. To think in terms of a recruiting campaign is to think of multiple strategies and different sources that can be used to fill a volunteer position efficiently and in a timely manner. The examples discussed in this section are those that you need to refine for your community. Your community may have two online newsletters, an online bulletin board, an alternative newspaper, an ethnic paper, and a general community online volunteer website.

You cannot expect to know all the community resources, so brainstorm with supervising staff, library managers, and volunteers. A lunchtime brown bag brainstorming session can provide a good list of suggestions. Is a posting on Craigslist (www.Craigslist.org) effective for the position in question? If the library technical services manager is looking for an Arabic translator to volunteer to assist in reviewing and cataloging English-Arabic juvenile fiction, where would you find such a person in your community? Recognize that many members of local mosques do not read Arabic, for they come from diverse non-Arabic-speaking countries. This is where the brainstorming process can pay off.

With a list of potential resources derived from brainstorming, your initial effort at this point is to identify what you think are the top possibilities. Next, start networking the top choices to succeed. This does not ensure final success, but your efforts are focused rather than scattered. The brainstorming session may also have identified the best approaches to connect with these community resources. This does not always happen, but if you are successful you will now have ideas on how to make the connections. This might mean an e-mail to a contact on a website, a telephone call to a networked friend in the community, a conversation with a staff member who knows someone who might be able to help, or a posting for information on a statewide electronic discussion list.

To make the most of your time, you should always ask follow-up questions: Do you known anyone who might be able to help me locate a volunteer with these skills? Where else can I look for a person with this set of skills? In other words, even when you initially run into a dead end with the original contact, you can get suggestions on where to recruit. This is where it pays to be flexible in your thinking.

You may, for example, have tried all your sources to find an Arabic translator, and by happenstance you mention your volunteer need to a longtime friend at lunch. She just happens to have a cousin who teaches Arabic at a university, is about to visit for a couple of weeks, and would certainly help the library. You think of all the effort you put in to find someone, and a good friend provides a solution. This is sometimes the way recruitment happens, by planning and by luck.

SECTION 18 | # VOLUNTEER APPLICATION FORMS

THE VOLUNTEER APPLICATION form is an important, multipurpose tool. It serves to let potential volunteers know that there is a process that matches their skills and experience with your library requirements. A well-written application form allows you to conduct better recruiting interviews because you can use the application information to discuss prior work and volunteer experiences. When the application form includes a section of interests that also relates to library needs, you can ask more in depth questions that can help to better match the volunteer to a position.

Most important, a good form allows you to screen individuals who do not meet the job requirements. In addition, application forms can be used to collect volunteer statistics. You can tabulate the number of applications received versus the number of volunteers accepted and determine which recruitment approaches work best for which types of volunteer positions.

How many volunteer application forms does your program require? There is no standard answer to this question. At one extreme, some libraries have distinct application forms for adults, youth, court-directed applicants, interns, and one-day volunteers, as illustrated by the samples in this section. At the other extreme are libraries that combine these into one application form. Advantages and disadvantages exist for both. Depending on your library jurisdiction and policy, you may not have a choice in this matter.

The option of a single, generalized application form ranges from relatively simple versions that use check marks to indicate the type of volunteer and reasons for volunteering to more complex forms that ask numerous background questions and contain additional legal acknowledgments. A single application form reduces the number of forms to track, reproduce, and explain to volunteers and staff. If there are a small number of new volunteers every year, this option is probably sufficient. As the numbers and types of volunteers increase, undoubtedly some type of visual coding on the forms will be necessary to facilitate filling, tracking, and identifying the types of volunteer applicants and their files for reporting purposes.

If you have the authority to decide on the number of application forms, consider the type of information you need in order to make informed selection decisions. Does a young adult application require as much information as an adult form? Should court-directed community service individuals have a simple form that identifies only key contact information because they will be short-term volunteers? In some jurisdictions, court-directed people bring a court form that indicates hours worked and requires your signature. What other information do you need? Further, do you want court-directed forms and files kept separate from regular adult community volunteer files for added personal privacy and confidentiality? Do you have a different retention time for holding court-related applications and file information?

WEB-BASED VOLUNTEER APPLICATION FORMS

At present, three approaches are used on volunteer services web pages. One is a statement to pick up a volunteer application form at one of the libraries in the system, which harks back to traditional ways of doing business and is not a customer-friendly approach considering today's online world. There should be volunteer application forms at the information, circulation, reference, and children's service desks for customers who are at the library and ask for application forms.

A second approach, widely used, is to post a PDF or HTML version of the volunteer application on the volunteer services pages that can be printed out by the volunteer applicant, completed, and either dropped off at the library or faxed to the library (see samples 18-1–18-7). As noted above, there can be different versions of volunteer application forms depending on the type of volunteer. Your web specialist can easily scan and upload your form(s) to the website. The key here is to give the customer specific directions about who to fax the form to, the street address if sent by mail, or where to drop off the application. This seems obvious, but there are volunteer services pages currently on public library websites that do not provide this basic information. Also, check to make sure the e-mail address is current.

A third approach is to provide an online application form that is completed and submitted online (see sample 18-2). This is a customer-friendly approach as long as there are places for explanations on the form as a way to provide additional information. Instructions on the acceptable use of scanned signatures should be stated.

Depending on your community, changes in the economic cycle, or seasonality, you can be overwhelmed with application forms. It would certainly be advantageous to have a volunteer assistant acknowledge receipt of volunteer applications via e-mail. Completed application forms can either be printed out for your review or maintained as electronic files by volunteer positions. These can be selectively forwarded to supervising staff as requested.

Volunteer application forms can be either simple or complex depending on the information you need to gather to satisfy library requirements. It is possible for volunteer applications to ask more specific personal questions than an employee form because the latter must comply with the requirements of federal and state employment laws. However, some libraries closely follow affirmative action employment laws relative to volunteers. Library system differs on the types of questions they include on forms, so be sure to get your forms reviewed and approved by library administration before using them.

If you begin the process of developing an application form or revising an existing one, consider these questions:

- Who gives final review to volunteer application forms?
- Can there be two or more forms, such as one for general community volunteers and one for court-directed individuals?
- Can there be a simplified volunteer form for one-day or special event volunteers?
- Can a simplified version of the form be used for youth volunteers?

KEY COMPONENTS OF AN APPLICATION FORM

The complexity of library volunteer application forms varies greatly by jurisdiction, and in general online forms are much simpler. In recent years, safety and security requirements have added to background consents for volunteers with additional screening questions. Some volunteer application forms are mirror images of paid employment application forms and others are simplified forms to collect general information. No single library uses all the categories shown below, nor do we endorse every category for volunteer forms.

VOLUNTEER APPLICATION

Please return this application to:
Volunteer Office, East Library, 5550 N. Union Blvd.
Colorado Springs, CO 80918 (719) 531-6333, x1251 http://library.ppld.org

VOLUNTEER POSITION: _____ Date: _____

Name _____ Other names used _____

Address _____ City_____

State _____ Zip _____ Home Phone _____ Work Phone_____

Email address _____ Date of Birth _____ / _____ / _____

For how long do you wish to volunteer at the library?
- ❑ Less than a month
- ❑ While I am seeking employment
- ❑ Less than six months
- ❑ More than six months

Library Location Preference (check all that apply)
- ❑ Briargate
- ❑ Cheyenne Mtn
- ❑ East Library
- ❑ Fountain
- ❑ Monument
- ❑ Old Colorado City
- ❑ Palmer Lake
- ❑ Penrose
- ❑ Rockrimmon
- ❑ Ruth Holley
- ❑ Sand Creek
- ❑ Ute Pass

Availability (check all that apply)
❑ Mon | ❑ Tue | ❑ Wed | ❑ Thu | ❑ Fri | ❑ Sat | ❑ Sun | Times Available_____

Work Experience (include volunteer and military service)
Last or present position
Employer_____Position_____City & State_____

Previous position

Employer_____ Position _____City & State _____

Education (check highest level)
| ❑ Elementary | ❑ High School | ❑ Some College | ❑ Area of study or training |
| ❑ Middle School | ❑ Technical School | ❑ College | _____ |

Personal References (not present employer or relative)

1. Name_____Phone_____Relationship_____

2. Name_____Phone_____Relationship_____

Have you ever been convicted of or pled guilty to a felony? (Please check one) NO_____ YES _____
If yes, please give date, place and nature of the charge for which you were convicted.
_____

I certify that the answers contained in this application are true and complete to the best of my knowledge. My volunteer service is conditional upon completion of the application and verification of the references and criminal background check. I am offering my services as a volunteer. If my offer is accepted, I will not be entitled to compensation for any services I provide.
Signature_____ Date_____

Sample 18-1.   **Adult Volunteer Application Form**

SKILLS /AREAS OF INTEREST

(Check all that apply)

Adult Literacy & English Language
- ❑ One-to-one tutoring
- ❑ Talk English! Facilitator
- ❑ Learn English! Classroom aides

Clerical/Office Work
- ❑ Answering phones
- ❑ Clerical/office work
- ❑ Filing
- ❑ Photocopying
- ❑ Record keeping
- ❑ Telephoning
- ❑ Envelope stuffing
- ❑ Shredding
- ❑ Sorting/organizing

Communications/Information
- ❑ Brochure/newsletter
- ❑ Editing
- ❑ Public Speaking
- ❑ Video
- ❑ Photography
- ❑ Writing
- ❑ Displays/bulletin boards
- ❑ Community Events
- ❑ Opinion surveys/polling
- ❑ Receptions

Computer Work
- ❑ Data Entry
- ❑ Database searches
- ❑ Desktop publishing
- ❑ Excel experience
- ❑ Word processing
- ❑ Other software: _____

General Library Work
- ❑ Shelving books
- ❑ Adopt-a-Shelf (shelf-reading)
- ❑ Holds/bin processor

Library/Research
- ❑ Archives/manuscripts
- ❑ Genealogy
- ❑ Local history
- ❑ Oral History
- ❑ Photocopying

Friends of the Library
- ❑ Book sales at author signings
- ❑ Semi-annual Book Sale
- ❑ Book store
- ❑ Book sorting in basement/warehouse

Volunteer Opportunities for Teens Ages 12-17

There are a number of opportunities for young people to serve at the library. They are listed on the PPLD Teen Volunteer Application. **Volunteer applicants ages 12- 17 should complete the Teen Volunteer Application form and return it to the branch library where they wish to volunteer.**

Thank you!

Public Library
PLCMC of Charlotte & Mecklenburg County

ESPAÑOL | FRANÇAIS | DEUTSCH | PORTUGUÊSE

MAKE A DONATION

CATALOG   LOCATIONS   CLASSES / EVENTS   RESEARCH / HOMEWORK   SERVICES   KIDS   TEENS   ABOUT US   CONTACT US

○ Catalog ● Website SEARCH   My Account | Get a Card | Pay Fines | Classic Catalog | Mobile

Home > About Us > Get Involved > Charlotte Mecklenburg Library: Volunteer Application

The Classic Catalog will be unavailable from 8am-Noon on Sept. 27 while we perform maintenance.

ONLINE VOLUNTEER APPLICATION

Print This Page

Use the form below to submit your volunteer application to the volunteer coordinator. Some positions may require a background check.

*(Items marked with * are required)*

Last Name:*	First Name:*
Street Address:*	City:*
State:*	Zip:*
Phone number:*	Cell phone number:
Email address:	Re-type Email address:
Emergency Contact Name:*	Emergency Contact Phone:*

Gender:*   ○ Male   ○ Female

Birthday: Birth Month: [   ]   Birth Day: [ ]   Birth Year: [ ]   * Volunteers must be at least 14 years of age.

Is this a community service requirement?   ☐ School ☐ Work ☐ Other ☐ Court Assigned

(*** Court Assigned requirements must be assigned by Mecklenburg County Court System ***)

If yes, total number of hours required: [   ]

To be completed by: [   ]

Availability: What days are you available? (may vary by branch)*

☐ Sunday ☐ Monday ☐ Tuesday ☐ Wednesday ☐ Thursday ☐ Friday ☐ Saturday

What time during the day are you available? (may vary by branch)*

☐ Mornings   ☐ Afternoons   ☐ Evening   ☐ Other

If you checked "Other" above, please provide details.

[   ]

Volunteer location: At which libraries would you prefer to volunteer?

First Location Choice: [Choose a Library ▼]

Second Location Choice: [Choose a Library ▼]

Sample 18-2.   **Adult Online Volunteer Application Form**

Why are you interested in volunteering?

What appeals to you about the position?:

Please let us know about any special skills or interests:

Current Employer:

Please note:Background checks may be required for some positions.

Have you ever been convicted of an offense against the law other than a minor traffic violation? (A conviction does not mean you cannot be selected as a volunteer. The offense and how recently you were convicted will be evaluated in relation to the volunteer opportunity for which you are applying.) * required ○ Yes ○ No (if yes, explain fully)

Your selection as a volunteer may be contingent upon a successful background check.

May the Library access your police records?* required ○ Yes ○ No

What specifically would you like to contribute to the library?

I understand that it is the Library's policy to protect the privacy of those who use the library. I agree to hold information about patrons in complete confidence and to access this information only in the course of performing my volunteer assignments. In addition, I understand that a breach of confidentiality is grounds for dismissal from the volunteer services program. I also understand that background checks may be necessary for some positions. My submission of this application to the Library indicates an agreement with these terms and conditions.

[Submit Application]

Pima County Public Library

Teen Volunteer Application Form

Name: _____ Phone: _____ Email: _____

Address: _____ City_____ Zip_____

Are you 14 or older? Y   N   Birthdate: _____/_____/_____ School: _____ Grade: ___
                                        (month) (day) (year)

Emergency Contact: _____ Phone: _____

Give two personal references we could call and talk to about your abilities (teachers, counselors, or other adults not related to you).
Name: _____Position:_____Phone:_____

Name: _____Position:_____Phone:_____

1. Have you volunteered before? Yes_____   No_____   If yes, where?_____

2. Please list the skills and experience that you possess which can be utilized in your volunteer service with the Library.   For example, can you speak Spanish?

3. Why do you think you want to volunteer at the library?

4. Please list any interests, hobbies, clubs, activities, or special skills:

5. Are you required to fulfill a specific number of volunteer hours? _____ If yes, how many? _____

At which branch do you want to volunteer? _____

Days you can volunteer: (circle) Sun   Mon   Tue   Wed   Thu   Fri   Sat
Times you can volunteer: From_____am/pm to _____am/pm
First day you can volunteer: _____Last day: _____

List any days you will not be able to volunteer for special reasons: _____

_____

Signature: _____Date:_____
(I attest that all information above is accurate and true to the best of my knowledge)

Parent Signature: _____Date:_____
(Required if teen is under age 18)

Sample 18-3.   **Teen Volunteer Application Form**

APPLICATION

Please print clearly & complete each section.
Applicants 17 years & younger must have a parent's signature.

**Metropolitan Library System
Volunteer Services Office**
300 Park Avenue, OKC, OK 73102
(405) 606-3762
E-mail: volservices@metrolibrary.org

TODAY'S DATE: ___/___/___   ☐ ADULT   ☐ TEEN

☐ Form signed
☐ Parent Signature (if applicant is 17 years or younger)
☐ Court Liaison phoned
☐ Interview completed
☐ HIPAA Training completed & sent to HUM
☐ Copy made & sent to Volunteer Services

NAME: _____
LAST   FIRST   MIDDLE INITIAL

ADDRESS: _____

CITY: _____ STATE: _____ ZIP: _____

PHONE (H): (___) _____ PHONE (W): (___) _____

E-MAIL: _____ Birthday: _____ PHONE (C): (___) _____

Please provide the name and phone number of your court-appointed contact. Court papers, court assignment, deadlines, and any information related to your community service requirements must be provided before volunteer service can be approved.

AGENCY / ORGANIZATION: _____

CONTACT: _____

ADDRESS: _____ PHONE: (___) _____

NOTE: A library supervisor will contact this person/agency to confirm information. Potential volunteers must have a background free of felonious incidents or history of violence and must be deemed appropriate and trustworthy by conference between the library system and the court-appointed person you list above. Six to eight weeks notice is required before your court date, and you may not be able to accomplish all your required hours with this organization.

TOTAL NUMBER OF COMMUNITY SERVICE HOURS ASSIGNED: _____

TOTAL NUMBER OF HOURS YOU WOULD LIKE TO SERVE AT THE LIBRARY: _____

DEADLINE *(must be a minimum of 6-8 weeks from time of application; please provide day/month/year)*: ___/___/___

Do you need confirmation in writing of your hours served with the Metropolitan Library System?   ☐ Yes   ☐ No

If you answered "Yes," please provide the name and address of the person to whom your confirmation letter should be sent:

AGENCY / ORGANIZATION: _____

CONTACT: _____

ADDRESS: _____ PHONE: (___) _____

CITY: _____ STATE: _____ ZIP: _____

PERSON TO CONTACT IN CASE OF AN EMERGENCY:

NAME: _____ RELATIONSHIP: _____

ADDRESS: _____ CITY: _____

STATE: _____ ZIP: _____ PAGER #: _____

PHONE (H): (___) _____ PHONE (W): (___) _____ PHONE (C): (___) _____

MLS #638   Rev. 11/04

Sample 18-4.   **Court-Appointed Community Service Application Form**

I certify that the statements made in this Volunteer Application are true, correct, and given voluntarily. In addition, I understand that this information may be disclosed to any party with legal and proper interest, and I release the Metropolitan Library System from any liability for supplying such information.

I understand that the Metropolitan Library System reserves the right to screen volunteers, and the Metropolitan Library System will not accept as a volunteer anyone who would jeopardize any aspect of library service or the safety of library customers and staff.

I understand that if I am unable to show up for a scheduled time for any reason, I am to notify my library supervisor as soon as possible.

I understand that if I miss my scheduled date and time of service without prior notification, my volunteer opportunity may be terminated by the affected library site and supervisor.

I understand that I will not be paid for my services as a volunteer, and I am giving my time freely to the library to which I am assigned. I will also not abuse any information, materials, or hardware I may use or obtain while volunteering.

I understand that by volunteering, I am not guaranteed any special consideration for any future permanent job positions with the Metropolitan Library System, should I ever apply for one.

APPLICANT'S SIGNATURE: _____ DATE: ____/____/____

PARENT/GUARDIAN'S NAME* (please print): _____

PARENT/GUARDIAN'S SIGNATURE*: _____ DATE: ____/____/____

If applicant is 17 years or younger.

LIBRARY USE ONLY

DATE: ____/____/____

LIBRARY SITE: _____

VOLUNTEER
SUPERVISOR'S NAME: _____

COMMENTS: _____

_____

_____

_____

INTERVIEW DATE: ____/____/____

TRAINING DATE: ____/____/____

STARTING DATE: ____/____/____

ENDING DATE: ____/____/____

DVS NOTIFIED
ABOUT END DATE: ____/____/____

MLS #638   Rev. 11/04

Sample 18-4.   **Court-Appointed Community Service Application Form** *(continued)*

We present the components of current library volunteer application forms here as tools in your review of your applications to determine what categories might be revised, eliminated, or retained. Some of these components may be included as policies in a volunteer services handbook and agreed to and signed for by the volunteer. Local and state laws vary in terms of how unpaid volunteers are addressed, and they are subject to change under new legislation and court rulings, so ask your library human resources administration and attorney to review the final versions of your application forms.

Typical Application Form Components

Name. Last name, first name, and middle Initial. The full name is important if a background check is performed.

Address. Include street address, apartment number, city, and zip code. Post office boxes alone may not be acceptable for background checks.

Length of Time at Present Address. If less than one year, you can request previous address and length of time at that address.

Telephone and E-mail. Home telephone, work and mobile phone, and e-mail address. Be sure to verify current accuracy, especially with people who have moved recently. (Note: Many people are using mobile telephones and keeping their mobile telephone service when moving across country. Local interested volunteers may have mobile telephone numbers with out-of-state area codes.)

Social Security Number. The social security number is required if the volunteer position requires a background check. Many volunteer forms do not have this category. Alternatively, social security numbers can be collected on a separate background check form.

Driver's License Number and Related Documents. Information required for driving positions and for background checks. Check driver's license number, state of issue, and expiration date. For a driving position, have applicant bring a current copy of the motor vehicle record from the state driver's license bureau and review applicant's driving history for tickets and accidents. Review proof of current automobile insurance coverage.

Emergency Contact. Name and contact telephone number for emergency notification.

Current or Most Recent Employer or Occupation. This can be a part-time or full-time paid employment position currently held by the volunteer. Provide a check box to indicate if the applicant is not currently employed.

Previous Employment. Brief listing of previously held paid positions.

Retired from and Title. Used to identify a past employer that makes charitable donations to nonprofit organizations if a person is volunteering, whether an active employee or retired.

Spouse's Employer. Used to identify an employer that makes charitable donations to nonprofit organizations if a family member is volunteering.

Parent or Guardian's Employer. Used to identify an employer that makes charitable donations to nonprofit organizations if a family member is volunteering.

School. For youth applicants, list the current school attending.

Current School Grade. For youth applicants, the current grade enrolled.

Time Availability. Most often a checklist or short-answer section indicates the applicant's availability, particular hours of the day (or morning/afternoon/evening preference) and days of the week. Some libraries ask about the number of volunteer hours per week. A checklist of daily times can be put into two- or four-hour regular shift periods. Alternatively, the applicant can use a blank space to write in the best days and times. For volunteers with specific dates of completion, such as students meeting civic requirements for graduation or court-directed community service individuals, the important information is the completion date.

Skills from Work or Volunteer Experiences. Use a checklist of specific skills based on work or volunteer experience as well as avocation skills or unusual talents. The indicated skills can be matched to library requirements for specific jobs. This list can be expanded to include a self-rating level of competency for each skill area. If you have a skill-based test related to the volunteer position, use it to determine

Court-Directed Community Service Volunteer Application

Last name _____ First _____ Telephone (home or cell) _____

Street Address _____ City _____ Zip Code _____

Age Categories:
___ under 16
___ 16 – 18
___ 19 – 24
___ 25 – 39
___ 40 – 54
___ over 55

Education:
Highest Level Completed:
___ Grammar School
___ High School
___ Technical School
___ Some College
___ College Degree in:
_____

Availability:
Monday _____
Tuesday _____
Wednesday_____
Thursday_____
Friday _____
Saturday _____
Sunday _____

Professional training in: _____

_____ Total hours needed? _____ Completion deadline? _____ Which court system?

Please describe why the court directed community service hours:
_____

In case of an emergency contact:
_____

(name and phone)

Do you have any physical limitations restricting your activities? _____ Yes _____ No
If yes, please explain:
_____

Is there any medical information that you wish to share that would be helpful for the staff to know for a medical emergency?
_____

I understand that, as a court-directed community volunteer, I will be assigned to perform whatever duties the library considers most necessary and helpful to its operation. I also understand that my work will be reviewed and, at any time, the library may terminate my services.

Signature: _____ Date: _____

Complete the skills / interest inventory on the back, sign both this application and the agreement form, and return them to the library or mail or fax them to:
_____

Sample 18-5. **Court-Directed Community Service Application and Agreement**

Skill / Interest / Inventory

Instructions: Indicate those areas of skill / interest which pertain to you. Mark as many as are applicable.

____ art design	____ displays/bulletin boards	COMPUTER SKILLS
____ crafts	____ clerical/office work	____ data entry
____ cartooning	____ outdoor plant care	____ web page
____ filing	____ indoor plant care	____ desktop publishing
____ baking	____ carpentry skills	____ word processing
____ photocopying	____ used book sales	____ spreadsheets
____ shelving books	____ handyman skills	____ database
____ painting	____ sewing skills	

Other: _____

As a court-directed community service volunteer with the library, I agree to the following guidelines:

The library agrees:

1. To provide you with a safe work environment.
2. To provide supervision and training by a member of the library staff, who will answer your questions and provide feedback regarding your work.

As a Court-Directed Community Service Volunteer, I agree:

1. To accept the guidance and decisions of the staff.
2. To recognize the function of the paid staff and stay within the bounds of a community service worker's responsibilities.
3. To always wear a volunteer badge. (They are kept in the file box with the time cards.)
4. To report on time, as scheduled, and check in with the supervisor or staff upon arrival. Failure to do so can result in separation.
5. To fill out and have a staff member sign my time card each shift I work.
6. To inform my supervisor as soon as possible if I am unable to keep my schedule.
7. To notify my supervisor and the volunteer services department if I do not intend to complete my hours at the library.
8. To dress appropriately and act courteously to patrons and employees. (The library is a public place where attitude and appearance are important. Things need to be done accurately.)
9. To maintain the dignity and integrity of the library with the public and patron confidentiality, which is guaranteed under state law. I will not discuss any patrons by name or their reading selections outside of the library.
10. I understand that upon completion of my hours, it is my responsibility to see that my final time card is sent to the Volunteer Services Department. The Volunteer Services Department requires seven days to process my confirmation papers after receiving my final time card. My signed papers will arrive via the postal service unless special arrangements have previously been made.

Court-Directed Community Volunteer Signature _____

Staff's Signature _____

Sample 18-5. **Court-Directed Community Service Application and Agreement** *(continued)* whether to train or reject the applicant. A skill-based test might be word processing a document, putting information into a spreadsheet, or putting books on a shelf cart in Dewey Decimal order; these are not personality tests.

Special Interests and Hobbies. Use a checklist or a place for applicants to write about their areas of interest (not demonstrated skills). Someone who has not read to children's groups before can still be interested in trying it out.

Library Job/Tasks Interest. Use a checklist for applicants to indicate which library volunteer jobs or tasks they prefer. Be sure to add an "Other" category to allow applicants to identify a type of task that is not listed, because this can lead to a new volunteer job. For example, a skilled recreational photographer may be willing to take pictures for the library website, volunteer web page, or Facebook.

Language Skills Other than English. Allow space for applicants to indicate what language(s) they are fluent in, including speaking, writing, and reading. Some libraries in heavily multilingual communities provide a checklist for applicants to indicate their languages and skill levels.

Computer Software Skills. Allow space to indicate any special software proficiencies or competencies.

Library Card. Applicants are asked if they have a library card or use the library.

Location Preference. If you have more than one library in your system, it is a good idea to let the volunteer indicate which library is preferred for volunteering. Some applicants may want to stay close to home; others are open to volunteering wherever there is a need. Some volunteers do not like to drive at night, so they want to stay near their local library.

Previous Volunteer Experience. Provide space to list organizations and assigned duties or tasks. A separate question can inquire if the applicant had previous volunteer experience at the library.

Reasons for Volunteering. Provide either a simple checklist of reasons for volunteering or an open-ended question about what the applicant would like to contribute, accomplish, or get out of the volunteer experience. This category can open up useful discussion during the interview process.

City of Carlsbad
One-Day Volunteer Application

DATE: _____

VOLUNTEER PROJECT: _____

NAME: _____   _____   _____   AGE:_____
              (Last)   (First)   (Middle Initial)

ADDRESS: _____   _____   _____   _____
              (Street)   (City)   (State)   (Zip)

PHONE: _____   _____   _____
             (Home)   (Work)   (Cell/Pager)

EMAIL: _____

EMERGENCY CONTACT: _____   _____   _____
                      (Name)   (Relationship)   (Phone)

VOLUNTEER SERVICES
AGREEMENT AND RELEASE

I, _____, hereby acknowledge that I have voluntarily applied to participate in performing certain services for the City of Carlsbad. I am voluntarily participating in these activities with the knowledge that there is some risk that I may be injured in the course of performing these services. I understand that the City's policy is to cover volunteers of the City through Workers' Compensation insurance. I also understand that under Workers' Compensation laws, Workers' Compensation benefits will be the sole and exclusive remedy in the event I am injured while performing these volunteer activities and services. I further understand and agree that I will only be entitled to medical expenses under the City's Workers' Compensation. I will not be entitled to any other Workers' Compensation benefits which may include, but are not limited to, permanent or temporary loss of use damages, replacement income or vocational rehabilitation benefits. With the exception of Workers' Compensation benefits as set out above, I hereby agree that I, my heirs, guardians, legal representatives and assigns will not make a claim against or file an action against the City of Carlsbad or any of its agents, officers, employees or other volunteers, for injury or damage resulting from negligence, howsoever caused, by any employee, agent, officer or volunteer of the City of Carlsbad as a result of my participation in this volunteer activity or service. In addition, I hereby release and discharge the City of Carlsbad, its agents, officers, employees and other volunteers from all actions, claims and demands that I, my heirs, guardians, legal representatives or assigns now have or may hereafter have for injury or damage resulting from my participation in these volunteer activities or services. In the event of an emergency, I hereby give the City of Carlsbad permission to seek medical attention for myself or my child, if volunteer applicant is less than 18 years of age. I give the City of Carlsbad, free of any compensation, unlimited permission to use, publish, and republish for such use as it may determine, information and reproductions of my likeness and my voice related to my volunteer work with the City. I hereby waive my right to first review the use of my likeness or voice before any use of publication.

I HAVE CAREFULLY READ THIS AGREEMENT AND FULLY UNDERSTAND ITS CONTENTS. I AM AWARE THAT THIS IS A PARTIAL RELEASE OF LIABILITY AND A CONTRACT BETWEEN ME AND THE CITY OF CARLSBAD AND SIGN IT ON MY OWN FREE WILL.

Signature (Parent or Guardian if volunteer is under age 18): _____
Date: _____

We look forward to working with you and appreciate the generous offer of your time and skill.

Creating community for those who live, work and play in Carlsbad.

Sample 18-6. **One-Day Volunteer Application Form**

Storytelling/Read-Aloud Volunteer Application

Name _____ Birthday Month/Day _____

Address _____

City _____

State and Zip Code _____

Telephone (h) _____

(w) _____

E-mail: _____

Emergency contact: _____

Name: _____ Phone _____

Occupation: _____

Languages You Speak Fluently _____Languages You Read Fluently_____

Skill/Talents (please describe) _____

Experience with children (please describe) _____

Are you interested in storytelling? Reading stories? Both?

Availability

- Days (Please circle all that apply)? M T W Th F
- Times? Mornings _____ Afternoons _____
- How often are you available to read? Weekly? Once a month? Please be specific:
- Can you make a one-year commitment?

Are there two people you know well, either professionally or personally, who can talk about your ability or experience in working with children?

Name: _____ Phone # _____

Name: _____ Phone # _____

The safety of children in this program is the first concern of the library. We require every prospective volunteer to pass a police background check. Please complete the attached form and return it with your application.

I have read the job description and guidelines and understand the responsibilities and duties of this position.

Signature of Applicant _____ Date: _____

Signature of Parent/Guardian if under 18 _____ Date: _____

Sample 18-7. **Storytelling/Read-Aloud Volunteer Application**

Education Level. A checklist or "fill in the blank" indicates the highest level of education completed, whether a high school diploma, GED, or one or more college degrees. A separate question can obtain information on relevant training and additional coursework. This information can be used to place applicants. Libraries are staffed with a high percentage of college-educated individuals, many with advanced degrees. Mature volunteers may not have the educational level of some of the current staff members, but they have life experience and on-the-job training that will certainly enrich and diversify library services.

Gender. Gender information is used primarily as a source of statistical information and on background check forms.

Date of Birth/Age. Date of birth is required for background checks. This category is most often used to indicate if a person is under age eighteen. Age categories are a source of statistical information and may provide information that indicates volunteer interest and assignments that are attracting them.

Convicted of a Felony or Misdemeanor. Asking about an arrest is not permitted, but asking about a conviction for a crime is. Minor traffic offenses can be omitted. Provide space to indicate the date of conviction, type of offense, and outcome. You can ask if the applicant is presently under charges for a felony or misdemeanor and about convictions resulting from a military trial.

Incidents of Child/Elder Abuse or Neglect. Information on any incident, with space for an explanation. The key is the circumstances, the time since the incident, and the type of volunteer position being considered.

Physical Limitations. If applicants have physical limitations that would restrict them from performing the volunteer jobs, it is important to know in order to provide reasonable accommodation.

Medical Conditions. The supervisor should have information on medical conditions because they can affect the type of volunteer position assigned, such as an allergic reaction to particular chemicals.

How Referred to the Library. This can be a checklist of ways the applicant learned about the library volunteer services program. Be sure to provide an "Other" category to identify an unexpected path to the program.

References. The number of requested references varies among library systems, from none to three. Some libraries specify who references must be from, such as business/professional reference, work supervisor, personal reference, or volunteer reference. Unless specified, references can include people who know the individual through membership in a professional, service, civic, or religious organization, because these are usually voluntary groups. It is often easier to conduct reference checks with these organizations than with larger companies or public agencies. Be sure to indicate that immediate family members and other relatives cannot be listed as references.

Photograph Permission. Applicants grant permission for library to use any image or audio recordings of them, including photographs, videotapes, digital video, and sound recordings, for publicity and promotion purposes in print and electronic formats. This is an area of growing importance as digital photographs and videos are uploaded to library websites and third-party sites such as YouTube and Flickr. If a photograph is taken of a group of volunteers receiving certificates at the annual recognition luncheon and posted the next day on the volunteer pages of the library website, this can be interpreted as promoting the library and volunteer program. Some libraries indicated that any identification of a volunteer is only by first name; others do not make this restriction.

Hold Harmless Statement, Medical and Property. This legal statement is used to protect the volunteer services manager, staff, administrators, library trustees, and the library from a lawsuit by a volunteer injured or suffering property loss while working at the library. In most library jurisdictions, volunteers are not covered by workers' compensation laws because they are unpaid. Any medical attention or costs of an injury are the responsibility of the volunteer. Local and state laws vary on the medical protection of volunteers, so this wording should be reviewed by the library attorney. Property can include a personal laptop being used as part of the volunteer assignment. In some jurisdictions, the hold harmless statement is required on the volunteer application form.

Although there are numerous variations, a typical hold harmless statement is in the form of "I hereby agree to indemnify and hold harmless the library and its officers, agents, employees, advisors, customers, and volunteers from any liability or claims of loss, costs or expenses including attorney fees, or personal injuries to me or damage to my property or theft or loss of my property in connection with my participation and work as an unpaid volunteer at the library."

Limits to Workers' Compensation. A few libraries specifically state on the application form that a volunteer is covered by workers' compensation and limits any payments for treatment to coverage under the existing workers' compensation program. In other words, a volunteer cannot ask for more than the program allows.

Background Investigation Consent. This statement gives permission for the library to obtain information related to the applicant's background and criminal history record. Some libraries state that criminal background checks can be repeated during the volunteer's time with the library and indicate a procedure to clarify any information obtained from the records. Alternatively, a separate criminal background investigation is applied only to those applying for sensitive volunteer positions.

Employment History Review Consent. In this statement the applicant allows the library or a third-party company used by the library to investigate employment history and work experience. Some volunteer applicants may have purposely omitted previous employers for reasons that might be relevant to volunteering at the library. Such statements also include a release from liability for damages resulting from providing the requested information.

Privacy and Confidentiality. This statement requires the volunteer to protect the privacy and confidentiality of customers, staff members, and other volunteers and any proprietary information of the library, subject to dismissal for violation. A volunteer privacy statement is most likely the same as that agreed to by paid staff.

Agreement or Certification Statement for Application. This section is an agreement that the applicant has provided accurate information without omissions and understands that tasks are assigned on the basis of library needs and requirements. Additionally, it states that if misstatements are found on the application form, if the assigned tasks are not done to library standards, or if the volunteer violates library policy, then the volunteer relationship can be terminated. The agreement implies that the library takes volunteering seriously and that the volunteer agrees to provide accurate information and follow all library rules and procedures.

Signature and Date. Signature line and date line are provided for the applicant eighteen years or older to sign. An additional signature line is provided for a parent or guardian of youth under eighteen years.

For Library Staff/Office Use Only. Used by staff to indicate specific information such as date application received, interview date, start date, training date, placement, supervisor, and comments. Only a small number of libraries use this component. (Note. Although there may be some efficiency gained by writing such information on the application form, it does not add to the friendliness of the form and can lead to a feeling of just one of many being processed along. Further, it is important that inappropriate staff comments do not appear in the comment section.)

PRIVACY AND APPLICATION FORMS

The more information you collect on a volunteer applicant, the greater your responsibility to protect the privacy and confidentiality of the information. Human resource professionals are trained and accustomed to protecting great quantities of personal information about paid staff. Volunteer services managers with limited prior experience and staff members assigned to manage library volunteers on a part-time basis are not used to being responsible for personal confidential files. It is easy to slip up. For example, having social security numbers on completed volunteer applications and sharing these with staff or sorting them in a semipublic area exposes the volunteer applicant to possibilities of identity theft. Passing such application forms on to supervising staff also requires that these staff members recognize the confidentiality of the information. Having the forms lie around the back room just because they are from "volunteer applicants" does not demonstrate a high level of professionalism in maintaining confidentiality and can open the library to legal actions if personal information is compromised.

Recognize that all personal information collected on current and past volunteers, including those not accepted into the program, requires protection. This means keeping records in secure files until destroyed by shredding or deletion from electronic storage. This is part of your volunteer services program responsibility. See more on retention of older volunteer files in section 36.

| # INTERVIEWING AND SELECTION

AN INTERVIEW IS a focused conversation, in the context of this book one designed to elicit responses that help you make a decision about inviting an individual to become a volunteer with the library. From your initial introduction to your final departing comments, you are representing the library and setting the tone for any future relationships. If you are new to conducting interviews, you may find it difficult to adopt a relaxed, conversational style. This is not as important as making sure you focus on the skills and qualities needed for the volunteer position, because losing your focus here can result in an individual being improperly selected for the job. Think of the interview as a focused conversation that is partially scripted, in both your words and your behaviors. Your personal script needs to concentrate on specific points of information that should be given to the volunteer applicant, along with key questions.

TYPES OF INTERVIEWS

There are two types of interviewing modes you are likely to use: telephone and face-to-face. (Video and electronic interviews exist but are uncommon in a library setting.) Telephone interviewing is useful to screen out potential volunteers who may not have the appropriate library interests, time commitment, or motivation. This can also be a time to recommend, in a positive manner, other organizations and agencies that accept volunteers. Through this conversation, you can also encourage individuals to come in for further information and at the same time create enthusiasm for the available volunteer job or tasks.

Face-to-face interviews are used to make either a final decision about hiring a volunteer or, more commonly, to screen volunteers for a supervising staff member. In other words, this is the first step in a two-step process, with the supervising staff member making the final decision. Both of these interviewing functions are important to the total process of finding an acceptable volunteer for the position. For volunteers under your direct supervision, this is a one-step process.

When you screen a potential volunteer, your effort is to find the kind of volunteer who has the skills and abilities to do the job and who will fit the departmental subculture and management style of the supervising staff member. A loud, fast-talking, highly animated individual is not likely to work out well with a staff supervisor who is quiet, deliberate, and soft spoken, regardless of the volunteer's skill level.

The end of your interview will most likely go in one of three directions: (1) "Yes, you have just the skills and interests and time commitments we are looking for, and we would like you to begin on Wednesday." (2) "Thank you for coming in, but at present there is no match between our library volunteer needs and your skills or time requirements. Have you considered this list of other community groups that need volunteers?" (3) "You have the volunteer background and skills we would like to have, but at the moment there are no appropriate openings. I would like to keep you on my calling list so I can place you in one of our future openings." Be honest with each volunteer applicant.

VOLUNTEER SELECTION

Every once in a while, more than one capable volunteer passes your screening process. Each is eligible for consideration, but only one position is available. If you cannot expand the volunteer hours or offer alternative volunteer tasks, then it is important that the selection process be based on specified selection criteria. The criteria may be the number of weekly hours, scheduled availability, time-off requests, skill mix, the ability to handle task demands, or fitting into the organizational culture. The latter criterion is less specific but just as important.

At the selection stage, detailed conversations about the job description, actual demonstrations of what is expected, or observations of another volunteer performing the tasks can make the decision easier. Be honest, realistic, and up front about the expected duties. Not only is this candor fair to the applicants, it allows them time to reexamine their decisions and decide if this job is really what they want. And remember that, when you are fortunate enough to have more qualified candidates for a position than you need, you can promise the candidate not chosen that he will be the first considered if another position of this type opens up.

After offering a position to a potential volunteer, allow her to think about the work overnight, or set a follow-up date to meet and discuss the tasks more fully. After talking about the library opportunity with family members, she may find that the scheduling demands will not work out or that this is not quite what she had in mind when she decided to volunteer at the library. A good interview leads to a self-selection process in which the potential volunteer opts out, wishes to do something else, or comes back excited.

An important part of the interview process is to find out what the volunteer likes to do or wants to avoid. Some people do not like to make telephone calls; others avoid a lot of people contact. It is important not to oversell a position to a marginal volunteer just to get someone to do the job. A bad fit between the volunteer and the position will likely leave negative feelings among staff, managers, other volunteers, and the misplaced volunteer.

Few people enjoy being rejected, especially for volunteer positions, yet using good interviewing skills may lead you to such a decision. In structuring the interview questions, you can assist unqualified people to self-select out. This is easier done with objective job conditions, such as "You must be here by 4:00 p.m. each of the assigned days" or "The library expects a full six-month commitment up front" or "Three consecutive days of volunteer orientation and required training must be completed first." These types of conditions can lead some applicants to have second thoughts and decide to volunteer elsewhere. If this does not happen, then you have to "reject" the volunteer for the position.

Inherent in the general process of volunteer interviewing, selecting, and rejecting is the library's community relations function. In turning down people because of lack of skills, interests, attitudes, personal schedules, or "fit" with the library organization, it is essential to recognize that these people are probably library customers and tax-paying citizens. A positive rejection may do little or no harm, but a negative one can generate intense, nasty comments about the library in general or you as the volunteer services manager.

Ideally, you can match a rejected volunteer with another library position, which converts the rejection into a new opportunity. If this is not possible, you might suggest that the person explore other community groups by drawing upon any skills sets in the application form that might fit another organization. It is useful to have a list of other agencies, even a printout of the list on your website, just to hand to the applicant. Certainly you can refer a person to your counterpart in a community organization, but beware that the expectations of all parties might not be met. Nevertheless, your rejection can lead to another contact name. If you feel a referral is inappropriate or not allowed by library policy, then reject the individual as politely as possible.

SCRIPTING

New interviewers fumble for words. Experienced interviewers use a variety of personal scripts to keep the conversation focused, mutually useful, informative, and friendly. Depending on your library administration, you may be required to follow strict hiring guidelines that include not asking illegal questions on race, religious affiliation, national origin, sex, age, disability, marital status, childbearing plans, or arrest record. Your human resources manager likely has a list of "not to be asked" questions, or you or a reference staff member can go online and find these on human resources websites.

Since employment affirmative action laws do not directly cover volunteers, your administration may not care what questions you ask potential volunteers, giving you more leeway to ask a wider range of questions. However, in most cases there is little need to ask questions in the interview that touch on any of the just-mentioned topics. Whether one is married, divorced, legally separated, or living with someone has no bearing on how well they can answer library telephones, shelve books, provide computer training, or any other tasks.

A useful script includes several topic categories and types of questions: introductory, background, skill-based, time and schedule, attitude/culture, and probing (see box 19-1). With experience you can learn to blend and script these types of questions into your interviews.

Introductory questions help establish a friendly, interested, and positive tone. They can be asked on your way to your office or as the applicant is getting seated. Moreover, in some more extreme instances you may quickly discover that the applicant is not appropriate for the library just with the answers to these questions.

Background questions verify what you read on the application form while providing the applicant the opportunity to clarify information and discuss it further. If the applicant skipped a question on the application form, this is the time to inquire about the omission. Asking about a recent move or place of

Introductory Questions

How is your day going so far?

Did you have any problem finding the volunteer services office?

Focused Background Questions

What types of work or volunteer experiences have you had that would make you a good library volunteer?

What is it about our library that makes you want to volunteer here?

Have you used our library services? Which one(s)?

When you are in a library, where do you usually go first? Second?

What kinds of jobs have you observed in the library that most excite you?

If you are assigned to a job that requires us to have a copy of your driving record and/or have a criminal background check on file, what would these records show?

Skill-Based Questions

What are the top three skills or talents that you would bring to our library volunteer position?

Are there any of these skills you are trying to improve?

Have you taken any recent workshops or classes?

What lifelong learning experiences can you bring to the job?

Describe your computer experiences, whether at work or home.

Some of our volunteer jobs require precise work and others are more general. Which of these types of work do you feel more comfortable with?

What types of volunteer jobs or tasks do you like to do the most?

What types of jobs do you least like to do?

Tell me about one of the most challenging volunteer or work assignments that you had to perform?

Which of your work or volunteer positions had tasks that required a high level of detail and accuracy?

If you could design your ideal volunteer job for the library, what would it be like?

Box 19-1. **Sample Interview Questions**

Time and Schedule Questions

Are the days listed on your application form the only times you can volunteer?

Which days of the week are the best for you?

What times of day are best for you?

How long per day can you volunteer for us?

What time of day do you do your best work?

What time and/or days during the week are definitely out for doing volunteer work?

Do you have any foreseeable scheduling problems if you started with us next week?

How long a commitment in months are you willing to give to the library?

When can you start?

Attitude and Organizational Questions

What prompts you to want to volunteer at our library?

Describe a group in which you were a volunteer that you think is most similar to the library environment?

What kinds of volunteer work have you done over the past five years?

In what type of group settings do you enjoy doing volunteer work?

If you could choose the kinds of people you would work with, what would they be like?

When you have a problem in accomplishing a task, what do you do?

Are there any problem situations that might interfere with your library volunteer duties?

Probing Questions

Why?

What do you mean?

When did that happen?

How?

Where?

Tell me more.

Can you please expand on that point for me?

I am not sure that I understand.

How do you think that experience might relate to our library?

Paraphrase an answer, then ask, "Is this what you mean?"

Box 19-1.　**Sample Interview Questions (continued)**

employment creates discussion and a further opportunity to establish rapport while you get useful information.

Skill-based questions determine how well the applicant's skills and abilities meet the specific skill requirements of the position. If the task requires finger dexterity, as in book mending, you can ask about the types of paid and unpaid positions a person has held that required the use of his hands, or about hobbies and recreational activities that involve finger dexterity. Anyone who knits, makes porcelain statues, or repairs their own household furniture demonstrates the skills necessary for mending. This does not mean they can do materials mending or even that they want to, but it certainly shows the capability to do this and similar tasks.

Interviews for a volunteer job that requires public contact, such as assisting at the circulation desk, can be asked about current or former paid or unpaid positions that required contact with customers. You can ask the applicant if in contacting a stranger she would prefer to write a letter, send an e-mail, or call on the telephone, and why? People who do not like to talk to strangers may prefer to write a letter or send an e-mail and wait for a response. Someone more comfortable talking to strangers might well be at ease telephoning customers or community organizations.

Time and schedule questions reduce potential conflicts or misunderstandings later on. They may be used to verify application information, with pauses to allow added explanations. If the individual has travel plans, as many retired or semiretired persons do, you need to be honest about library expectations. If a potential volunteer has a three-month travel plan, you may be able to inform him that you will be glad to schedule volunteer work upon his return.

Some library volunteer tasks are fluid and can be adjusted to an applicant's schedule. Other tasks have to be performed at certain times of the day, week, or month, or when a particular staff member is present in the library and can supervise the volunteer. You might ask whether the days and times of the week noted on the application form are the only times an applicant is available to volunteer. The applicant may be responding to a position opening but actually have other times during the week available which, in fact, would work better. This opens options for you as well as the candidate and may allow scheduling adjustments.

Questions on attitudes and organizational culture cover the "soft skills" of relating to and working with others in a library setting. Even in a relaxed interview situation, there is a formality that can camouflage how an individual may actually work with other volunteers and staff members. Questions here attempt to get at a person's temperament (intense, easygoing), expectations about others (demanding, supportive, participative), outlook on life (optimistic, pessimistic), disposition (sense of humor, humorless), and motives for volunteering in a public library. Along with the questions in sample 19-1, you might use any of these: "What is your reaction when a project you are working on goes wrong and you have to redo the work?" "When someone wrongly accuses you of making a mistake, how do you handle the situation?" "When you have a bad day, what do you do to cheer yourself up?" "In what paid or volunteer positions have you worked in a team environment, and how did those situations work out for you?" A good response to such questions would demonstrate a positive attitude under what can be stressful circumstances.

Probing questions help you get more in-depth answers. Poor interviewers often take the first answer they hear without asking a follow-up to obtain more information. A volunteer applicant may give quick responses to your questions because she is nervous. If you take these at face value, you may be disappointed later on. Learn to probe. Two easy-to-use nonverbal probes are waiting out pauses to let the person speak further on the topic, and giving a slight positive nod of your head and simultaneously making eye contact, which prompts the applicant to continue.

As in any good conversation, there is give and take in the flow of words, but you should limit your side of the dialog to about 25 percent talking and 75 percent active listening. Remember to listen for behavioral and attitudinal examples that give clues to the type of person applying for volunteer work. A behavior example is an action the person took in response to something that happened. The action taken ("I went to the supervisor" or "I talked to the person during our break period") is an indicator of how the person might act as a library volunteer. If you do not hear examples, just ask the applicant a situational question such as "Can you give me an example of when you enjoyed volunteering your time?

An attitudinal example shows positive or negative statements toward a person, object, organization, or issue. A statement such as "I just hate computers" is attitudinal. Remember, though, that context matters. Said in a moment of frustration, as many of us have done, such a statement has a different interpretation than it does within an interview. An applicant who claims to enjoy the orderliness of the library or friendliness of the staff is also making attitudinal statements.

Libraries have organizational cultures that include values, beliefs, and rules that guide staff and administrators in day-to-day interactions. Some library systems are administratively formal and require staff and customers to observe well-defined and posted rules. Other libraries are guided by flexibility in pleasing customers, stretching the rules when necessary, and have the open friendliness of a community library. Within a library, different departments often have their own subcultures. There may be ongoing laughter in the back work area as the children's librarians and assistants practice a new hand puppet show; at the same time, you can hear a pin drop in the back room of the reference department as they do searches or read e-mail. Additionally, under different department heads department subcultures can change, although changes to the overall library culture are less obvious and slow at best.

An important aspect of your interviews is determining whether an applicant with the required skills and interests can successfully fit into the subculture of the department. An applicant might causally mention that what made volunteering at the community winter clothing drive fun for her was being able to sort clothing while meeting and conversing with a lot of new people. Although qualified in others ways, she might have difficulties if placed in a library department that expected limited personal conversations during work.

If you must reject a candidate for any reason, have a script prepared for that too. Here is one example: "You and I have discussed our volunteer program, and I do not see a fit between your skills and our current library requirements. I think your desire to do community volunteering is commendable. Here is a list of community organizations prepared by our reference department that regularly look for good volunteers. The current contact information is shown, and our reference librarians can help you locate their websites if you like. Again, thank you for thinking about the library." In the behavioral part of your script, you are standing up and moving the person toward the door. Remember, friendliness is important throughout the process.

SCRIPT SOURCES

Your library may have used a structured interview when you were hired for the volunteer services manager position; the human resources person or your manager may have used a written set of prepared questions that they asked you in sequence. This is one type of formal interview script. Other hiring managers have a semiformal script that may ask follow-up questions based on the written answers on the application form first and then use a few of their "standard" questions during the interview. These "standard" questions are not written down, but they are regularly used by these managers during interviews. Still other interviewers "wing" the interviews on the basis of the applicants' answers and follow up on different responses. Questions for a structured interview should come from the job description so that they are relevant and consistent for all applicants to a particular volunteer position.

Writing down answers and following up with probing questions provides you a basis for selecting one volunteer over another or for finding a different volunteer job for an applicant.

In thinking about your interviewing approaches, consider two warnings. First, if you choose to use only the application form as the basis for structuring your interviews, be aware of omissions. If the application form covers a range of volunteer positions and you do not bridge to the specific requirements of the position you are filling, omissions can result in problems later. To illustrate, assume that you accidentally forget to tell an applicant for a storytime helper position that duties include shelving picture books, which requires bending, stooping, and kneeling. If the volunteer is expecting only to assist reading books to children and knows nothing about the other duties, this can lead to dissatisfaction and accusations that you were not up front about the job demands.

Second, just "winging" interviews is not recommended. You can find yourself asking illegal or inappropriate questions and not treating volunteer applicants consistently. There will certainly be times when you find yourself on conversational tangents, but having a structured interview brings you back to the questions and topics at hand.

SECTION 20	# BACKGROUND AND REFERENCE REQUESTS

SOME VOLUNTEER JOBS at libraries require background investigations. Most often, they involve vulnerable customers (e.g., children), at-risk individuals (homebound customers), or sensitive or confidential customers or library information. Today, public institutions and nonprofit agencies must be careful to ensure that they hire responsible individuals with a past record of honesty and integrity. Background and personal reference checks protect you and the library as well as the volunteer and library customers from potential problems.

BACKGROUND INVESTIGATIONS

Background investigations are part of the screening and selection processes of recruiting volunteers. There are numerous types of background checks including current and previous employment, current and prior residences, criminal history, lawsuits, sex offender checks, credit checks, and financial stability. If your library system requires a basic criminal background investigation of all volunteers, either at the time of hire or on an annual basis, then your procedures are established.

If you are setting up a volunteer program or reassessing your current back-ground investigation requirements and procedures, then the first question is why do you need background checks for volunteers? Just because another library system is doing them does not mean that you should have them. The other library may have volunteer positions that differ from yours. If your volunteers are always working directly under the supervising staff and are always in sight or in public places within the library and never alone with vulnerable customers, then your volunteer program may have little if any need for background checks.

Background investigations may also provide a feeling of safety and security for the staff and customers. The associated costs of investigations in this case are understood as part of workplace safety. This can lead to a false sense of security (see below). Another justification for background checks is that they are part of the libraries' due-diligence effort when hiring new volunteers. In the event of a major problem, such as a sexual offense against a minor or a theft from the circulation desk by a volunteer, the library can demon-strate that background checks were in fact conducted on the volunteers. The emphasis here is to reduce the risks, liabilities, and potential legal costs to the library of using volunteers and at the same time to do damage control from a community relations viewpoint. Finally, background checks are a way to scare off people you would not want as volunteers; in more formal terms, they self-select out of applying for your positions. Although each of these reasons may be a legitimate basis for conducting background checks, there is a cost factor that has to be weighed against the benefits.

Type and depth of background investigations are also relevant. If paid staff and unpaid volunteers have similar hiring criteria and these include a basic criminal background check as issued by the local police department, then the rationale for these expenses is that they are part of the budgeted costs of providing a safe work environment. However, when these checks cover only your state databases, and not national databases, this can create a feeling of security that is not warranted. A person who may have been convicted two years ago of purse snatching in one state would not show up on another state's database. Although this crime does not put this person on the top ten wanted list, in the large female demographics of libraries this is someone who can make many staff members feel unsafe.

Commercial background investigation companies draw upon public, mul-tistate, or national databases, but the expenses increase. Even so, if a volun-teer will be working with children or youth alone, as might be the case for homework helpers, then there may be good justification for the added costs of a multistate criminal check and a multistate sex offender database check as well. Determine how many volunteer positions you think should have more extensive background checks and the yearly turnover of these volunteers to get an approximation of the yearly costs for these checks. If out of one hundred volunteer positions only six positions require in-depth checks, but you have a low turnover, the actual average yearly expense for the added checking may be less than a couple of hundred dollars. Some library application forms indicate that, if a more detailed criminal background check is required, the applicant is responsible for the costs; this is one way to reduce these expenses for the volunteer services department.

With the rapid expansion of personal information on the Internet, there is a lot of competition from background investigation companies, which can keep expenses down. Just remember that all criminal and other background investigations are not equal; it is important to understand the limitations of any report information you receive. Even on national database reports, not all states contribute information equally. As an aside, human resources departments often conduct online name searches for applicants being considered. If you have not done a name search on yourself, you might be surprised at what you find.

Before you initiate or reevaluate current background services that require more information from the volunteer, talk to the library administration, library attorney, or city or county legal department. Make sure that you and the library administration have a basic understanding of the state's statutes on offenses against individuals. The state law can act as a guide to help you write the volunteer policy on this issue. Conviction of crimes against children, driving while under the influence of drugs, substance abuse, sexual abuse, elderly abuse, domestic violence, fraud, burglary, and theft, among others, can preclude acceptance for a volunteer position.

Background investigations must be done with the consent of the individual. Whether on the volunteer application form or on a separate criminal background investigation form, you require the signature of the applicant (see sample 20-1 for an example). Make sure you check with the police department or commercial investigation service to find out what personal and demographic information is necessary to complete a background check. Some checks require fingerprinting and photographing.

A background investigation may be less on the criminal side and more intended to verify the information supplied on the application form, such as current and previous employers, dates of employment, and current and past home addresses. Confirmation of the information submitted on the application and in interviews gives a sense of confidence about an applicant's honesty.

At some point you may have concerns that cannot be written into your volunteer policy statement but need to be considered, such as when a background check suggests the possibility of irresponsible behavior, a violent

Metropolitan
LIBRARY SYSTEM

Authorization for Background Check
(For persons 18 years and older.)

During the application process and at any time during the tenure of my volunteer service with the Metropolitan Library System, I hereby authorize LexisNexis Screening Solutions Inc., on behalf of the Metropolitan Library System to procure a background report that I understand may include information regarding my character, general reputation, or personal characteristics. This report may be compiled with information from court record repositories, departments of motor vehicles, past or present employers and educational institutions, governmental occupational licensing or registration entities, business or personal references, and any other sources required to verify information that I have voluntarily supplied. I understand that I may request a complete and accurate disclosure of the nature and scope of the background verification to the extent such investigation includes information bearing on my character, general reputation, or personal characteristics.

If a conviction record is found on an individual submitting an application, the applicant will be considered individually based on the following:

- The length of time since a conviction
- The nature of the crime
- The relationship between the job to be performed and the crime committed
- The number of convictions
- The rehabilitation efforts
- Subsequent employment history

Based on these criteria, possibility of service and volunteer placement will be decided by the administration of the Metropolitan Library System.

_____   _____
Applicant/Volunteer Name and Signature   Date

Oklahoma Residents please note: Under Oklahoma law, you have a right to receive a free copy of your background report by checking the appropriate box below.

☐ YES, I am an Oklahoma resident and would like a free copy of my background report.

Please Print

Last Name_____   First Name_____

Middle Name_____   Name Suffix_____

Other Name_____   Social Security #_____

Date of Birth _____   Home Phone_____

House Number _____   Gender ☐ Male   ☐ Female

Street Name_____   *(Physical address only, no P.O. Box number)*

City_____ State_____   County_____

Zip_____

All information on this form will remain confidential.
Metropolitan Library System Volunteer Services Office, 606-3762

Sample 20-1. **Authorization for Background Check**

nature, or unsafe habits. What if an individual applies for a position in home-bound services and the background report comes back with an arrest but no conviction for elder abuse or domestic violence? What are your options, and how can this situation be addressed? At this point you need to require more information and clarification from the individual concerning the arrest. Keep the discussion confidential and always keep detailed records. You may want to seek administrative or legal counsel before deciding to use this individual as a volunteer.

Will you have a formal or informal procedure by which an applicant can review or clarify information found on a background investigation? Will you require the applicant to put in writing the part of the report that is in disagreement or in need of more clarification in order to become part of the file. This is an area for which you should seek guidance from the library administration or attorney.

PERSONAL REFERENCE CHECKS

Calling a volunteer's personal references can help you learn more about the personality of the individual, verify some of the supplied information, and give you a feel of how the applicant relates to other people. Unless these references are current supervisors subject to policies of their company that limit what information can be provided, most people share a lot of useful information if you give them the chance. Remember, they are trying to be helpful to their friend. This is the plus side of reference checks and can make you feel that you accurately assessed an applicant during an interview. On the down side, if the references are close friends of the applicant, they may not be as forthright about any limitations of the applicant.

Briefly explain the reason for your call. Typical opening background questions are "How long have you known _____?" "In what capacity have you known _____?" Provide a brief explanation about the volunteer assignment and time commitments. Keep your questions focused on the volunteer position. You can ask how the reference thinks the applicant would perform volunteer tasks as described. Be sure to pause and let the reference do most of the talking. You can ask a follow-up question if you feel the information is inadequate or does not complete the information you need or if you have certain reservations. You can ask what reasons, if any, would prevent the applicant from being able to perform the described volunteer duties. Again, it is important to pause and allow the reference to think about the question. It is useful to have a set of prepared questions or a standard reference form so that you can be consistent and not forget to ask important questions. If your library uses a written form for paid staff applicants, you might be able to modify it for your use.

The challenge in conducting volunteer reference checks is that, for most libraries, volunteer services managers do not have their own staff and thus have little time to conduct reference checks. This is especially problematic when quite a few volunteers are brought into the library every year. One option is to hire a volunteer as an assistant to be trained to conduct reference checks. There are people with extensive administrative backgrounds who would like to volunteer their time in your office rather than shelve books. Another option is to send a written reference form with a stamped return envelop to the references (see sample 20-2). Using this approach requires collecting address information on the volunteer application form. A more expensive option is to have a commercial investigation company conduct the reference checks as part of a general background investigation. Essentially, the company runs the applicant's name through a set of public databases and then makes telephone calls to the listed references to verify applicant information.

A last option is to identify the positions that should have reference checks as a precondition of hiring, which limits the number of reference checks needed. This can be done if your library policy is flexible and requires volunteer positions to be reference-checked only under specific conditions. For example, a person recently moving to the community might constitute an adequate reason to conduct a reference check. Or, if you feel an applicant's answers are not consistent and you need additional information, a reference check might be justified. Guard against any patterns that can be interpreted as discriminatory, such as doing reference checks on one ethnic/racial group and not another or one age group and not another.

Quick Overview on Reference Checks

1. Reference checks need to be done on individuals who will be working with vulnerable customers (children, the elderly, or the handicapped) and in sensitive areas of the library (with computerized customer records or money).

2. The authority to request background and personal reference checks must come from the volunteer services policy.

3. Determine the types of convictions that are acceptable and unacceptable for purposes of having individuals in particular volunteer positions.

ALACHUA COUNTY LIBRARY DISTRICT
Headquarters - 401 East University Ave.
Gainesville, FL 32601-5453

Reference Form
(Reference should not be related to the volunteer applicant.)

This reference is for_____, who is applying
$\qquad$ *first and last name*
to be a volunteer at the Alachua County Library District. I have known this young
person for_____through_____
$\qquad$ *period of time (days, months, or years)* $\qquad$ *name of school, church, etc.*

This young person has demonstrated that s/he is responsible, dependable, and

would be a good candidate for a Library volunteer.

Additional information you would like to give about this young person (optional):

_____

_____

_____

Name of person submitting reference:

_____
Please print

Daytime phone number_____

Signature: _____

Date:_____

Please return to:
Alachua County Library District Volunteer Program Specialist
401 East University Avenue
Gainesville, Florida 32601
(352) 334-3943

ACLD Volunteer Program Handbook—Reference Form (Minors) $\qquad$ August 2001
Revised: August 2004
Revised: November 2004

Sample 20-2. **Youth Reference Form**

4. Prior conversations with your administration and attorney need to be done on the legal ramifications of an individual with a criminal background who applies for a volunteer position.

5. All background investigations must be done with the prior consent of the individual. Acquire or develop appropriate forms. Check with your local police department or commercial background investigation company for procedural details.

6. Identify the administrative review process you will use when there are gray areas found in completed background reports or telephone reference checks.

7. Call personal or professional references to get more personalized, job-related information. A minimum of two references is usually adequate.

8. Information received from background checks and personal references must be kept strictly confidential, and files must be maintained in a secure file cabinet.

| # VOLUNTEER AGREEMENTS AND RELEASES

VOLUNTEER AGREEMENTS ARE used to add legal formality to the relationship between the volunteer and the library organization by defining their mutual obligations. Essentially, in exchange for the library providing a volunteer opportunity, the volunteer agrees to specific conditions. For some libraries, the conditions are primarily those of a "work" relationship as identified in a volunteer manual or list of volunteer policies and rules. Other libraries expand the agreement to include the volunteer's acknowledgment of the risks and liabilities. Volunteers agree to release and hold harmless the library and its paid and volunteer staff from costs of legal actions, including lawsuits in the event of injury or loss or damage of personal property. Although this seems on the surface a clear statement, in practice the issue of negligence can come into play. One library includes on its application form in capital letters with reference to claims, "Including those based on negligence," to try to address this legal concern.

Suppose you ask a volunteer to bring a laptop to the library to help you write invitations to a volunteer reception. Walking across the floor with the computer, the volunteer trips and falls, breaking her laptop and twisting a knee. The estimated repair cost for the laptop is $400. In addition, the doctor states that a minor operation may be required if the injury does not heal. In

Parental Permission Form

Nashville Public Library
615 Church Street, Tennessee 37219
Young Adult Volunteer Program
Ages 13 - 17

Parent/Guardian Agreement

BRANCH/DEPARTMENT_____

We are pleased that your teenager has expressed a desire to be a volunteer for Nashville Public Library. As a parent or guardian you will play a very important part in the success of the program. This program will provide young adults with work experience and skills that will be of benefit during college years and thereafter.

The following criteria will help to bring an understanding of what Nashville Public Library will expect of young adults.

Young Adults between the ages of 13 and 17 may apply.

Volunteers may work a maximum of four hours a day, twice a week.

Volunteers will be supervised by a staff person and should keep that person advised when a change in scheduling is necessary or if the volunteer is unable to come to work. Repeatedly not showing up for an assigned shift will result in dismissal from the program.

Volunteers will dress appropriately and wear a Volunteer Badge while working. They will be permitted to take breaks in the staff lounge.

When not on duty, volunteers will be treated as patrons. They will not be supervised and will not be allowed to enter the staff lounge.

For safety reasons, volunteers must not leave their assigned department once they have started to work unless in the company of a Parent/Guardian or with the permission of staff. This is a public building and the library is not responsible for the behavior of public patrons. If volunteers have any concern for their personal safety they should immediately report to staff or to a security guard.

Parents/Guardians must be aware of library closing times and understand fully that library staff will not remain after hours or keep the building open for teens awaiting transportation.

Our Pledge to you: Young Adults will have a productive and positive experience while volunteering for the Public Library. The staff looks forward to working them.

If the above guidelines are acceptable to you and _____

Please sign below

Volunteer _____ Date of Birth _____
         Signature

Sample 21-1. **Parental Permission Form**

Parent/Guardian _____ Phone # _____ Date _____
            Signature

Parent/Guardian Address: Street _____

City _____ State _____ Zip_____

Staff Supervisor _____ Branch/Dept: _____

Completed form to be sent to Volunteer Services. Keep a copy at work location for records.

June 2006

this example, there is no standard administrative practice that specifies the outcome. On the surface, a signed release or waiver would seem to prevent the volunteer from suing the library for computer repair and medical costs. Some volunteers would just admit they were clumsy and pay for the repair themselves (possibly from homeowner's insurance) and file a medical claim with their own heath insurance program. If the fall was caused by a step stool accidentally placed in the way by a paid staff member, then there could be an interpretation of negligence on the part of the library. A volunteer in this case might want to sue the library to recover costs. Even with the signed release, because you asked the volunteer to bring the laptop to the library to conduct volunteer work, the legal outcome is ambiguous.

A specific type of release found in library volunteer programs is used when a minor wants to volunteer and needs the approval of parents or legal guardians (see sample 21-1 for an example). The age for parental signatures varies from under fourteen to under eighteen. Again, these parental releases can be merely work agreements acknowledging and giving approval for the minor to volunteer in the library. Expanded versions require the parents to hold the library harmless in the event that the minor has an injury while volunteering at the library. Again, these releases serve as legal protections for both the library and the parents. You are encouraged to use these forms. For young volunteers, an additional type of agreement is a consent given by the parents to allow library staff to obtain necessary medical emergency care in the event of an accident.

In the case of volunteers twelve years old and younger, you might want to require the presence of a parent or guardian to monitor the child's work performance. An additional paragraph on the parental permission form (sample 21-1) can be added, worded something like this: "The library is more than happy to provide your child with a positive volunteer experience. The library staff are very busy and, while they do appreciate the help a young person can provide, they will take no responsibility for them should they decide to leave the job assignment or library facility."

An increasing number of libraries use the volunteer agreement to allow a background criminal check or investigation as part of the application process. On some application forms the agreement is merely a check box with words approximating "I agree to a background check"; on other forms a small, legally written paragraph specifies details and requirements for a background check.

An agreement to submit to a substance abuse test is part of the application process at some libraries. This agreement can be part of the application form or handled on a separate form provided by the testing laboratory.

As an option to having agreements on the volunteer application form, libraries create separate agreements and release forms (see sample 21-2). These forms combine "work" expectations and "risk and liability" releases into a series of agreements that are acknowledged by signature and date. How much of the work-related conditions are part of such agreements varies by jurisdiction. To illustrate, the confidentiality requirement as a work expectation is a typical part of a volunteer policies handbook, but for some volunteer services programs confidentiality is a separate agreement. Similarly, the use of a volunteer's image or voice can be part of the library work conditions as stated in the volunteer policies or separated out as a specific agreement. For this particular policy, you must be sensitive to needs of particular volunteers who do not want their pictures posted, even using only their first names, as for example those who have restraining orders in effect.

The use of legal language, whether on an application form or a separate release form, is not user friendly, but such language does shift the agreement to volunteer from a casual "drop in when you can" approach to an expected set of mutual commitments and obligations.

What is critical to these agreements is that you are up front with your library policy requirements so that potential volunteers are not blindsided. Further, if your library administration requires you to initiate one or more of the above agreements retroactively or test existing volunteers for substance use, you must again be up front with the issue. First, hold general meetings, communicate in small groups, or conduct one-on-one sessions with the volunteers to explain why they need to sign agreements or submit to background investigations or substance abuse testing. Your explanations may be in terms of overall library safety, customer safety, and personal safety. It helps to have one or two case examples drawn from local or national sources related to

City of Carlsbad

VOLUNTEER SERVICES AGREEMENT AND RELEASE

Confidentiality Agreement

I respect the confidentiality of City information and will discuss or give official information only as directed by a supervisor. No confidential information will be provided to the public except within the guidelines of the City.

Photo Release

I give the City of Carlsbad, free of any compensation, unlimited permission to use, publish, and republish, in any media now in existence or that may later be developed, for any lawful purpose as it may determine, information and reproductions of my likeness and my voice related to any aspect of my volunteer service for the City. I hereby waive my right to first review the use of my likeness or voice before any use or publication.

Volunteer Handbook

I acknowledge that I have received the City of Carlsbad Volunteer Handbook. I further understand that, by signing this statement, I have read or will read the Volunteer Handbook and that I understand its contents, or will discuss all questions that I have with my supervisor or the Community Volunteer Coordinator on the first day of my volunteer service. I also realize that this statement will become a permanent part of my volunteer personnel file.

Reference Verification and Background Checks

I authorize reference and employment verification as necessary for specific positions that I have volunteered to perform. I authorize fingerprinting, photographing and criminal background checks and Department of Motor Vehicles checks as necessary for specific positions that I have volunteered to perform. On behalf of myself, my heirs and representatives, I hereby release the City of Carlsbad, its elected officials, employees and agents from all liability for any damages that may result from my reference verification and background check(s). The background check policy is available upon request.

Permission to Seek Medical Treatment

In the event of an emergency, I hereby give the City of Carlsbad permission to seek medical attention for myself or my child, if volunteer applicant is less than 18 years of age.

Insurance Information and Release

I understand that there are some risks and that I may be injured in the course of performing these volunteer activities or services for the City. I understand that the City's policy is to cover volunteers as "employees" of the City for sole purpose of California Workers' Compensation benefits. I also understand that under Workers' Compensation laws, Workers' Compensation benefits will be the sole and exclusive remedy in the event I am injured while performing these volunteer activities and services. I further understand and agree that I will only be entitled to medical expenses under the City's Workers' Compensation. I will not be entitled to any other Workers' Compensation benefits which may include, but are not limited to, permanent or temporary loss of use damage, replacement income or vocational rehabilitation benefits. With the exception of Workers' Compensation benefits as set out above, I hereby agree that I, my heirs, guardians, legal representatives and assigns will not make a claim against or file an action against the City of Carlsbad or any of its agents, officers, employees or other volunteers, for injury or damage resulting from negligence, howsoever caused, by any employee, agent, officer or volunteer of the City of Carlsbad as a result of my participation in this volunteer activity or service. In addition, I hereby release and discharge the City of Carlsbad, its agents, officers, employees and other volunteers from all actions, claims and demands that I, my heirs, guardians, legal representatives or assigns now have or may hereafter have for injury or damage resulting from my participation in these volunteer activities or services.

I HAVE CAREFULLY READ THIS AGREEMENT AND FULLY UNDERSTAND ITS CONTENTS. I AM AWARE THAT THIS IS A PARTIAL RELEASE OF LIABILITY AND A CONTRACT BETWEEN MYSELF AND THE CITY OF CARLSBAD AND SIGN IT ON MY OWN FREE WILL.

Name (please print) First Middle Initial Last	Age if under 18 years old	Date

Signature

Signature of parent or guardian if volunteer is under 18 years of age	Date

Address (Street/City/Zip)

Phone	Email address

EMERGENCY CONTACT NAME	EMERGENCY CONTACT PHONE

Please bring this application with you to a library volunteer orientation or, if requested, return it to
Amy Bennett, Volunteer Coordinator, Georgina Cole Library, 1250 Carlsbad Village Dr. Carlsbad, CA 92008
Fax (760) 434-9975 Phone: (760) 434-2877 email: abenn@ci.carlsbad.ca.us rel rev 11-6-06 vol packet 1-26-09

5

Sample 21-2. **Volunteer Services Agreement and Release**

libraries, schools, or similar organizations to support the decision. You can mention other libraries that have such policy requirements or bad incidents where agencies had no similar policies. If you have a volunteer who is an informal leader and understands the reasoning, this individual can explain from her own perspective why such agreements or testing are important. You can also expect some of your long-standing volunteers to resign. To initiate such agreements after the fact may seem to be to question the trust between them and the library. Try to emphasize that it not a lack of personal trust in any single volunteer but a matter of being consistent in carrying out library policy requirements among all volunteers or those who hold particular volunteer job positions.

Ideally, the library administration will let you phase in a major change in policy over a twelve-month period. Over this period, established volunteers have time to reconsider and discuss the policy with new and existing volunteers while getting comfortable with it. In addition, there is the normal attrition over the twelve months; by the end of the period, you may have very few volunteers quitting.

SECTION 22 | **TIME FORMS**

TIME FORMS ARE used to keep track of volunteer hours. They are an important part of your record-keeping activity. As your volunteer pool grows, record keeping can also become a problem. Volunteers who need credit for working in the community (e.g., for school, social service organizations, or religious groups) tend to record their donated time faithfully. They have a good reason to keep track of their hours. Volunteers who see themselves freely giving their time to the library do not always see the need for signing in or out on time forms. They do not feel that recording their time is necessary if they are volunteering for a couple of hours a week.

REASONS FOR TIME FORMS

There are many reasons for tracking volunteer hours and keeping accurate records: rewarding and recognizing your volunteers; crediting supervising staff; evaluating your volunteer program; justifying your program to the administration and staff; effectively publicizing community involvement; supporting an individual's donated time for such things as tax purposes and school credit; and documenting your volunteer program trends and achievements.

Your monthly or yearly reports are enhanced by the number of hours contributed by volunteers. Although volunteer hours capture only one aspect of a successful program, showing upward trends in the amount of time volunteers work lends additional credence to the value of your program. Some libraries share these numbers on the library website and others as part of annual reports. By multiplying the total yearly hours contributed by volunteers with an estimated dollar value of volunteer time, you can demonstrate a bottom line indicator of the impact the program has on the library (see section 4). This dollar figure can, however, be a double-edged sword. If too much emphasis is placed on the positive value of volunteer dollars, administrators can use these figures during tight budget periods to replace paid staff or not hire additional staff. These decisions can encourage negative perceptions of volunteers by the staff, which in turn can make your job harder.

Calculations of year-to-date and lifetime volunteer hours either individually or collectively are popular ways of recognizing volunteers and their contributions. Which hours to count can be somewhat ambiguous. For example, how do you track an individual's time spent on a project at home or baking a cake for a volunteer recognition event? In either case, the volunteer may not think about recording time worked at home. The library may actually "lose" hours relative to this volunteer. One option is to have volunteers record their work at home if it exceeds four hours a month.

A volunteer who does not record all time worked at the library may require an additional brief one-on-one discussion on the importance of reporting hours. In the end, you may have to adjust the hours to add realism to the totals.

Staff supervising volunteers can be given special recognition for the number of hours they supervise volunteers over the course of a year. Even if the task of supervising volunteers is part of their job descriptions, they can still be recognized for what they do. This can include written comments as part of their yearly performance evaluations as well as thank-you notes and small gifts.

Time forms are particularly important for documenting the hours of court-directed community service volunteers and youth volunteers working for school graduation or civic, religious, or institutional credits. Also, there are programs that need documented time for an individual to purchase food at a discount in community programs or receive tax relief in those jurisdictions that allow volunteer credit. In each case, the time form acts like a legal document by providing proof that the volunteer worked the assigned hours.

To maintain accuracy, it is important to have the volunteer and supervisor sign the form to verify that the hours were completed as assigned. In large libraries, security issues may also be a concern, so having accurate time forms can tell which volunteers were in the building at a certain time and where they were working.

By tracking volunteer hours you also find out who is not coming in as scheduled. This is important if you have multiple departments or multiple locations and the volunteer or library staff do not call you with the information. By reviewing time forms, you can see a pattern of absences. You can use this information to find out why a volunteer is not coming in and, if necessary, take corrective action.

TYPES OF TIME FORMS

There are three types of time forms. One is the daily or weekly sign-in roster, on which volunteers sign in and out on the dates they work (see sample 22-1). One variation is to list the tasks worked as well as the name of the assigned staff supervisor. From the volunteer's perspective, this is an easy process as long as the sign-in sheets are readily available. Some libraries have electronic versions of these sheets. From yours or the supervising staff's perspective, it takes only a glance to know which volunteers are working. The downside of this form is that it can result in a loss of confidentiality, since anyone can review the names and hours. Furthermore, it is more difficult to sort out the total number of hours by volunteer if you use a sheet that covers a week at a time, especially if you have many volunteers working on different days. Electronic versions can, however, be quickly sorted.

Another type of time form is the monthly calendar. This form has the volunteer's name written next to the date and time he is expected to work. A check mark next to the name indicates that the volunteer reported for work. This system works if volunteers are on a regular schedule with a set time each month. Again, electronic versions can be set up to accomplish this process.

A third approach is separate timesheets or time cards for each volunteer. The volunteer is expected to complete the time card and put it back in the file box on the dates worked. If a volunteer does not want to keep the hours, you may have to fill in a timesheet to complete your reporting requirements. Again, an electronic version of an individual timesheet can be used; a good example comes from the Multnomah (Oregon) County Library (www.mult colib.org/vol/Volunteer_TimeSheet.html).

Volunteer Sign-in Sheet

ORIGINATING BRANCH/DEPT: _____

PLEASE PRINT _____

Date	Time In	Name of Volunteer	Activity/ Assignment	Time Out	Total Time

Please return to Volunteer Office at the end of each month.

Sample 22-1. **Volunteer Sign-in Sheet**

SETTING UP TIME COLLECTION PROCEDURES

It is important that you specify whether the time forms are to be completed on a daily, weekly, or monthly basis and how these should be submitted to you. In multiple branch library systems, if you have paid branch volunteer supervisors, they can take responsibility for getting the time forms to you and new ones distributed to the volunteers. Volunteers reporting directly to you must take responsibility for getting the total hours to you. Additionally, you need to ensure that forms for the next time period are available to volunteers in a timely manner, or that electronic forms are ready to accept data for the next period.

Calculating volunteer time is labor intensive if done manually. If you are able to use a volunteer assistant who enjoys detailed work and is accurate, this becomes a good monthly project. If you develop statistical reports from the time data, the volunteer assistant can also perform this duty for you.

TYPES OF VOLUNTEER TIME STATISTICS

There are no standard statistical reports among library volunteer services departments to use for comparisons or set goals. Monthly reports of hours and number of people by department, library, or library function are typical. This information provides time series data that can be used to compare volunteering across each library unit on a monthly basis. You may find seasonal variations in volunteering or growth or decline among departments or branches over the course of a year to be useful information. Aggregating the data at the end of the year provides yearly totals of volunteer hours and numbers of volunteers. This information can be converted into percentages of volunteering by department or library. For example, the circulation department may have 30 percent of all the volunteer hours for the year but only 20 percent of the total volunteers. This means that fewer volunteers are putting in more hours. Technical services may have only 10 percent of the volunteer hours and 5 percent of the volunteers.

Another useful statistic compares number of volunteer hours to number of paid staff hours. The payroll department receives reports of total worked hours by library departments and branches per pay period as part of routine payroll calculations. At the end of the year, the aggregate number of total hours worked is also part of most payroll reporting. Just divide your total annual volunteer hours by the staff hours worked and you have another useful percentage as an indicator to demonstrate the importance of volunteers.

One way to indicate the cost effectiveness of volunteers is based on your budget. Given that most yearly volunteer services budgets are small, you can demonstrate some impressive numbers. Your volunteer services department budget may be your salary and benefits, mileage reimbursement, awards and recognition dollars, supplies, and any allocated costs assigned to your department. Your accounting staff can help you. Divide your total department costs first by the total yearly volunteer hours and second by the number of volunteers you had for the year. The first calculation gives you the costs per volunteer-hour of your program and the second gives the cost per volunteer. Everyone should be impressed by how much gets done with so few dollars.

Library operations are organized around quantitative measurements such as customer counts, circulation numbers, reference questions answered, summer reading program participants, number of special events, and new material purchase costs. The volunteer services program is often seen as the "soft" or nonquantified part of library operations. As a volunteer services manager, you may be a "people" person who finds it hard or does not have the aptitude for creating program statistics. You can use a volunteer who has such talents. Using statistical measures to describe your volunteer services program helps establish legitimacy and respect for you and the program, especially when the statistics are part of the library reports presented to the trustees and community.

PART 3 | **TRAINING AND DEVELOPMENT**

SECTION 23 | **ORIENTATION TRAINING**

MANY PEOPLE FIND new work experiences disorienting and confusing. This holds true for new volunteers, especially when they are placed in jobs with few or no introductions to staff or other volunteers, no discussion of library policies, or no instructions about where to put their personal belongings. Orientation training bridges the gap between being an outsider and being a member of the team. When orientation is done properly, new volunteers develop camaraderie with staff and other volunteers and understand how their efforts fit in with the mission of the library. Moreover, orientation time excites and motivates volunteers and reaffirms that agreeing to be a library volunteer was a good decision.

Orientation training can be either informal or formal, as you deem necessary to acquaint the volunteer with the job and the library adequately. If you work for a small library, the first day can be as simple as making introductions to staff and other volunteers, providing a brief tour of the library, including the location of the restrooms, and explaining where to put personal items. In a large library with many volunteers and job opportunities, orientation can be done in a group setting on a weekly, biweekly, or monthly basis.

ORIENTATION FORMAT

Orientation training should not be confused with skill or job training. Orientation gives volunteers their first general introduction to the "behind the scenes" operations of the library. It also enables volunteers to meet the staff. As you plan the format for the orientation session, decide on the length of the session and the time and day during the week. These decisions often depend on the number of new volunteers and whether they have paying jobs. If you have a large number of new volunteers, you can hold a monthly orientation for about one to two hours. You may want to include additional time for refreshments and a tour of the library. If you have a large number of young volunteers, you can hold an afterschool orientation with fewer handouts and more food. When there are a few new volunteers, you can conduct personal orientations at the time they join the library. The one-on-one orientation can be up to one hour or less in length, including time for questions and answers.

Orientation training may include PowerPoint slides to identify key points, but these can be boring if overdone. By using Flickr, you can enhance the oral information by showing photographs of library branches, supervising staff, backroom work areas, and volunteers performing particular duties. A picture might show a volunteer storing her personal items in a locker, which you can tie back to orientation information about personal effects. Orientation training can include streaming video about general orientation topics or library specifics that new volunteers can watch on their own at computer workstations or public access computers. Visual learners are able to learn faster by seeing a demonstration or picture of what they are supposed to learn and know. As the volunteer services manager, you can use volunteers with digital cameras, camcorders, and with computer editing skills to put these types of programs together.

As you finalize the format for either a large group or individual sessions, it is important to decide which library handouts, brochures, manuals, task lists, and other information the volunteers will need to be well informed. Too much information means information overload, with much of it not being remembered a week later. Uploading the information to the library intranet can reduce some of the handouts and the amount of paper. Whether hardcopy or electronic, these materials should be viewed as reference items for the future.

As you prepare the handouts, ask the supervising staff members for input on the content and professionalism of the material. Poorly copied or hard-to-read materials do not make good first impressions. Whether you use flipcharts or PowerPoint slides during your group presentations, be sure the information is current and accurate.

Finally, think through the session by writing notes for yourself, mentally orchestrating the meeting so that you can see the flow from topic to topic. It is important that your new volunteers leave feeling they made a good decision in becoming library volunteers and that library volunteering will be an enjoyable experience.

ORIENTATION SESSION

You should cover several areas in every orientation: general welcome, staff/volunteer introductions, library expectations, library tour, completion of required forms, and key library policies and procedures. Information materials can be put in an orientation packet or uploaded to the library intranet for easy access and reference.

General Welcome

Your welcome should express genuine sincerity and friendliness. This is important because it leaves a lasting impression and makes new volunteers feel immediately appreciated and part of the library team. A welcoming letter is a good beginning.

During a group session, keep your opening comments brief and to the point. Give a general overview of the orientation to keep yourself and the group on track. Time is valuable to you and the new volunteers. In addition, they are probably eager to get started with their new jobs or specific training.

Introductions

New volunteers need to be introduced to the supervising staff, staff members who will work with the volunteers, and other volunteers. You can have several of these people available at the meeting or introduce them later during the tour. The supervising staff should include the immediate supervisor and the department manager. Introducing these people gives volunteers a sense of the library's organizational structure and how they fit into the larger picture and operations of the library.

When volunteers are going to work with specific staff members, it is important to have introductions so that the volunteers are acknowledged as part of the group. This is also important for security reasons because the staff members now know that someone new will be in their work area. Finally, if there are other volunteers working in the same area or at the same time, it is a good idea to connect them with the new volunteers; this makes the adjustment period more comfortable and completes the picture of a volunteer-friendly library.

Forms of Identification

A name badge gives volunteers an immediate sense of identification with the library staff as well as identifying them as volunteers. The word "volunteer" on a badge is an easy, inexpensive form of identification. Adding a first name personalizes the identification. Badges can be collected and in some cases reused later. A more expensive option is the volunteer vest, which is worn over street clothes. Having a formal form of identification allows volunteers to move about freely, especially in staff-only areas. It also gives customers an idea of the level of assistance being offered. An important side benefit to special volunteer identification is the positive publicity it generates in a public area.

Facility Tour

Provide a tour of the library that includes both the public and staff work areas. This gives new volunteers a sense of the backroom library operations that few have any knowledge of. Tours assist individuals to transition from outsiders to insiders and make for more effective volunteers.

ORIENTATION PACKET AND CHECKLIST

An orientation packet can include library brochures, information on library services, and a handbook. A volunteer handbook is a good way to demonstrate professionalism in a volunteer services program. The handbook can be used as an orientation outline when you go over the various sections with new volunteers. In addition, an orientation checksheet is useful in helping you make sure you cover all the pertinent points.

A handbook can be as simple as a few pages stapled or bound together in a colorful booklet. It can be posted on the intranet so that it is available to all volunteers as a reference. Recognize that people learn differently and that some volunteers prefer hard copies and others an electronic format. Pictures and other graphics help make text more inviting. If there is a sign-off agreement that the volunteer handbook has been read and policies understood, then you need a hard copy of this sign-off form for your files. You can also invite volunteers to read the electronic version, print the acknowledgment page, sign and date it, and return it to you.

The handbook contains both general information and specific procedures that affect the volunteer work experience. Any of the following might be included under "general information":

Library history

Volunteer mission statement

Library services and events

Confidentiality policy

Rights of a library volunteer

Organizational chart

Key contacts

Key telephone numbers

Glossary of library terms (jargon)

Emergency procedures

Map of library (including location of restrooms and break rooms)

Some general library information can come directly from staff handbooks, library brochures and handouts, training manuals, or the library policy and procedure manual; appropriate sections in this book also suggest ideas about what to include in the volunteer handbook.

Procedural information that is useful for new volunteers includes the following:

Volunteer schedule

Volunteer assignments

Sample time forms

Absence and late notification procedures

Identification policy

Storage of personal items

Parking

Use of the telephone for personal calls

Breaks

Performance appraisal

Volunteer benefits

Volunteer awards

In this section of the handbook you can parallel the staff handbook and find additional ideas from relevant sections of this book. A volunteer will not remember all of this information, so design the handbook as a guide that can be referred to for useful information when necessary.

If you do not choose to use a handbook, you can collect a packet of information in a looseleaf folder for each volunteer or have a package at the library available to all volunteers. In libraries with an intranet, this information can be posted electronically. Pertinent information includes job descriptions, a map of the library, and one or two pages on general volunteer policies. Some libraries post these polices on the library website under the volunteer services program. If you are required to have only electronic postings of the volunteer materials as part of overall library cost savings, you may still need to print hard copies for those volunteers who learn by and require hard copies.

ONE-MONTH FOLLOW-UP

It is important to follow the initial orientation, around one month later, with a telephone call or meeting to find out how the ongoing volunteer is doing and the level of job satisfaction. In addition, you can get an evaluation from the supervising staff. These will give you a clearer picture of how the volunteer is performing. One month gives the volunteer time to fit into the library organization. If the volunteer/library relationship is not working out, you can head off future problems that reflect poorly on the volunteer services program. This period also allows you to decide to either retrain or reassign a volunteer to another library job. In the extreme case, if the volunteer is not working out you may have to devolunteer. Setting up a tickler file or a reminder on your computer is a way to keep track of the timing of follow-ups.

| # CUSTOMER CONFIDENTIALITY

NEW LIBRARY VOLUNTEERS rarely get to see a copy of the American Library Association's Library Bill of Rights or Statement of Professional Ethics or learn about the library's obligation to ensure that the records of a customer are kept confidential. Many do not understand that sharing information with a friend about someone's request for a certain book or discussing what a particular customer is checking out raises privacy issues. Some have no concept of confidentiality issues even though they are explained on the volunteer application form. When designing your volunteer program, you must be cognizant of the library's policy on confidentiality, training for and restrictions on tasks that access customer information, and procedures for responding to requests for customer information by law enforcement agents.

CONFIDENTIALITY POLICIES

Your library probably has a written policy on customer confidentiality (also known as patron privacy), generally found in the staff employment handbook and the library policy and procedural manual. If this is the case, you should include it as part of your volunteer orientation program or volunteer handbook or prepare a separate handout for new volunteers during orientation training.

When you discuss the privacy policy, it is important to provide a few examples of preventing customer confidentially from being compromised by specific volunteer duties. Remind volunteers that they cannot share customer information with friends and family or use information about staff or volunteers for personal gain or to benefit other organizations. If your state has a customer privacy/confidentiality law with stated financial penalties for violation, it is useful to remind volunteers about this penalty.

As the volunteer services manager, your job is to make sure that all volunteers understand the importance of this policy and the consequences of not following it, including devolunteering. If you do not have centralized orientation training, then it is important that the volunteer supervising staff be delegated the duty of explaining this policy.

ADDITIONAL CONFIDENTIALITY TRAINING FOR SPECIFIC JOBS

Some libraries restrict volunteers, by policy or practice, from any positions that require working with customer records. In these libraries, volunteers are required to direct customer assistance questions to paid staff. The reasons for restricting trained volunteers who work in and around the service desks are quite diverse. If your library restricts volunteers from customer records, you still need to provide confidentiality training to reduce the chance that a volunteer unwittingly shares information about a customer.

In other libraries, volunteers who work at circulation or readers' advisory desks or with homebound delivery of books or books-by-mail programs often have access to customer records or privileged information, including current and past materials checked out as well as specific contact information. Does the library or particular branches restrict or allow trained volunteers to access any customer records?

Volunteers agree to protect customer privacy and are trained to recognize their obligation to maintain confidentiality, be discreet, and use professional objectivity. Thus, if a customer who is well known to the library staff and volunteers leaves his library card at home, volunteer circulation assistants may be allowed to access his customer file to review holds, check for fines due, and the like under the umbrella of providing quick and efficient customer service. Or, while working at the children's desk, a volunteer may be asked to check family files on books still out or holds. Thus, working with customer files requires further computer training and mentoring to ensure accuracy with few errors.

A difficulty may arise when staff members interpret accessing customer files as a key difference between themselves and volunteers. In such an instance, capable volunteers may be prevented from assisting customers if the task entails calling up customer information. A similar difficulty can occur if different branches, departments, or shifts allow volunteers to access customer's files differently. For one thing, customers who use two or more libraries or departments may recognize the inconsistencies and face longer wait times if paid staff members are busy. Similarly, volunteers who help out at different libraries and are used to assisting customers by accessing customer accounts in one library may face strong negative comments from staff members at another branch that does not allow volunteers to access the records. If you have volunteers working at different branches, you may have to do extra training on the different library rules and volunteer expectations. Doing this up front can save many tension-filled conversations later.

LOCAL LAW ENFORCEMENT AND THE USA PATRIOT ACT

Customer confidentiality training should also cover the procedures a volunteer is to follow if a law enforcement officer asks to see a particular customer's record. Paid staff members receive information and training on such situations, which may be nothing more than for them to direct the officer to the department supervisor, library manager, or library director. You or the supervising staff member should make sure your volunteers understand this too.

The USA PATRIOT Act allows appropriate federal agents access to library customer's records without notification to the customer. It is highly unlikely that a volunteer will be faced with a federal law enforcement officer demanding a particular library customer's records or information under the Patriot Act, but you should consider addressing during orientation what a volunteer should do in such a situation. A federal law enforcement officer holding a national security letter can be intimidating, so it is best to explain the library procedure to volunteers working at service desks. Your library procedure may be to call to the service desk the highest ranking staff member on duty, or direct the federal officer's request to the library manager or director. If your library has a staff policy on Patriot Act procedures, you can adapt this for the volunteer handbook and orientation information.

| # VOLUNTEER TRAINING AND TESTING

THE BASIC COMPONENT of every assigned task is the element of job skill training. Even the most mundane task can be done incorrectly without proper training.

TRAINER IDENTIFICATION

Determining how volunteers are to be trained is an important part of the volunteer services manager's job. Selecting good volunteers but providing poor training leads to dissatisfaction and high volunteer turnover. Who should train the volunteers is the first question to be answered. Library branches and departments differ in their approaches to training. A supervising staff member in one library might do all the training, while at another library or within another department training is delegated to another paid staff member. Knowledge, available time, willingness, mentoring abilities, patience, and the desire to help volunteers succeed are important traits that make for a good trainer. In some instances, it is the assigned staff person and not the supervising staff member who is the better volunteer trainer. But just having specialized library knowledge on the volunteer's task does not automatically make that person a good trainer. Some paid staff can become curt when volunteers do not immediately understand what to do after a quick explanation; some are not good at explaining the details of a job or how to handle exceptions. Some staff members may even feel it is not their job to train others, including volunteers.

Thus, it is important to identify people in the library branches or departments who are willing and able to be good volunteer trainers. When this happens, the staff trainers are also buying into the success of your program by working to make the volunteers successful. Without the feeling of comfort that comes from gaining skills with support of a trainer, new volunteers can easily get off to a poor start.

Your duties as volunteer services manager may encompass the role of trainer for volunteers who report directly to you or for those who do routine library jobs such as shelf maintenance or magazine sorting. The challenge is to find high-quality training time to give to each volunteer. This endeavor may require you to block out specific training times.

DEFINING THE SCOPE AND LIMITS OF THE JOB

One of the purposes of a job description is to ensure that volunteers understand the scope of the work. Consider, for example, volunteers assigned the job of answering all directional questions at an information desk. The specific duties must first be defined in a written job description. Then the assigned supervising staff must train the volunteers to distinguish between directional, reference, and ready-reference questions and how to refer customers to the appropriate area of the library or to a specific staff member. A volunteer should be well equipped to answer questions and stay within the scope of the assigned task, namely, answering directional questions. If she ignores the job limits and tries to answer other kinds of questions, the results are likely to be poor customer service because of her lack of specialized knowledge. Mistakes here are most often caused by new volunteers trying to be extra-helpful to customers.

Volunteers, like paid staff, need to understand why such job limits exist. If they have difficulty grasping this concept or working within their assigned job boundaries, you may have to train them for another job or devolunteer them.

ON-THE-JOB TRAINING

Most volunteers learn on the job. Adults learn better if they have a chance to practice their new skills after the initial training period. The volunteer who is shown the procedures to follow in selecting and processing donated paperbacks, inspecting audiovisual materials for damage, or running a complex photocopier will retain information and be more successful if he has a supervised practice period. Moreover, it is important for the equipment, tools, and workspace to be available from the beginning. It is difficult for a volunteer to be successful if there is no room to work or if a piece of needed equipment is unavailable or broken.

Volunteers who arrive with specialized skills, such as knowledge of specific databases or desktop publishing packages, still need to be trained to understand library terminology and project expectations. In this case, the training is not about specific skills but about project goals or outcomes and why these are important to the library.

SPECIALIZED TRAINING

Some volunteer positions require additional specialized training. Mending books, literacy tutoring, or processing archival material usually requires training by an appropriate staff person. In this type of training, it is useful to review the volunteer's work early in the process to make sure the job is being done correctly and to correct any problem areas quickly.

In any specialized job, it is important to make sure your selection process identifies volunteers who are not only willing to work but have the skills and aptitude to perform at the standards set by the library. If volunteers do not work at acceptable levels, it is better to offer them other volunteer opportunities than to hope for long-term improvement.

If the job requires public contact, such as greeters at an information desk or children's program assistants, it is important to include some training on what volunteers can say and how to say it. By preparing scripts and practicing different scenarios, you can make sure there is some consistency in training. If you write the script, it is a good idea to have the appropriate department manager review it first before using it to train the volunteer. Remember, too, that scripting cannot cover all the situations a volunteer will experience. Do not forget to include in your training session what *cannot* be said to the public. For example, you probably do not want a volunteer to say, "I understand that you're upset that the library does not have your book. They don't seem to want to order the kind of books that I think you and I like to read." The volunteer in this instance may have good intentions, but the phrasing certainly does not help the image of the library. Good scripting and practice can usually prevent this kind of unfortunate exchange. When volunteers enjoy working with customers, they can usually learn the script quickly and adapt to changing circumstances.

YOUNG ADULTS AND TRAINING

Successful young adult volunteer programs require a variety of available tasks and some choice of assignment. This approach allows young volunteers to assist the library while exploring their interests and testing their talents. Training necessitates relatively simple, user-friendly demonstrations with explanations of why the tasks are important for the library. Young adults want to know that they are making a difference and not just being assigned what they see as "make-work" duties. This requires a lot of patience from the supervising staff.

Young adults want a variety of assignments, so it makes sense to allow them to shift from one task to another at regular intervals or when they have completed an assignment. In turn, this rotation requires ongoing training, which for some staff members can become a problem. Many junior and senior high schools offer advanced computer courses. Some young adults may want to extend this skill to their volunteer work. With some demonstrated training, they can help with the public access computers in the children's or young adult areas. In the latter, a peer helping a peer can be effective under the general supervision of the young adult librarian. Honor students may be excellent tutors with younger children or enjoy reading to them. Others would just as well stay away from the public and are content preparing for storytimes or children's programs. Still others have great graphics skills and enjoy making creative posters to announce new programs. Training and assignments need to alternate between entertaining jobs and those less so, such as shelving juvenile nonfiction, so that there is a feeling of fairness in the assignments and a variety of duties.

Staff training for a library youth advisory group includes mentoring and coaching in emerging leadership skills such as planning, collaboration, and decision making. The personality and skill set of the young adult librarian are critical in making this a successful functioning group, especially since members come and go over the course of a year.

TRAINING AIDS

A variety of training aids can help you, the supervising staff, and volunteers track what needs to be accomplished and how to do it. Both you and the supervising staff have busy schedules, and it is easy to forget part of the training. The volunteer is new to the library and can easily get information overload. If you are fortunate enough to have a professional trainer as part of your library, this person will likely have additional suggestions to those noted below on how to develop specialized training aids to assist your volunteers to do the best jobs they can.

ORIENTATION CHECKSHEET A checksheet enables you or a staff supervisor to make sure a new volunteer has the necessary information and equipment to begin the job. This form may list such items as volunteer badge, restroom locations, storage areas for personal belongings, name and phone number of the supervising staff member, introductions to staff and other volunteers, trainer, date of training, and time forms.

WRITTEN SCRIPTS Scripts are useful when a volunteer is assigned to a task that needs uniform and consistent statements, particularly when working with the public—for example, greeting customers at the library entrance or answering telephones. A script can be as simple as "Home Town Public Library. How may I direct your call?"

PROJECT AND TASKS COMPLETION CHECKLIST This is a list of subtasks that need to be completed as part of an assigned project that stretches over many days or weeks. The list has a place for the volunteer to check off or initial so that progress toward completing the whole project can be monitored and the volunteer knows where to begin the tasks on each workday. A library community-wide marketing effort, for example, has numerous subtasks that need to be accomplished over a set period of time.

SHORT DEMONSTRATIONS WITH PRACTICE SESSION "Showing by doing" is one of the best forms of training because it gives a volunteer a chance to practice a new skill. For example, donated books can be divided into categories such as textbooks and general nonfiction books. You can demonstrate to the volunteer which category each book belongs to and then let the volunteer practice the sorting technique. This exemplifies applied learning.

MENTORING An experienced volunteer or staff supervisor can mentor volunteers. A new volunteer assigned to substitute during storytime puppet shows can be mentored in the art of providing an entertaining show using different hand puppet characters.

CHEAT SHEETS AND TASK CARDS These task aids are written in an abbreviated format to assist the volunteer's recall in the performance of occasional tasks. For volunteers who enter data into a monthly report, commands can be listed on a sheet so that they can remember the nuances of inputting the information.

VISUAL DISPLAY OF A JOB These are pictures of how a set of tasks needs to be accomplished. For a volunteer assigned to set up a community meeting room, labeled pictures of the various room arrangements can be posted so that a group can ask for configuration number 1, 2, or 3. This reduces the chance of error and increases the sense of accomplishment. A new volunteer can be asked to set up a room based upon the pictured configurations.

GRAPHICS AIDS These are often illustrations from graphics software packages that are used to help explain a set of tasks. A volunteer who is teaching library customers Internet search techniques, for example, can have a prepared set of graphics to use as a way to be sure to cover all the points.

SIMULATIONS: SECOND LIFE Online multilevel virtual games such as Second Life can demonstrate library tasks through actual librarians teaching in a virtual environment. These librarians, represented by avatars, can give online workshops to library volunteers, also represented by avatars, on shelving, customer service, or storytelling techniques, thus mimicking real-life situations in a nonthreatening atmosphere. Volunteers can practice techniques and skills virtually and eventually transfer them to real life.

DVDs "How to" DVDs and CDs are training aids that can be reviewed to help learn skills. For example, a volunteer who is going to be a reference assistant can watch a DVD on how to help customers with ready reference books. Usually these kinds of videos include written instructional aids that can be used separately.

INTRANET TRAINING PAGES A library can place training and task information on the staff intranet with a password security to the volunteer's training pages. In this way, a volunteer can review what was explained during training.

FLIPCHARTS A simple flipchart is useful to list or diagram key points of a task or locations in a building. If a volunteer is assigned to help shift books, the flipchart can show where the books are to be relocated.

RECORDED TUTORIALS Software programs often come with tutorials. Volunteers can be asked to use the tutorial to learn a software program they will be working with as part of an assigned duty. Remember, not all people learn well with computer tutorials, since these often assume levels of information a volunteer might not have.

REMINDER SIGNS These are briefly worded signs to serve as memory aids, such as "Wash hands after using cleaning solvents," "Return office equipment to supply room," or "Did you sign in?" These signs, sealed in plastic, can be posted or given to a volunteer on a job assignment.

TWO-MINUTE TRAINING SESSIONS Quick training requires spoken words to be supplemented with one or more training aids, such as a demonstration or short practice session and a follow-up. This allows the introduction of a task, the practice of performing the task, and some tool for remembering the order of activities to complete the task. For example, asking a volunteer to make two-sided copies and collating the pages into a booklet on a large office copier is best accomplished with a demonstration, short practice session, and cheat sheet on what to do when the copier jams.

TRAINING AND TECHNOLOGY One current training trend in libraries and other organizations is the use of online training formats including webinars, online professional and academic university courses, commercial web-based skill training courses, in-house intranet training, and web video training. Application of such tools to library volunteer training still lies in the future.

With increasing numbers of people taking online high school and college courses along with business online training courses and webinars, future library volunteers will come with the knowledge to access and make effective use of these tools. Ready examples for a volunteer program could include intranet web demonstration videos on shelf maintenance, cleaning DVDs and CDs, preparing for a storytime session, assisting with ready reference questions, and customer service. Virtual volunteers can utilize this kind of online training.

TESTING AND DEMONSTRATIONS The word *test* is often upsetting to adults. What a test does is demonstrate skills or knowledge about something. Instead, think in terms of demonstrations rather than testing, and you can relieve a lot of anxiety. In a simple version, a new volunteer shelver, after being trained on the Dewey Decimal system, is asked to put a book cart in Dewey Decimal order—in other words, to demonstrate that he can do it. A new volunteer brought in to set up a database or update a statistical report can be asked to demonstrate these skills by setting up a simple database or updating a sample spreadsheet.

This type of skill demonstration can give you clues about a volunteer's ability to perform the job well. If the demonstration is not successful, you need to ask if this is a case for retraining or reassignment. Allowing for volunteer nervousness, ask yourself if the skills are demonstrated within a reasonable time? Even though the volunteer is unpaid, the assignments may have deadlines.

SECTION 26 | SAFETY TRAINING

SAFETY TRAINING MUST be part of your volunteer orientation and part of the ongoing practice of updating information. Training does not necessarily mean formal classroom instruction; it can include informal conversations on correct safety procedures. Many managers often assume that everyone knows how to perform a task safely, forgetting that they too were once taught how to perform tasks safely.

Just getting volunteers recruited, selected, oriented, and trained is demanding, so thinking about safety is probably far down a busy volunteer services manager's list. Often safety awareness is the critical component of safety training. An enthusiastic volunteer ready to get the assigned job done is not necessarily thinking that there are safe and unsafe ways to do it. A volunteer assigned the simple task of using a paper cutter to cut sized paper for a children's program may not think about safety. But if the supervising staff member merely tells him, "That cutter is sharp and the handle does not stay up, so make sure your fingers are on this side of the paper," and gives a quick demonstration, an accident may be prevented. Safety training does not have to be elaborate to be effective.

The first step in training is to look over your volunteer jobs or particular tasks and determine which kinds of safety training information should be shared with the volunteers. Then review the library's safety manual (if there is one) to see if there are sections that relate to tasks performed by volunteers. Copy this information for your volunteer handbook or use it as a separate handout as part of your orientation training. If there is no safety manual, you can draw upon safety websites or ask a reference librarian to identify safety sites from which materials can be printed out and used by volunteers. Also, other libraries in your area may have already created safety information that you can use or draw upon for your needs. As you assemble this information, there are five key areas: library safety policies and procedures, accident notification and reports, protective equipment, specialized safety training, and health and wellness information.

LIBRARY SAFETY POLICIES AND PROCEDURES

Your library probably has a formal safety policy statement. This statement can set the tone for your conversations with volunteers. Safety practices are inherent in every job. An awareness of safety issues is extremely important in preventing accidents. You may have an accident-prone volunteer, but in most instances an accident is a momentary lapse in doing a job correctly—something that can happen to anyone. For example, a capable volunteer carelessly puts the book cleaner down and the solvent splashes in her face.

Regardless of who is responsible for an accident, you or the supervising staff person must deal with it, and your first focus should be on prevention. If the library has safety procedures for each department, you may find it useful to review these and provide handouts with your comments to volunteers working in those departments. What would be most useful to you is to take a few minutes to go over the safety aspects of each volunteer's job. This may be as simple as showing a volunteer how to adjust a chair properly, including the back support, at a computer terminal. If you do not feel comfortable training a volunteer in safety techniques, ask the immediate supervisor to work with the volunteer. In this way, the volunteer knows that the library takes safety procedures seriously.

ACCIDENT NOTIFICATION AND REPORTS

When an accident happens to volunteers in most public libraries, they do not come under the workers' compensation plan and thus do not follow the usual accident procedures of paid staff. If you do work in one of the few public libraries where volunteers are covered under workers' compensation, then your procedures are well established and you follow the same emergency procedures that apply to paid staff—including telling a volunteer which clinic to visit and which forms to complete.

When volunteers are not covered by workers' compensation, in cases of a minor injury they typically go to their clinic or doctor's office for treatment. They can call a family member for transportation if necessary. If the volunteer is incapacitated, the best option is to call 911 while another staff member calls or tries to locate the emergency contact person identified on the volunteer's records. First responders generally take a person to the closest hospital.

Even if you are not required to complete any forms for a volunteer accident, it is important to have an in-house incident report that you and the supervising staff member complete. It may prove useful in the event of later legal action taken against the library that you have documented the time of the accident, the sequence of events, the actions taken, and the names of any witnesses. Even though volunteers sign waivers, these do not eliminate lawsuits. Information on the report can also be used to determine if any conditions in the library led to the accident. In most cases it is volunteer carelessness, but not always.

Many volunteer services managers do not work full time or are not around in the evenings when some volunteers are working. In any circumstance, you need to have emergency contact information on each volunteer available in a confidential computer file or physical file so that supervising staff can access the information quickly.

PROTECTIVE EQUIPMENT

Most library tasks do not require protective safety equipment or clothing. If volunteers are using glue and cleaning solvents, you can have disposable non-latex gloves available to protect their hands. You can also provide wrist support pads to place under computer keyboards, or work gloves for pulling weeds, or a sturdy ladder for hanging pictures.

After a disaster such as a flood, protective aprons, boots, gloves, and disposable respiratory masks must be made available to everyone, including volunteers, involved in the cleanup process. Also, a volunteer who is sorting through a pile of donated books should be provided gloves and a disposable mask to address the possibility of dust and insect excrement. Many people do not like to wear masks, but if you make them available and explain their purpose your volunteers may accept the need for them.

If you have a safety officer in the library or local government jurisdiction, or have access to a risk control specialist from your workers' compensation insurance carrier, you can get free advice on workplace safety as it relates to any of the volunteer tasks.

SPECIALIZED SAFETY TRAINING

Specialized safety training is the exception in libraries. Cardiopulmonary resuscitation (CPR), first aid, and learning to use a fire extinguisher come closest to what is considered specialized training. If this type of training is available to the staff, it might be important to include long-term volunteers in the training, but first talk to your safety officer or key administrator to find out how emergencies are handled in your library. It is essential to know if a trained library volunteer, such as a registered nurse, might expose the library to legal risk if he provides emergency first aid to a customer or staff member. Your state may have a good samaritan law that protects a volunteer and the library from legal actions in such cases.

HEALTH AND WELLNESS INFORMATION

If your library has a wellness manual for staff, it is useful to share this infor- mation with volunteers, especially long-term volunteers. Some manuals show the proper way to lift boxes and illustrate quick on-the-job-exercises to reduce fatigue and body stress. Even though your volunteers may work only a few hours a week, offering this kind of information shows you care about their well-being and want to help them prevent personal injuries. The following topics are typical of wellness brochures as applied to library volunteers:

Breaks

Taking breaks can actually help increase productivity. When feeling stressed out, fatigued, or as if you are moving in slow motion after doing the same task for a long period of time, it is time to take a short break.

Micro-breaks are useful when working at a computer screen for an extended time on a concentrated project such as a spreadsheet. Give the eyes and muscles a change of pace by focusing on some distant object for five seconds. During this time, take a few deep breaths and shift position.

Short, five-minute mini-breaks can include stretching or changing job tasks to use different sets of muscles. Use a mini-break to stretch the muscles after unloading book carts, answering telephones, or performing any other task for an extended period of time.

Use regularly scheduled break times to reduce stress in one of the following ways: slowly and deeply inhale through the nose and then slowly exhale through the mouth; read a joke book; progressively tense different muscle groups for five seconds and let the body go limp for thirty seconds; visualize a peaceful scene, a fun event, or a pleasant activity.

Handling Books and Materials

Handling library materials can involve lifting, bending, pushing, carrying, and reaching. In particular, lifting library materials from a bookdrop or shelves or moving tables to set up for meetings can involve back, legs, shoulders, and arms. Good lifting techniques require the following: (1) plan before lifting; (2) keep the back in a natural, upright position; (3) bend and lift with the legs, keeping the items lifted close to the body; and (4) if turning is required, pivot with the feet without twisting at the waist. If an object is heavy or looks heavy, ask for assistance.

Practice Safe Work Habits

Remember to practice basic safety techniques such as these:

- Use step stools for books and objects in high places.
- Use only the top two shelves of a book truck to avoid back and arm strain.
- When moving and shifting books, use both hands and do not over-extend the grip and reach.
- Do not stack books and other items on the floor or on top of computers.
- Keep often used equipment within easy reach. Remove clutter from the workspace.
- When sitting, turn the chair rather than twisting the body.
- Do not rest the wrists and forearms on sharp edges.
- When using the telephone, be careful not to bend the neck.

Computer Workstations

When working at the computer for a long period of time, your neck, back, shoulders, legs, hands, wrist, fingers, and eyes are the areas of the body where most of the activity (or inactivity) occurs. If others also use your computer, learn how to make the necessary adjustments in chair height and tilt of the screen to prevent glare. Request help if necessary.

Reduce Life's Stressors

Minimizing stressors is a skill that can be learned and practiced. The sources of most stressors are burnout from too much activity, interpersonal relationships and conflicts, and personal worries, feelings of inadequacy, or being too demanding on oneself or others. There are various ways to reduce stress:

Quiet time

Plan a quiet period in the day without noise or interruption.

Stay a few minutes in the car without using the radio or cell phone.

Do something different in the daily routine

Take a different way home or take a walk in a new area of town.

Visit a friend not seen for a while.

Do something that is fun

Try a new hobby or participate in a sport or recreational activity.

Read books or magazines you have not seen or read before.

Get outside help

Seek help from a counselor, the clergy, or other professional.

Find someone to do jobs that are causing the extreme stress.

Personal practices and outlooks

Establish realistic daily schedules, accepting the fact that unexpected events will occur.

Realize that for most activities adequacy, not perfection, is the goal.

Practice positive self-talk: "I can do this." "I look good."

Find the humor in situations and remember to smile.

PERFORMANCE MANAGEMENT AND EVALUATION

IN RECENT YEARS there has been a growing emphasis on performance management in private, public, and nonprofit sectors, with applications to volunteers. In the most succinct version, performance management in this context means that volunteers are performing tasks that are necessary to achieve library goals, and the tasks in turn are associated with performance standards the volunteers are held accountable for meeting.

Using a simple, hypothetical example, assume your library has a shelving rate for nonfiction books of one full book cart per hour, and a trained and experienced volunteer is expected to meet this performance standard. A performance evaluation of the volunteer's work may show that the volunteer is meeting, exceeding, or not meeting the shelving standard. Viewing this example from a nonperformance management approach, volunteers are not held accountable for the number of nonfiction books they shelve during their shifts. Their shelving work is merely supplementary to that of paid shelvers.

Performance management is defined by and ultimately intended to meet the library's goals. In this example, your library may have the goal of improving customer satisfaction by having nonfiction books on the shelf when customers arrive at the library or when holds are placed. If the library standard is to have all returned nonfiction books back on the shelf within 24 hours of when they are checked in, then the shelving standard for nonfiction books of one cart per hour was calculated to meet this goal. Thus, the volunteer who is meeting this operational standard is achieving the library's larger goal of customer satisfaction.

Behind performance management is the notion that there are particular direct costs associated with each volunteer. This includes the cost of the manager's time in hiring, selection, and orientation as well as the supervising staff member's time in training, supervising, and evaluation. When the volunteer is meeting or exceeding the job standard, the costs are offset by the benefits of meeting one or more library goals. Taking this one step farther, customer satisfaction translates into more public support for the library. When a volunteer is not meeting the job standard, the costs associated with the volunteer are not contributing to the library's goals.

Although a lot of effort has been expended in recent years to establish performance standards for various library positions, in practice this is difficult. If your library is one that does have job performance standards attached to particular paid positions, and these positions are similar to volunteer positions, then one of your hiring and selection aims must be to find volunteers who are able to meet the standards. Most community volunteers want to do their best, and if given proper training and encouragement they will likely achieve the standards.

Performance evaluation with a volunteer is a two-way conversation designed to elicit and share information after a designated period of time on the job. The first conversation needs to be about one month after hire, and the next about three months later. The bigger issue, however, is whether to evaluate library volunteers and who needs to do it. This can be a touchy subject. Most volunteers want to do a good job. If they are told their work is subject to a written performance evaluation, they may reconsider volunteering.

Written evaluations can be useful in helping volunteers improve or enabling you to find a better job fit for them. They can also provide the basis for volunteers to leave the library gracefully. A written evaluation can further serve the needs of a volunteer who is in career transition by providing a written record of accomplishment.

If volunteers are going to be given performance evaluations, they should be informed of this at the beginning of the interview process or at least during the orientation training. This can be positively phrased in the following manner: "All employees, including volunteers, must go through a performance evaluation process. This is done to show areas of individual strength and indicate areas that need improvement in order to optimize your performance in helping us at the library." If a potential volunteer does not wish to work within this type of structured environment, it is important to find this out as early as possible.

PURPOSE OF EVALUATIONS

Performance evaluations are an important part of any job. They are one way to measure the career growth and productivity of an individual as well as to provide accountability for time and effort. For volunteers, evaluations can be used to

- Provide feedback about task performances and meeting standards
- Learn about a volunteer's experience and feelings about the volunteer services program
- Develop positive comments about a volunteer for use in a recognition program
- Explore new jobs in the library that may be more suitable to an individual's skills or interests
- Suggest other organizations that might provide a better volunteer fit
- Provide feedback to the originating agency for volunteers performing court restitution or service learning for schools and civic organizations

PERFORMANCE EVALUATION PROCESS
Formal Evaluations

Formal evaluations are done after a volunteer has spent one to three months on the job, depending on the type of volunteer and time commitment. If a volunteer has a commitment to work six months, a one-month evaluation followed by a formal evaluation after the third month can provide necessary mutual feedback and information from the volunteer. A general form can be provided to the supervising staff person for writing brief comments about the volunteer's job performance (see sample 27-1). A second form can be given to the volunteer to determine if the training is adequate, if there are enough supplies to get the job done, if the assigned day and time are working out, and whether necessary assistance from supervisors and staff is being provided and is useful. After reviewing the evaluations, you can call a meeting to go over the results. At this time you can include an open-ended discussion on any concerns or questions the volunteer may have, and then at a later date you can follow up with a written note or a second meeting to clarify any unanswered questions raised during the meeting.

With your busy schedule, performance evaluations may have to be delegated to library supervising staff members. More often than not, evaluation sessions are friendly and positive conversations, with volunteers wanting to know what they can do better. The training challenge here concerns the supervising staff; unless they have been trained to conduct performance evaluations, conversations can get sidetracked.

If you receive any negative comments from supervising staff, your job is to share this information with the volunteer in a positive and constructive manner. It is not uncommon in this situation to ignore or talk around problems of performance. If you need to discuss a problem, do it factually. Concentrate on job performance and job behaviors. If job standards are not being met, this should not be new information to the volunteer. It might help to script the conversation first so that you can think carefully about what you are going to say and how to say it. Be as positive as you can.

Performance evaluation forms come in many variations and ranges of complexity. They can be as simple as three to five questions with spaces

---

One-Month Telephone Volunteer Evaluation Form

Name _____ Work Location _____

Assignment _____ Staff Supervisor _____

Beginning Date _____ Date of Orientation _____

Daytime Phone _____ Best Time to Call _____

E-mail _____

- Relationship to supervisor:
- Relationship to team members:
- Response to work load (too much or too little):
- Response to hours:
- Quality of on-the-job training:
- Job strengths:
- Job weakness or areas of improvement:
- Concerns:
- Overall job satisfaction:

NEED FOR FOLLOW-UP?   NO_____ YES_____ (if so, when?) _____

Telephone Interviewer _____ Date _____

Sample 27-1. **Volunteer Evaluation Form**

for comments. They can be more complex with statements that require the supervising staff member to check off ratings in boxes under evaluation categories and options for writing comments. This type of evaluation form is easy to use and provides general information about a volunteer, but it can lead to ambiguous interpretation of the answers. For example, you cannot be sure what one staff member means by the words "seldom" or "always" or "meets standards" or "occasionally meets standards." More sophisticated evaluation forms list a range of specific performance behaviors associated with the positions along with rating scales and space for required written assessment of the behaviors. Although these latter forms are useful, they may be too extensive for volunteers.

There is a shift in recent years to the use of online evaluations for paid staff in some library jurisdictions. If your library is using such evaluation processes, it may be possible to develop a simplified volunteer evaluation form that could be printed out or posted on the library intranet for a supervising staff member to use. In this way, you would just send an e-mail to notify both the volunteer and the supervising staff member that an evaluation is due.

Informal Evaluations

If you do not use formal evaluation forms, let the volunteer know that the purpose of this meeting is to share information and get feedback about the overall volunteer experience. Indicate that this is a routine conversation with all volunteers after one to three months of working at the library. Your goal is to seek ways to improve the volunteer experience and to make sure that your recruitment statements about the volunteer tasks still hold true. In this way, both you and the volunteer can learn and contribute to the evaluation conversation.

Acquiring information about a volunteer's performance can be gained by asking the supervising staff person key questions about the volunteer's work performance. Your notes then become the basis for the evaluation conversation. It is important to frame your questions to the staff person in a neutral manner so that you are not biasing the responses. Ask questions such as "Can you tell me how the new volunteer is working out?" If the staff member merely says, "Doing okay," then use a probing question to find out more specific details. To illustrate this point, you can ask, "What examples do you have that the work is okay?" and "What could the volunteer do better?" These types of questions can lead to specific examples and a discussion of the volunteer's performance.

LIBRARY STAFF AND OUTSIDE EVALUATIONS

Who should evaluate a volunteer working off-site? It can be you if you are overseeing the volunteer, or it can be the supervising staff member who has regular contact with the volunteer. However, if the volunteer is working under a staff supervisor but performs the job off-site, such as taking books to senior centers or reading to children at a local childcare center, you should try to get input from an outside evaluator. Such an off-site supervisor many be a program director for an agency receiving library services, someone who is likely familiar with completing evaluation forms for a variety of purposes. This can be an e-mail with attached evaluation form or a mailed form with return postage paid.

The evaluation can be used in two ways: to evaluate individual volunteers and to evaluate the library services provided with a component for volunteer evaluations. Either approach is useful, but both have difficulties.

In the first approach, any "problem" volunteers will likely be brought to your attention, but this is not a foregone conclusion. Even if you ask for honest evaluations, a person in another organization may be hesitant to criticize library volunteers for fear of losing the services provided. Another concern with assessing volunteers is that you may not be getting information about the program as a whole. The volunteers may be doing a great job, but the outreach program may have outlived its usefulness or need revamping. It is important to have good rapport with the agency representative. Recognize that in some instances the agency representative may be the problem, not your volunteer or the program. Your knowledge about the relationship is important in interpreting the returned evaluation form.

The second evaluation approach is to focus on the outreach program's strengths and weaknesses, with a secondary emphasis on the volunteers. This information is useful for planning changes in the program and services but may not give you adequate feedback about each volunteer.

If you conduct a third-party evaluation, decide how much weight to place on library staff evaluations versus the comments of the outside evaluator. Probably only a small number of volunteers will be involved in off-site work; still, you need to know how they are doing.

FREQUENCY OF EVALUATIONS

If you conduct an initial evaluation after one month, you should plan on some form of follow-up evaluation a few months later. You may want to review your records to determine how long most volunteers stay with the library. If the majority of the volunteers leave after six months, you may want to perform only one formal performance evaluation. If you have a core group of individuals who have been working for several years, a yearly formal evaluation may be adequate. Recognize that this should be high-quality, one-on-one time with the volunteer. Even if all the comments are positive, this focused conversation can be a good way for volunteers to share ideas with you about the volunteer program or their evolving interests in other jobs within the library or personal plans. Just taking the time to conduct a performance evaluation demonstrates that you and the library respect a volunteer's freely given skills, talents, and energies.

PART 4 | **AWARDS AND RECOGNITION**

SECTION 28 | VOLUNTEER RECOGNITION POLICIES

MOST VOLUNTEERS LIKE to receive some form of recognition for their contributions to your library, yet many libraries have little or no budget to sponsor a formal volunteer recognition program. How then do you thank your volunteers for the work they do?

It is important to think through your recognition policies and get comments from administration and staff as you develop them. Will your recognition program include the Friends group, or will they have their own recognition event? Will this be an affair within the library or a community event? Will there be one major event for the entire library system or separate library events? These are some of the policy questions that need to be addressed, though you must stay flexible to accommodate changes in your volunteer services program over time. Whatever your recognition policies, they need to be written clearly so that you can articulate them to volunteers, administrators, and potential donors.

If recognition is not given consistently to everyone in your program, you may create tension and conflict even with the best intentions. If one volunteer receives a verbal thank-you and another is ignored, or one receives a small gift and another a certificate of appreciation, you may find increased dissatisfaction as an unintended consequence. The forms of recognition do not have to be the same for everyone, but you need to be consistent within each volunteer category. Young volunteers may appreciate a pizza party and a certificate at an informal gathering; some seniors may not want to venture out at night for a recognition program but might enjoy a noontime luncheon.

Obviously, all library volunteers can be given informal verbal recognition, even if they are in your library for court-directed restitution. It does not take much to tell a volunteer who is cleaning DVDs or mending books or assisting with a spreadsheet report that you appreciate the great job they are doing. Similarly, volunteers using the library as a way to earn service credits can be given recognition with a note on their sign-off form or as a separate letter of thanks. People remember these comments, and this is part of the community relations aspect of your job. In this regard, your recognition policy can include a statement that supervising staff will make an effort to acknowledge good volunteer work.

CRITERIA FOR RECOGNITION

On what basis will you give formal recognition? Some options include

- Number of hours worked in a given period, such as six months or a year
- Lifetime volunteer hours
- Number of months volunteering for the library, regardless of hours contributed
- Completion of a project or important endeavor
- Measurable accomplishments such as number of telephone calls made, number of customers assisted at an information desk, or dollars collected during a fundraising campaign
- Recommendations by supervising staff members

From a policy point of view, you need to consider whether you will award volunteers on the basis of one of these criteria or others, and whether the recipients will receive the same kind of recognition awards. Do you want your volunteers to perceive the awards as having the same or different values? If everyone, regardless of category, receives the same colored certificate, the perceived recognition is seen as equal. If some people receive a small plaque or their names on a large volunteer plaque in the library and others receive a certificate, then you are clearly differentiating by the type of award. Do you want to build on the same award theme every year? For example, you can award volunteer pins the first year and then add a bar for every year of additional service rendered.

A second policy issue is whether to honor past achievements, current activities, or both. Do you invite only those volunteers to a reception who worked a set number of hours over the past year, even if they are no longer active, or do you limit your invitations to those currently active who worked the requisite number of hours? Do you invite all currently active volunteers, even those who are new to the volunteer recognition event? Good arguments can be made on all sides of these issues. The size of your volunteer group may force you to choose an option on the basis of room size, costs, or other administrative considerations.

SELECTING OUTSTANDING VOLUNTEERS

Do you want to select a single "volunteer of the year" for the entire system, for each library, or for a category of volunteers (adult, youth, Friends)? These important issues, if not thought through, can lead to unnecessary tensions.

Choosing the specific criteria can be a challenge. If you use only the number of hours volunteered, then the majority of volunteers are out of luck. If you use a criterion such as the degree of commitment and dedication, you have to decide carefully how to measure this so that others perceive the selection as fair. If you use a committee, who selects the committee members and what criteria do they use to make their recommendations?

Should individuals be named "volunteer of the year" only once, or can they be selected again? If you decide there is no limit, then how do you address the issue of fairness and objectivity? As you make your final set of decisions, it is a good idea to get comments from the library staff, including volunteers.

INVOLVEMENT OF PAID STAFF

How do you involve paid supervising staff in recognition events? Will you give a "volunteer supervisor of the year" award? Are there staff members who deserve special recognition for supporting the volunteer services program? This is both a policy issue and a financial issue. On the policy side is whether you should award all supervising staff or only those who supervise the volunteers receiving the awards? By integrating both in the same event, you can develop a feeling of partnership in the volunteer services program, since both groups see themselves as a part of the whole library team. The financial side relates to the budget you have for these recognition events.

BUDGET

It is not uncommon for libraries to set aside funds for staff and volunteer recognition programs. Ideally, your volunteer program has a yearly, separate budget that you manage, with recognition funds as part of your budget. This gives you a dollar amount that can be used in your event planning. Alternatively, libraries roll volunteer services program funding into an administrative library budget item, and volunteer recognition event funds are provided if available. In this circumstance, you have to identify the expected costs for your event and make a case for the funds with a library administrator.

As you think about library funds, there is another important policy issue. Will your library support the use of taxpayer funds for recognition events for staff and volunteers? Some libraries do not see this as a problem. Others view it as a potentially negative community relations issue, especially in tight budget times. It is important to discuss this with the library administration before any event is planned, and keep in mind that the official position on this matter may shift over time.

A large formal volunteer recognition affair that includes library staff and the community can be costly. More people means more food and drink and a more complicated event to organize. Invariably there are unforeseen additional costs, and allowances for these must be made. Budgeted funds serve as a beginning point. This is when creative thinking may be necessary. Numerous local businesses including grocery stores, bakeries, and coffee shops are often willing to donate or discount food and gifts or provide small dollar amount gift certificates for the event. Then there are both staff members and volunteers who like to bake and see it as an honor to be asked to make something special for the recognition event. They can receive acknowledgment for what they do. The real balancing act is between your recognition policies and the amount of funds, gift and food donations, and space available. As times and budgets change, you need to stay flexible and innovative to provide successful recognition events year after year.

Underscoring your recognition planning must be the intent to see the event as a sincere thank-you from the library and the community. The sincerity of volunteer recognition is not dependent on or measured by the funds available or the number of people invited. When your volunteers go home after a successful event, what they will remember is the way you, the top administrators, and the paid staff showed honest appreciation for the work they did for the library. The small gifts, certificates, and awards may be stored, but the feelings they hold will linger. Your goal is to reinforce a feeling of continued commitment and thanks for library volunteering.

PUBLIC AWARENESS OF VOLUNTEER RECOGNITION

Decide to what degree you want your recognition event to be an internal affair versus a community relations event. You can make a good case for either side. If you have volunteers who are easily embarrassed or uncomfortable in the limelight, a small internal event is less stressful for them. Alternatively, free advertising generated by an article about the annual recognition event for library volunteers is a good way to get the word out about your program to the community. Posting information about the recognition event and later pictures on the volunteer services web page also gets the word out that volunteers are valued by the library. This rationale underscores the view that, the more people learn about the volunteer services program, the more likely you will attract qualified volunteers.

Remember that once you choose a direction, it is not irreversible. As with all policies, you should review this policy periodically to make sure that earlier decisions still make sense considering changes within your library, your volunteer services program, and the community.

Volunteer Recognition Policy Statements

In appreciation of our volunteers' contributions of time and skills, the library will provide a yearly recognition event and adequate funding for the purchase of special awards and recognition gifts for all volunteers.

The library will formally recognize outstanding volunteers of the year as voted on by staff members who work with them.

The library will recognize outstanding volunteers from all libraries based on the number of hours contributed over the past year.

Community volunteers who provide more than five hundred hours of service to the library will have their names placed on a volunteer plaque.

Library trustees are recognized as important community volunteers who give their time freely to act as advocates for library services within our community.

The staff is encouraged to give informal thanks to our community volunteers as an acknowledgment of their many services to the library.

Young volunteers will be rewarded on a periodic basis for the services they provide to our library.

The library encourages staff members who regularly work with volunteers to attend the annual volunteer reception.

The library will honor one volunteer staff supervisor of the year with an award at the volunteer appreciation event.

SECTION 29 | RECOGNITION PROGRAMS

AMONG THE TYPES of recognition programs you can choose from are acts of informal recognition, informal events, and formal affairs. And once your recognition program has been designed and implemented, you will want to evaluate its effectiveness.

INFORMAL RECOGNITION

An informal verbal recognition program can be as simple as making sure you and the supervising staff members give praise for work well done. This is one of the strongest forms of recognition and especially useful for a volunteer services program with limited funding. You can let the volunteers know they are contributing members of the team by simply saying that you heard great things about their work. A thank-you card or note from you or the supervising staff members also goes a long way toward recognizing a volunteer's time and effort. The cost of buying note cards is minimal, but the impact is significant.

You can use your library services web page to provide informal recognition by posting pictures of volunteers performing their work with short captions or articles about each volunteer. Even if your library has a written agreement that allows you to use volunteer pictures for promoting the library, it would be respectful to get informal acceptance by the volunteers for the pictures and the articles and, of course, identify them by first name only.

Youth volunteer pictures are more often found on the young adult services web page than on the volunteer services page. However, if young adult volunteers are performing jobs also performed by adults, there is nothing wrong with having their pictures and short write-ups on the volunteer services web page.

INFORMAL EVENTS

Slightly more formal than verbal or written recognition is a morning breakfast or coffee, a brunch, or a casual potluck luncheon. Having the library director or president of the library board attend and acknowledge the work of the volunteers adds importance to the recognition. At these events you can recognize and thank all the volunteers and any special volunteers. There is no need for certificates at these informal events, and rewards are in the form of peer recognition. Such events serve to strengthen volunteers' commitments to the volunteer services program and the friendships among volunteers. They also allow you to get to know the volunteers in a more informal setting. The costs of these events can be quite moderate.

There are other times when informal recognition events are appropriate and meaningful, such as a milestone birthday, achieving five hundred volunteer hours by a long-term volunteer, or completing specialized training. You can make these informal occasions extraordinary by inviting a top administrator and the supervising staff to the celebration. With a little planning, costs for these informal affairs can be minimized if held in a library community room. In some jurisdictions, a historic house or similar structure can be available to the library with the only financial requirement being a refundable cleaning deposit. This adds to the specialness of the occasion.

FORMAL AFFAIRS

At the other end of the spectrum is a major affair with local dignitaries, formal presentations, and possibly the local media. Formalizing the recognition program requires funds and advance preparation time to make the event successful (see sample 29-1). The basic structure of these affairs is familiar, though the variations are almost endless. A typical formal recognition event would go through key introductions, awards and gifts, special acknowledgments, closing comments, and social time with food and beverages.

These events can be held in the late afternoon, evening, or on a weekend morning when guests can attend. You can plan the program to coincide with National Library Week to bring special attention to the library. Other good times are early spring (March or April) and fall (October or November), when there are fewer holidays and less vacation travel.

The planning period begins a few months in advance to schedule a place; choose a theme; design invitations; invite dignitaries; print certificates; acquire awards, gifts, and prizes; and order or coordinate food deliveries and cleanup. This is usually the biggest volunteer event of the year. Even so, it is not likely that library staff will be assigned to work with you, but you can draw on the interests and skills of your volunteers to help make this a festive occasion.

The challenge in organizing a formal event is to keep it from becoming stuffy and obligatory. You want it to be enjoyable, lively, and desirable for each volunteer and guest so that they will want to attend. You may find that some volunteers still do not come because they view their work as a quiet service to the community. Others may feel uncomfortable in a large group of people. Still, it is important to acknowledge their work and contribution at this time.

EVALUATION OF RECOGNITION PROGRAMS

Evaluating your recognition program does not mean adding up financial costs or attempting to get more funds into your budget. Rather, it means asking the basic question, "Am I giving sincere thanks and recognition to the library volunteers?"

It is a good idea to do a "reality check" on how you and the paid staff are recognizing volunteers throughout the year—both informally and formally. Have you given a verbal or written thank-you to your volunteers at least once during the year? Do you know if the supervising staff recognize their volunteers? If so, in what ways? How many informal affairs did you sponsor over the past year? Did you get representative opinions, both good and bad, about any formal or informal events you organized? What would you do differently next year?

For small and medium-sized libraries, a survey is not necessary to get volunteer comments. Throughout the year, you can ask volunteers how they feel about working at the library and what they would like to see in the way of a thank-you and recognition. Volunteers' responses to this question will depend on whether they feel appreciated. In larger libraries, you may be able to post a survey on the library intranet for volunteers to print out and

Annual Volunteer Reception Planning Checklist

1. Identify respective/active volunteers in each area of library service.

   Bookmobile volunteers
   Friends of the library, unless they have their own recognition event
   Homebound delivery
   Library service and administrative departments
   Library board

2. Develop a list of those businesses that have donated in the past or have agreed to assist the library in the current year.

3. Check lists against lists from previous year to make certain that no volunteer or business is overlooked.

4. Ask designated members of Friends and supervising staff who have worked with volunteers during the year to review the lists to make sure that no one is overlooked.

5. Write to the local supermarkets and ask them to donate gift certificates for food at the awards program.

6. Send appropriate invitations to those identified in the lists above, dignitaries, library administrators, and supervising library staff.

7. Develop a program list of names with area(s) of service indicated.

8. Proof spelling of all names.

9. Develop an awards committee to plan and implement the volunteer awards program and select the outstanding volunteer(s).

   Speak with local florists about donating a floral arrangement.
   Schedule the room and complete reserve form.
   Order food and beverage.
   Identify cleanup group (check availability of community service
      volunteers).

10. Obtain a new guest book for those attending to sign.

11. Obtain nametags for volunteers to wear while at the reception.

12. Obtain gift certificates, gifts, and/or certificates for the outstanding volunteers.

13. As a community event, price advertising in the local newspaper. Post on library website. Submit announcement to community television and local community information web page.

14. Debrief after the event on successes and needed improvements to be incorporated into next year's planning effort.

Sample 29-1. **Planning Checklist**

complete. There are also relatively easy online survey sites, such as Survey-Monkey (www.surveymonkey.com), at which you fill in the blanks for the questions you want to ask, your volunteers go online and complete the survey, and you retrieve organized data. Before conducting this type of survey, you should check with the library administration to determine if using an external web-based survey is within library policy guidelines. A computer-literate volunteer can readily post your questions and retrieve data for you if this is not among your skill strengths.

Whether you are interpreting individual comments from a volunteer or survey data from many volunteers, there is always a context in which the answers are given. The physical context is the particular library or department where the volunteers work. The attitudinal and emotional feelings can relate to the relationships they experience as volunteers or in their personal lives. What you are looking for are patterns in the comments that can give you the big picture of the program from the volunteers' perspectives. Also, a review of their comments can identify particular strengths or weakness of the program. Both positive and negative comments can be useful.

RECEPTIONS AND NEW TECHNOLOGY

It is relatively easy these days to use camcorders to videorecord volunteer receptions and upload all or part of the event to the library website or Facebook. A speech about the importance of volunteers given by a top administrator can be a valuable video segment to upload for other volunteers and staff to view. So can seeing the "volunteer of the year" receive an award. For technologically advanced libraries, creating a video podcast or streaming video of the reception is possible. This is also a useful approach for acknowledging virtual volunteers and including them in an event.

When you first begin using this technology, expect amateurish quality. Even very good camcorders have built-in microphones with limited capabilities for picking up sound in a room full of talking people. To go beyond this level, you can seek professional advice. This can be done by asking paid staff and volunteers if they know an expert in the video recording business or searching local web directories and contacting start-up companies. The latter are usually one- or two-person businesses that may even offer to video your volunteer reception, add music, and work with your computer staff to upload to your library server for free or low cost as a way of marketing their business. They use high-quality microphones cabled into one or more video cameras, and the outcome is usually of high quality.

| # AWARDS, GIFTS, AND PERKS

What types of recognition items can you give to volunteers that are affordable and meaningfully tied to the program? This is a difficult question to answer. Awards are presented for accomplishments, gifts are given for volunteering one's time and effort, and perks can be used for either purpose. Usually what is important is not what you give to a volunteer but the thought behind it. In this section the emphasis is on recognition, especially on a limited budget.

RECOGNITION BUDGET

For many smaller and medium-sized libraries, the volunteer recognition budget for awards or gifts is nonexistent or very small. The amount available to spend per person may be less than five dollars. Based on your policies, you need to decide whether to award a few people or recognize everyone. If you present a recognition award to everyone, then you need to decide how much you can afford and what you can purchase for that amount. Presenting one individual with an engraved plaque for $35 may have to be offset by giving the others printed certificates of appreciation. Alternatively, a special commendation presented by the library director to each volunteer may take more time to organize but cost little. Creative brainstorming with supervising staff can bring additional ideas. There are also commercial catalogs online that display a variety of awards and gifts in different price ranges, and these can provide you with additional ideas (see Bibliography).

One option is to seek gift donations or gift certificates from local businesses. You can do this yourself or recruit a volunteer. To begin, write a form letter to initiate the contact, then make a list of potential donors. Call each business first to find out the name of the contact person. If you contact businesses a few months before you need the gift donations, you will probably be more successful because some stores require approval from higher management or their corporate office in another state. You need to be able to accept rejection, not take it personally, and move on to the next company. Be sure to write a thank-you letter to the donors.

If you do not have a policy for it, you can write a set of guidelines on acceptable donations. For example, will you take a $20 gift certificate from an adult bookstore or accept donations of merchandise that are not appropriate?

An alternative with limited funds is to use your computer to make bookplates and allow each recognized volunteer to place their personalized bookplate in a new book of their choice. Add a potluck dinner or provide certificates and personalized photographs to each volunteer, and this type of event can be as much fun as an expensive, elaborate reception. Making due with limited funds is part of the challenge of being a library volunteer services manager.

AWARDS

Certain items by their nature are not gifts but awards: certificates, plaques, written commendations, proclamations, and special logo pins. To receive one of these items, a volunteer has to earn it. That volunteers have to earn these items does not mean that they are working just to receive awards.

Almost any object can become an award simply by placing an inscription on it. A small glass globe of the earth becomes an award by adding the words, "In recognition of 10 years of volunteer service." Its value to the volunteer is tied to the social occasion and how it is presented. The globe given to a volunteer in your office becomes a nice paperweight, but presented by the library director or the president of the library trustees at a reception it becomes an object of prestige and honor.

Finding awards that relate to libraries can be a challenge. Engraved bookmarks, letter openers, library note cards, and books have been used successfully in the past. As noted above, a bookplate inscribed with the volunteer's name and placed in a newly purchased book makes a meaningful award. For a new generation of volunteers, the library is a place of numerous public access terminals, WiFi, rows of DVDs and CDs, online access, e-books, and blogs, so whether a traditional "book"-related award will mean as much is a question open for discussion.

Even when some engraved plaques and trophies cost less than ten dollars, the costs can add up when you have several awards to present. As an alternative, you can invest in one large wall plaque and add volunteer names as they reach a predetermined number of donated hours or some other achievement. Once you choose to use a wall plaque, it is important to keep up the program so that it does not end up looking like a dated relic.

GIFTS AND PRIZES

The category of gifts and prizes relates to a person's status as a volunteer rather than to a particular accomplishment. Gifts can include actual objects or gift certificates. Depending on your recognition policy and budget, you can give everyone a small gift or hand them out as door prizes. If you are crafts oriented or have crafts-oriented volunteers, small handmade gifts add a personalized touch at low cost. Any decision you make can be successful if done with a sense of respect for the volunteers and as part of an enjoyable activity. Attaching a personal thank-you card to each gift increases its value.

There are a wide variety of small thank-you gifts available. In addition to getting ideas from creative volunteers and staff, you can also go through volunteer gift catalogs and online websites. Think about seeking nonmonetary donations from local merchants such as gift certificates from grocery stores, hotels, restaurants, movie theaters, museums, zoos, and recreational centers or amusement parks. Also, try to get donated tickets to cultural programs, community festivals, or any library-sponsored events. Library branch managers often have community contacts that can lead you to people who are decision makers or know people who can access such donations.

Small, inexpensive gifts include baskets of candy, flowering plants, posters, balloons, specialty buttons, personalized photographs taken at the library, stationery, note cards, and decorative ceramic appreciation plates.

Common library theme gifts include logo T-shirts, sweaters, and sweatshirts; volunteer pins, logo mugs, and pens; and bookmarks and posters. Libraries can give certificates for merchandise at their gift shops. Finally, computer-generated bookmarks, note pads, funny cards, and similar items make inexpensive gifts you can give yearly or year-round.

Thinking of gifts or prizes year after year can be a challenge. Keeping an idea file of volunteer catalogs, notes on what other organizations and agencies have given, suggestions made by volunteers and staff, and websites where you see gift possibilities is one way to be able to plan ahead. As with most gifts, the dollar value is less important than the spirit in which the gift is given. The gifts are merely the symbols of your recognition and thanks on behalf of the library.

VOLUNTEER PERKS

Perks, short for perquisites, are a type of privileged benefit a person receives—in our context for being a library volunteer. Perks can add to the appeal of working in a library. Two issues need to be examined before you decide to implement any formal perks for volunteers. One is whether volunteers should receive the same perks as staff. The perk serves a status function in many organizations. If the staff perceives that their perks are diluted because volunteers are also getting them, petty conflicts can result. For example, if waiving overdue fines is a staff perk, then do you want to waive them for volunteers as well, and if you do will there be ramifications?

A second area of concern is establishing criteria for eligibility for different perks. Do volunteers receive perks the first day they start, or should they work a set number of hours or weeks first? Can they be eligible for parking privileges after one month and have overdue fines waived after six months? After every hundred hours of volunteering can a privileged benefit be provided to the volunteers?

Whether identified as perks or benefits, list what you are currently providing the volunteers and list what paid staff get as perks. Are there places that the two lists can overlap? For a volunteer, being able to add one's name near the top of a holds list for a popular best seller is a perk. For a volunteer with artistic skills or computer graphics knowledge, designing library posters or announcements and getting special credit can be considered a perk. A general perk for all volunteers is the ability to claim federal and state charitable tax deductions for unpaid expenditures while volunteering. This includes automobile mileage, bus fares, and parking costs. For some volunteers who are looking for work experience, a job recommendation is an important perk.

Awards, gifts, and perks are an important part of any recognition program. Some form of recognition—not necessarily tangible—is essential to good management practice. Showing appreciation for the work done encourages volunteers to continue to provide their time and services to the library, to share their experiences, and to show their awards and gifts to their family and friends.

PART 5 | VOLUNTEER RULES AND DISCIPLINE

| # LIBRARY VOLUNTEER RULES

LIBRARY VOLUNTEERS WANT and need guidance. Some staff members hesitate to enforce library rules with a volunteer, yet volunteers need to know what the work rules are so they can feel comfortable fitting in with the staff and the ongoing library operations.

From a library manager's point of view, volunteer work rules clarify which activities are acceptable and provide a basis for enforcing them if necessary. For example, is a volunteer breaking a rule when she puts her lunch in the refrigerator marked "staff only"? Is the refrigerator available for use by both staff and volunteers? As volunteer services managers know or find out quickly, no issue is too small to be blown out of proportion.

RULES IN THE VOLUNTEER SERVICES HANDBOOK

A volunteer services handbook often evolves from a single handout based on part of the general library's policies and procedures manual. A good handbook emphasizes the positive aspects of volunteering and puts a positive spin on the volunteer rules by using less formal terms such as "guidelines," "code of conduct," or "library expectations."

It is important to distinguish between general library policy rules and specific work rules. Library policy rules are broad categories of rules that cover all areas of library operations. These can be written under the heading "Library Expectations," as exemplified in the phrase "Library staff and volunteers are expected to . . . " Many of these policy rules can be taken directly from the staff handbook and then reworded for your volunteer manual. For instance, your library policy on sexual harassment describes inappropriate behaviors toward staff, volunteers, and customers. Similarly, a policy rule stating that the library is a nonsmoking workplace means that no one can smoke within the building. Other typical policy rules address illegal drugs and alcohol and customer confidentiality.

Work rules are more specific and pertain to behaviors such as dress codes, use of the telephones and lockers, and break times. Your volunteer services handbook may state that a volunteer must be dressed appropriately to maintain the professional environment of the library. However, a volunteer who is sorting donated books should not be expected to dress the same as a reference assistant working in a public area. It is important that the staff supervisors be allowed to interpret what "appropriate dress" means. For young adult volunteers with less experience in the work world, you may find it useful to have a one-page illustrated handout that specifically illustrates appropriate volunteer dress and reinforce it by explaining to the young adult volunteers why the dress requirements are important for the library.

When writing your handbook, you need to decide which general work rules or guidelines all volunteers must follow regardless of their assignments and which rules are specific to departments. The latter rules need to be explained by the supervising staff. A general volunteer rule is "All volunteers are expected to show up for their shift or call their staff supervisor if they are going to be late or absent." A specific department rule might be "A volunteer cannot use the department copy machine for personal use unless agreed to by the manager."

Throughout a large library system, you may not know the specific differences in the rules or their interpretations within the various libraries and departments. It is important that you decide how this information is going to be communicated and who is responsible for conveying it. These procedures should be spelled out before you place a volunteer to reduce the possibility of embarrassment, hurt feelings, or staff/volunteer conflicts. The best options for sharing specific library or department work rules with volunteers are staff supervisors. As a supplement, and not an alternative, these rules can be posted on the library intranet under the volunteer services section so that a volunteer can read what is expected. Again, recognize that volunteers, both young adults and adults, are picking up only a small part of the information that is shared during their initial orientation and training, so it is useful to provide access to what is expected in hard copy or in electronic form.

You also need to decide if you want the volunteer services handbook to serve as a recruitment and marketing tool or a rulebook. In the former case, the emphasis is on the enjoyment of volunteering, with photos or other graphics and a list of the kinds of opportunities available. In the latter case, the handbook is a list of work related "do's" and "don'ts." Some libraries put all or some of the handbook expectations on the volunteer services web pages. Currently, both recruitment/marketing and the work rule versions of handbooks are on library websites.

STATEMENT AND CLARIFICATION OF THE RULES

Ideally, the staff supervisor will take the time with a volunteer to clarify the department rules. In a busy library this may not be feasible. A positively written, one- to two-page list of important information and rules can supplement and highlight oral explanations (see sample 31-1). In either case, include some or all of the following points on your list or in discussions:

- Departmental dress code
- Lockers or storage space for personal effects
- Attendance, tardiness, or absences
- Designated smoking areas
- Parking
- Telephone, fax, computer, copier use
- Office supplies
- Reporting injuries
- Break times and break areas
- Holiday schedules and library closures

Most people do not read long lists of rules closely, and when they do they usually interpret them in terms of their own experiences. Volunteers do not know how specific rules are applied in the library. For example, a volunteer can read from a list of rules that telephones are not to be used for personal reasons unless in an emergency. With cell phones and smartphones now widespread, can the volunteer leave the work area to use his mobile phone? How much time away from work is seen as abuse of the telephone policy? At this point, rule clarification is important and a face-to-face explanation is required.

Volunteer Guidelines

Mesa County Public Library District Volunteer Guidelines

The following guidelines and procedures outline the essential expectations of your volunteer position. Please become thoroughly familiar with these expectations and be sure they are acceptable to you before making your decision to volunteer for the library.

1. Library user requests are always handled by paid library staff because of liability issues and because library staff are updated regularly on changes in our operations. We ask that volunteers refer all user inquiries to library staff without exception.
2. Privacy of library users' records is protected by Colorado state law. This means that you may not share any knowledge you may gain through your volunteer duties at the library of any record or other information that identifies a person as having used the library or requested or obtained specific materials or services at the library. To violate user privacy is to violate state law and is punishable by state law.
3. Volunteers and staff are expected to present a clean and neat appearance while on the job. Please dress comfortably but appropriately for your assigned task.
4. You will report to a designated staff person in the center or branch where you are volunteering and training is provided for all tasks performed. That staff person will issue you a locker for your valuables and a volunteer badge for identification. Please be sure to always use your locker and wear your badge. When questions arise, feel free to ask a designated staff person for further clarification.
5. Your volunteer time is an integral part of the coordination of staff hours and duties. If you are unable to come in at your scheduled time, please call your designated staff person or the center.
6. Be sure to sign in and out every day you are volunteering. Volunteer hour tabulation is an important part of the library's statistics.
7. Parking for main branch volunteers is in the public parking lot.
8. At the main branch, volunteers are invited to enjoy their breaks in the lounge at the back of the reference center. You may store your own cup in the cupboards if you wish. Please store all food and unsealed beverages in the break room and wash and put away any dishes you use.
9. If you have any comments or concerns not addressed by your designated staff person or branch manager, please contact the community relation's manager who is here for you!

Sample 31-1. **Volunteer Guidelines**

Who is responsible for clarifying and enforcing the rules? If you are in a large library system with several libraries, you are not in a position to enforce the rules yourself. Are the supervising staff members trained to correct volunteers tactfully? Enforcement needs to be the role of the supervising staff members, but some of these people have limited supervisory experience and find it awkward to correct a volunteer. Therefore, you might hear from a secondhand source that a volunteer is breaking a rule. Now you are expected to act. If this is the case, you need to become a "fact finder" by either observing the rule violation yourself or asking questions to determine the veracity of the accusation. You can take action only after you have verified all the facts.

UNUSUAL SITUATIONS

All rules are not clear-cut. They have gray areas that make it unclear how to proceed under certain circumstances. A large part of any volunteer services manager's job is interpreting ambiguous situations. Consider the example of a volunteer who is working in the back room and receives cell phone calls from an elderly mother. The staff complains that the volunteer is receiving too many personal calls during the shift. The volunteer claims to be receiving only one or two calls at the most from the parent; she also observes that certain employees are receiving personal calls from their children and other family members during their work time. What can you do to defuse this situation?

Set rules do not cover all contingencies. At times you have to interpret the rules as they apply to specific situations. In the example above, if the paid staff are allowed to receive personal calls, can the department rules be stretched to cover volunteers? Can you have the volunteer keep track of the number and length of calls received per shift for two weeks to help you decide if her phone usage seems excessive? Can you limit the incoming calls to two per four-hour shift? Each question offers several options; the best options are somewhere between the extremes of either setting a poor precedent or being too rigid to deal with an unusual volunteer situation.

With young adult volunteers the ubiquitous cell phones, iPods, and earbuds are part of the contemporary lifestyle—but they are often limited or forbidden by library rules. The key to getting these volunteers to follow such rules is taking the time to explain why the rules exist. Some young people will definitely "test" the rules and might say, "I am only texting my friend and I am not making any noise," when assigned a duty of cleaning puppets. Another wearing a volunteer nametag and shelving easy readers may ask, "Why can't I listen to music on my iPod?" From their view, these are legitimate questions and require thoughtful answers. Young adult librarians are used to such "testing the limits" questions and may respond with humor in correcting the behaviors. If shelving is considered a customer service function, earbuds do not allow customers to ask questions of a shelver easily. Alternatively, is there anything wrong with listing to an iPod while shelving in the children's area? Is the texting in the above example a set of short exchanges, or is it extensive and ongoing? These are the types of situations that lead to additional discussions that either reaffirm existing rules or establish different expectations.

Library policies and rules can change over time in response to evolving circumstances or at the discretion of the library director. Be sure to state this somewhere in your volunteer services handbook. In this way, you protect the library organization and managers when they have to make changes that affect volunteers.

ENFORCEMENT POLICIES

It is important to remember that most volunteers want to be effective at their jobs and follow library rules. Any enforcement is usually focused on additional clarification or explanation of the consequences to customers or the library of not following a rule. Suppose you are told that a volunteer is frequently using the backroom staff computer to check for personal e-mail related to a personal business. You or the supervising staff member needs to explain that this ties up the computer for other staff members and for library-related business. Luckily, most volunteers gladly change their behaviors to accommodate the library. It is the rare habitual violator who creates a problem. A problem volunteer may say, for example, "I'm not using the office computer any more than anyone else. I am being singled out because the staff does not want me to volunteer here!" In this situation, you are beyond the point of having only to give additional clarification and must take corrective action.

Generally, by the time you hear about a problem volunteer or have to deal with such an individual, the staff or other volunteers already know about the issue. Everyone is waiting to see what you, the volunteer services manager, will do. In other words, you cannot ignore the situation and hope the problem goes away, or that the volunteer does. You will seldom be this lucky. Whatever steps you decide to take, it is important that your actions are covered within the volunteer services handbook. This is easily accomplished with handbook statements that include the following points:

- The use of volunteers is subject to the changing needs of the library.
- Volunteers are responsible for following the library rules and policies as specified in the volunteer handbook.
- Volunteers are subject to corrective action that may include devolunteering.
- All volunteers serve at the discretion of the library director.

As the volunteer services manager, you are the representative of the library director for your department. These statements give you flexibility to take corrective actions when necessary and to devolunteer a person who is not working out. A volunteer services handbook that clearly sets forth a set of workplace rules goes a long way toward avoiding future disciplinary actions.

| # VOLUNTEER CORRECTIVE ACTION

FORTUNATELY, THERE ARE very few problem volunteers. Whether youth or adults, most individuals are supportive of library policies and conscientious about following instructions and rules. Problem volunteers usually have personality traits that are extremely difficult, if not impossible, to modify. It is a good idea to set up corrective action procedures and summarize these in your volunteer services handbook.

COUNSELING VERSUS CORRECTIVE ACTION

A key reason people volunteer their time and energy to serve the community is personal reward and satisfaction. Even those who are part of an assigned duty such as court-directed community service or school requirements also want to do a good job. There are few exceptions, although these are invariably the volunteers paid staff remember when they do not want any more volunteers in their department.

If selection is done correctly, there are usually few problems with task performance. When these do occur it can be quickly determined if this is a call for retraining and whether the problem is one of quality or quantity. A quality issue is typically sloppiness in doing the task and usually results from working too fast or careless inattention to details. This is a time for a short counseling session on why the outcome of the task is important to the library and must be done correctly to reflect positively on the library and serve the customers. A quantity problem might be "being slow as molasses." Here too a counseling discussion about what is expected in the time period and an explanation of why the outcome is important quite often are sufficient. If this does not fix the problem, then reassignment to a less time-demanding task may be the answer, recognizing that the volunteer was not matched with the right job. If the source of the problem is motivation because the volunteer does not like the assigned task, then this leads to an additional counseling session.

For young adult volunteers, building positive and fun relationships early on is the key to reducing the need for corrective actions. Asking about their interests, the reasons why they chose the library to do volunteer service, and what they hope to get out of their experience personalizes the relationships. When you demonstrate sincere respect for them as young adults and do not talk down to them, this goes a long way toward establishing a volunteer environment that encourages high performance. In this type of setting, peers can quickly control each other to support the job expectations. Surrounded by working adults also adds to the structure of their volunteer experience. This does not mean that there is never a need for counseling or corrective action, but these episodes will be greatly diminished. Young adults accept positive and negative feedback if it is given as constructive assistance to do their jobs better.

When a volunteer is not following or understanding a volunteer services procedure or library policy, this calls for a counseling session. In your mind, the question should be why this particular volunteer is not abiding by the requirement as other volunteers. Counseling involves listening and getting the volunteer back on track by showing empathy and helping the individual understand what behaviors need to change and why. You are working through a problem with an individual to achieve a behavioral change. Someone may, for example, not have understood the importance of signing in when arriving at the library. You can explain that this is important as a way for others to know who is in the work area. In most instances, once explained, the problem goes away.

LISTENING AND FACT FINDING

One of your first responses to a problem situation should be to verify the information. This requires a combination of active listening and objective fact finding to gain insights into the real problem and to show that you are open to differing opinions.

If you find the problem is with a volunteer and your advice and counsel are not followed, the next likely step is to issue a verbal warning and provide additional clarification of the rules. Most likely the volunteer is still not clear about the library protocol or about supervisory expectations. Be sure that you stay open to the volunteer's expressed concerns. Recognize that the first comments in this type of conversation are usually less important than what is said later in the conversation. For example, if a volunteer is verbally complaining that staff members do not want him around, you can ask the following questions to clarify the problem: "Who do you think does not want you to volunteer at the library?" The initial response might be "everyone" or "all the staff." If you pause and do not answer immediately, the volunteer will probably expand on the answer. If you find this approach difficult, you can ask a follow-up question to elicit a more specific answer: "Can you give me an example of why you think no one wants you to volunteer at the library?" You might find that only one staff member made a negative comment, which the volunteer generalized to everyone's feelings about his work. In this situation, you can offer to talk to the supervising staff member to get the other side of the issue clarified. You may likely find that the volunteer does not want to escalate the issue. You can offer to reassign him to another job or change his hours so that he is working with different staff members.

PROGRESSIVE CORRECTIVE ACTION

Corrective action is a focused sequence of steps taken when a volunteer chooses not to follow the task requirements or library rules and continues on the same negative path after counseling. Allowing the negative situation to continue can result in the disruption of departmental relationships. You recognize that at this point you need to take stronger measures to rectify the problem.

Progressive corrective action is a process of steps that starts with verbal warning, then written warning, then a leave of absence, and then devolunteering. Unless your library policy requires it, you do not have to go through the full sequence of steps against a volunteer. In fact, you may want to state in your handbook that if any corrective action is necessary it can result in devolunteering on the first offense. You might take such action, for example, if one of your volunteers comes to work under the influence of illegal substances or is caught taking money out of a cash drawer where fine money is collected. Fortunately, extreme cases such as these seldom occur in a library—but you do want to be prepared to take action if such a situation does arise.

Your volunteer services program probably has diverse types of volunteers, and the question here is how to provide progressive correction actions for these differing types. Although young adult volunteers, for example, need to recognize and follow library rules, you do not want to take such negative corrective actions that they never return to the library, even as customers. Similarly, an adult volunteer who leaves because of a corrective action is still a resident, a voter, a taxpayer, and, you hope, a library customer. Thus, sensitivity is required in how you conduct corrective action conversations and how you implement corrective actions.

In young adult situations, corrective actions are generally for not showing up or calling in when scheduled, not following instructions, having friends visit who interfere with volunteer duties, using profanity, violating the dress code, goofing off to avoid the assigned duties, playing computer games during volunteer time, or creating verbal confrontations. Whether a volunteer is young adult or adult, fact finding on your part is crucial for each situation. A typical example is that of a high school youth who agrees to volunteer from 4:00 to 6:00 each Monday, Wednesday, and Friday afternoon as a way to meet school graduation requirements. On the third week she does not show up on Wednesday and does not call in. The supervising staff member calls attention to the problem. An apology is exchanged. Two weeks later the same thing happens on Wednesday. At this point you are probably called into the conversation. The question that needs to be answered is why this youth is not following the agreed upon schedule? In conversation, you may find that there is overlapping time conflict with a softball coach who is holding extra practice sessions. The youth does not want to give up her volunteer position because of the required graduation credits and does not know how to handle this time conflict. Reaffirming the agreement on volunteer time is part of the corrective action. Asking the young volunteer what should be done could lead to a mutual acceptable solution, perhaps volunteering on Sunday afternoons rather than Wednesdays. Not all young adults have the maturity to address schedule conflicts between two people in positions of authority.

When corrective action is necessary in an adult volunteer situation, it is best to get a statement from the volunteer about the problem incidents. This is part of your fact finding with the supervising staff member and any other staff or volunteers to understand what has happened. A report, usually written, is presented to the library director or senior administrator to determine what action the library wants to take. You need to be specific and document everything that is said and every action that occurred. Suppose that a new volunteer has started working, and staff members allege that small items and pocket change are missing from their purses and lockers. There is no proof, and no one has seen this volunteer take anything, nor is it clear when things went missing. Careful fact finding is called for here without jumping to any conclusions. Even when your efforts lead to an ambiguous outcome, just asking factual questions often leads to the elimination of the problem. Staff members watch their personal effects more closely, lost items are found, and if the volunteer was the culprit he quits or ceases taking things. If there is still uncertainty, you can offer the volunteer the opportunity to work in another department and monitor the situation closely.

When the corrective action escalates to a written warning, it is usually because of a persistent problem. At the young adult level, this may mean bringing the parents into the conversation. Young adults work with the permission of parents or guardians and on a work schedule to which they have agreed. Although the supervising staff member may want to devolunteer and tell the youth not to show up anymore, it is more prudent to take one more step and talk with the parent or guardian. This conversation can be by telephone or face to face; be honest in explaining the problem. Whether the young adult is present during this conversation is a judgment call. You might, for example, be told that a youth who is not following instructions or completing assigned tasks suffers attention deficit disorder, and that the parents are hoping that volunteering in a nonschool environment will help their child. It is important to explain that the library cannot "babysit" volunteers, but a compromise may be reached by reducing hours or identifying more limited tasks that the young adult can do. Each situation is different, and it is always important to document your findings and your conversations.

Corrective action can also escalate with adult volunteers. Again these are extreme exceptions thanks in large part to the fact that people self-select to work in a library. Fact finding is critical. It leads you to an answer to why an adult volunteer persists in negative behavior that is detrimental to the department—and that answer will determine how you proceed. Recognize that there can be several different reasons for this behavior: a volunteer is hard of hearing and does not understand instructions, another does not recognize the limits of her authority, and still another does not realize that his behavior is abrupt or rude to staff and customers.

A volunteer who continually violates a minor safety rule may be subject to progressive corrective action. Consider a volunteer assigned to water the plants in the library who is found standing on a swivel chair to reach a hanging basket. The supervising staff member asks him to use the step ladder in the storage closet, but he continues to use the chair. This is an accident waiting to happen and exposes the library to an unnecessary safety risk. This is where progressive corrective action escalates. Keep a fact-finding perspective by asking why the volunteer is not using the step ladder. It may turn out that he understands and agrees that the step ladder is safer and that this safety concern was pointed out to him a couple of weeks back, but the step ladder is hard to get out of the storage room and too heavy to carry. Is there an alternative? Can the volunteer use a library stool to reach the plant or the stepstool in the work area? Put in writing what you agree to and let the volunteer sign it. If this does not work, you are justified in removing him from the task. If you place him in another assignment that requires following another safety rule (as well as other library rules) and volunteer refuses to do so, you can devolunteer him.

Typical situations where progressive corrective action applies to adult volunteers are repeated violations of library nonsmoking rules on or around library premises, taking small amounts of library supplies, violation of customer confidentially policies, having ongoing conflicts with staff or other volunteers, and abusing telephone, computer, or copy machine privileges.

CORRECTIVE ACTION STATEMENTS

It is important to plan ahead before you initiate a corrective action conversation. It should not be a spur-of-the-moment decision, for you may say something you wish you did not or forgot to cover a key point. Below are three sample statements that illustrate varying degrees of corrective action:

> *Informal.* You as a volunteer, and I as a staff member, both have to follow library guidelines. I know you did your best when you were told to straighten the newspaper shelves, but you threw out all the papers except last week's issues. You were previously told about this last month. The library's policy is to hold all newspapers for two months. What do you think the problem is? [long pause] If you do not know what to do, please ask for clarification from the reference staff or come to me. You can even give me a call at home if you do not understand something. I know you pride yourself on being fast and efficient, but please do not let something like this happen again.

> *Formal.* The rules and polices of the library are designed to support efficient operations to better serve our customers. As a volunteer, your cooperation in following the rules will make your experiences rewarding. It is not likely that you purposely violate the established library rule, so what do you think is the problem? [long pause] Additional training can be provided. You are encouraged to ask questions if you do not understand something. Any further violation will result in being reassigned to a more closely supervised volunteer duty or asking you to give up your volunteer position.

> *Disciplinary.* In order to serve our customers and the community and to meet agency requirements, the library has a set of expecta-

tions and rules that all staff and volunteers are expected to comply with while working at the library. A volunteer who violates the posted or written rules will be subject to disciplinary action. Disciplinary action may include (1) joint discussions with the volunteer services manager and library manager, (2) reassignment to a new set of volunteer duties, (3) a request for resignation, or (4) formal devolunteering. Any volunteer can appeal a decision to the library director, who will then review the circumstances and actions taken and make a final decision.

DOCUMENTING ACTIONS

During a busy day, it is hard to recall who said what and when, especially when there is a potential for conflict. It is a good idea to make written notes when you take an action that you feel might have broad ramifications for the library. One option is to keep a notebook and jot down what you did and the date. You can also write a note in your computer notebook or in the volunteer's file. In most situations, your notes are memory cues to help you act with consistency. If you tell a volunteer it is all right to change her work days during the week due to a family situation, your note is to remind you to tell the supervising staff member about the change in the schedule.

In the case of a problem volunteer, your notes serve as documentation of your conversations and decisions. Problem volunteers have a way of changing interpretations as they recall meetings or conversations. Your notes are written for your eyes only and help you clear up any confusion. You should be aware, however, that these notes can become matters of record in an administrative hearing in the library, or they may be used by a third-party agency if the volunteer takes legal action, for example, in response to being let go. You do not want to write something for the file that can reflect poorly on you or the library. In the case of devolunteering, these notes become part of the documentation that leads to the decision.

The most likely legal charge against you or the library would be discriminatory conduct as seen from the volunteer's perspective. Imagine that a volunteer privately tells you of a positive test for HIV, and four months later the supervising staff member wants the volunteer replaced because of numerous task errors. You have no other appropriate volunteer positions, so you devolunteer the individual. A week later you receive a letter from an attorney representing the local AIDS organization stating that you discriminated against this individual after you learned about the HIV test. Suddenly your notes become part of an internal library review. Similar issues can occur with individuals from any legally protected class within your community. Fairness and objectivity are important values to hold during your fact finding and corrective actions, whether or not the outcome is devolunteering.

SECTION 33 | DEVOLUNTEERING

MOST OF THE time, a verbal warning is enough to change the work behaviors of young adults and adult volunteers to be in line with library expectations. Writing warnings, reducing hours, or requiring people to take time off from volunteering usually eliminates most problems. If things get to this point, many volunteers quit. Even so, you need to understand devolunteering.

There is no requirement to keep someone on as a volunteer in a library. If an individual is not working out after you have tried progressive corrective action, then for the sake of the library, paid staff, customers, and other volunteers you need to initiate the process of devolunteering.

PRELIMINARY DEVOLUNTEERING ACTIONS

Once a decision is made to dismiss a volunteer, the key reasons for devolunteering are written down notebook style. This includes a summary of specific behaviors and dates. For volunteer services managers, the process of devolunteering is stressful.

In a young adult devolunteering situation, you want to include the parents or guardians in the conversation. If you devolunteer a youth without letting the responsible parent or guardian know, they may think that their child is still working safely at the library under adult supervision. This situation can lead to a much bigger problem for the library administration and director. You cannot assume that the young adult will tell the parents about being devolunteered.

For adult volunteers, your knowledge of the written files and understanding of the entire situation must be clear. Devolunteering is not done lightly. Consider the case of a volunteer who is conducting computer training for the public. According to the supervising staff member, she has excellent computer knowledge and a demonstrated commitment to the schedule and to the training. She provides extra assistance to paid staff members on personal computer problems and is a likeable person on a one-to-one basis. The problem is that she does not demonstrate the patience and empathy necessary to work with the diverse range of ages and computer experiences customers bring with them to public computer class. There have been "put downs" and "abrupt answers," and on occasion the volunteer has not responded to a particular customer's questions. These issues have been discussed on specific dates by the supervisor, who again pointed out the listed requirements of the position on the volunteer job description. Fact finding verifies these problems and is supported by customer complaints made on library comment cards. A written warning is given, along with additional training on customer relations. Complaints continue. The supervising staff member wants to devolunteer and asks you to start the process.

If this were your problem, then throughout the sequences of events you would be maintaining an informal diary of dates, conversations, and actions taken to resolve it. It is a good idea to review your notes with a library administrator to keep your decision making objective. As the volunteer services manager, you cannot ignore the situation and just hope the volunteer improves or leaves. Allowing the volunteer computer trainer to continue in the position will create more negative comments from other customers and possibly negative comments within the community. This can reflect negatively on the library's public training classes and your volunteer services program. If there are no other positions available that this volunteer can perform, then you need to devolunteer her. This requires a face-to-face conversation—but first make sure you have all your information and thoughts well organized.

Over time, there is a reasonable chance that you will have to devolunteer a court-directed volunteer. Court-directed individuals pose a slightly different problem because some of them choose the library as an "easy place" to perform their community restitution services. Again, remember that devolunteering of community service volunteers is infrequent because most are good citizens who got into legal difficulty and want to get their restitution time over quickly. Devolunteering here is mostly for volunteers who do not perform at an acceptable level or do not show up at their appointed times. You can immediately devolunteer them if you feel it is necessary. In these situations, it may be useful to get a second-party opinion. Introducing a second party into the devolunteering process gives you a cooling-off period and a chance to gather your thoughts before you take action, as well as a different perspective.

In circumstances that could involve a charge of discrimination, it is prudent to share your concerns with a senior human resources administrator, key library administrator, or legal counsel before you initiate any devolunteering action. The library policy in this area may be applicable to the procedures you use to devolunteer. Once you decide to devolunteer after a thorough examination of the facts, you can continue to set in motion the wheels to dismiss the volunteer.

DEVOLUNTEERING CONVERSATIONS

For almost anyone, devolunteering is a serious loss of face. It is difficult for most people to understand that they have been fired from a volunteer job. Therefore, to prevent unnecessary complications (such as lawsuits), it is a good idea to have someone else present, such as the supervising staff person. Ideally, you will meet the volunteer in your office, conference room, or a place that is private. It is also important to talk to the volunteer before he starts a shift. The conversation should take no more than ten minutes, but block out fifteen to twenty minutes to make sure you write any pertinent notes while they are still fresh in your mind.

In preparing for the meeting, run through a checklist of any library-owned items the volunteer may have including keys, instructional manuals, or borrowed equipment. Be sure to arrange to get these items back.

Keep in mind that devolunteering someone is an administrative decision based on objective facts. It is not a reflection on the volunteer as a person but on the individual in the position of a library volunteer. The objective basis for any devolunteering action is either job performance or violation of library rules. There may be other personality issues, but you need to stay objectively focused on performance and rules.

When devolunteering a young adult, state your case but stay positive, pointing out that the volunteer experience has not worked out for the library. This leaves the door open for a second chance at a later date. Depending on age or circumstances, you may want the parent present for this conversation. If a parent or guardian is not present, let them know that their youth is no longer a library volunteer. Be brief in your explanation and invite them to call back if they have questions after talking with the youth. Recognize that, as young adults grow up, most start learning to accept responsibility and have a better understanding of why rules must be followed. A difference of one or two years at this time in life is usually very telling. Even if the parents ask for a second chance, it would be best to require a minimum of six to twelve months before a volunteer reapplication. Over this period, the young person's interests in library volunteering may change and other activities may compete for the youth's time. If done well, the devolunteering is viewed as part of a learning experience for the young adult and neutralizes negative feelings about the library and the services it provides.

With adult volunteers you should script what you need to cover in outline form. You are not required to, nor should you, go into detail about the basis of the devolunteering. If there have been progressive corrective actions and prior conversations, the devolunteering conversation should not be a total surprise. You may not have another volunteer position open that fits this volunteer. If you do have another position open, you can keep this option open if the volunteer asks for a second chance.

Below are two scripts of possible scenarios, scripted to explain to a library volunteer the decision to devolunteer:

> *Script 1.* After four months with the library and three different assigned tasks, we made the decision that the library is not the best place for your volunteer efforts. The staff supervisors provided extra training, at your request. As you recall, you and I last met on the 21st of the month and discussed the problems with your perfor-mance not meeting library standards. As of this afternoon, you are no longer a volunteer with the library. We have appreciated your time with the library. I would be happy to help you identify other local community organizations that use volunteers.

> *Script 2.* Thank you for coming in today. I reserved the study room so that you and I can discuss your work as a volunteer. During the past two months, I have spoken to you about your rudeness to our customers. I also explained to you on two prior occasions how important our community residents are to the library. Last night you lost your temper and became rude to a family with small chil-dren. The library manager telephoned the family and apologized on behalf of the library. My only recourse now is to remove you from the volunteer schedule. As of this afternoon, you are no longer a library volunteer. I hope you will continue to use the library ser-vices as a community resident. There are many other fine volunteer

opportunities within the community and I am sure you will find one that is suited to your interests.

The volunteer may request a second chance or want to know specifically why devolunteering is occurring now. Your answer needs to be brief and to the point: "It is your overall performance that is not meeting standards. This is not related to any particular event or day." You need to be firm but always polite; stay in control of the conversation. Even if the issue is a personality trait (e.g., aggressive, domineering, or confrontational) or a communication style (e.g., boisterous or abrasive), your answer stays the same: "You are not meeting library standards."

After a brief explanation, your goal is to bring the conversation to a polite end. At this time, stand up and move to the door to indicate an end to the conversation.

DEVOLUNTEERING OUTCOMES

A volunteer may initially express feelings of disappointment, anger, or sadness or may merely take a stoic stance by saying "good-bye" and leave. In a few cases, volunteers are actually relieved because their interests or life circumstances were changing but they stayed on because they did not want to let you or the library down. For others, the loss of the volunteer position per se is less important than leaving a social group of other volunteers or staff members they came to know. Although you may anticipate a particular reaction, you will not know until the devolunteering conversation actually occurs.

No matter what your feelings are toward the volunteer or the reaction, it is important to stay professional throughout the conversation. This is not a time to think or talk of blame or fault; it is a circumstance in which a person did not match or continue to match the needs of the library. This same person may be successful as a volunteer in another community organization, and in the back of your mind this is what you can hope is the outcome. In the best scenario, after a few weeks the person is back in the library checking out books and stays a supporter of the library.

DEVOLUNTEERING AND THE TROUBLED VOLUNTEER

Troubled volunteers are those who have psychophysical conditions that were not noticed during the recruitment and placement process. For example, a person who is bipolar can seem quite normal when the medications are taken and the dosages are correct. Similarly, a person with seasonal affective disorder may not have symptoms on the sunny days of spring and summer. Mood disorders, depression, and other illnesses can be controlled through medication, and many people with these illnesses operate successfully in their everyday lives. Because they are unpaid staff, there is no legal requirement to provide reasonable accommodations in their volunteer work settings or to treat them in special ways unless your library jurisdiction has an administrative requirement that states otherwise.

As unpaid staff members, volunteers do not have access to the employee assistance programs offered to paid staff. There are, however, community mental health agencies in most library jurisdictions, and there may be free or low-cost services available depending on the needs of the volunteer. These agencies often have employer services that can provide you information and advice on how to handle a particular troubled volunteer with problem behaviors.

A volunteer's wide swing in moods can occur when she is not taking her medications because she feels good, or her doses are off, or something happens in the work setting that sets off a major reaction. When this happens, the workplace can become tense for both paid staff and other volunteers and possibly customers. Through the corrective action process, you probably have come to recognize that there are bigger issues with this volunteer than just task performance or relationships with others in the department. Some volunteers may have even explained their illness with you in confidence.

When a troubled volunteer needs to be devolunteered, you should prepare by talking to a human resources manager and other key library administrators on how to proceed. Could the devolunteering conversation lead to a violent outburst? Is there a better place to hold the conversation than your office? Who should be with you during the conversation? Will you need security? Should a family member be called? Will you need a cab to have the person taken home?

We hope you never have to devolunteer a troubled volunteer in your career as a volunteer services manager, but it is a reasonable idea to walk through the process in the event this ever becomes necessary.

DEVOLUNTEERING AND REFERENCE REQUESTS

If a devolunteered person asks you to be a reference, you can base your decision on library policy. In some situations, you may agree to be a reference if you know this is a hardworking individual who had difficulty learning particular library tasks or being able to work in a library setting. In other situations, you may agree only to complete a volunteer work verification form.

If you have devolunteered someone working for community, court, or high school service credit, you have to decide whether or not to indicate on the form that you devolunteered the individual. You may just indicate the hours volunteered at the library and leave the comment section on the form blank. Put the burden on the volunteer to explain why all the designated hours were not completed at the library. How honest and complete you are will probably depend on your library policy. If in doubt, get advice from the library administration or legal counsel.

APPEALS PROCESS

Volunteers who feel that they were treated unfairly by you, the staff, or the supervising staff member should have the right to appeal a decision that affects their status as a volunteer. Just having an appeals process, even though extremely few people will ever use it, gives volunteers the option to bring others into the conversation. The appeal can occur as part of the formal corrective action process or after devolunteering. Sometimes just talking with a top library administrator or the library director is often enough to diffuse a volunteer's anger. The volunteer is still a community member, and you want this person's continued support for the library in the future. The appeals process should be explained in your volunteer handbook.

The first step in the appeals process is typically a meeting with the immediate supervising staff member. The volunteer needs to bring a written memo (providing you with a copy) to the meeting outlining the felt grievance. This memo becomes part of the formal process. If the volunteer is not satisfied, then he can meet with you or your manager. The final step is a meeting with the assistant director or the library director. After this formal appeals process takes place, the volunteer may take the grievance to an attorney, though it would have to be extremely serious for this to occur. What is important is for you to keep a diary of the events and document everything. File your notes in a confidential folder, with copies of the pertinent information to your manager.

SECTION 34 | **EXIT INTERVIEWS AND REFERENCES**

AS YOU REVIEW your library volunteer services program over a period of time, you will notice that some individuals work for a month, others for eight to ten months, and some for many years. Whether a volunteer officially resigns or quits without notification, the person has information about the volunteer experience that can be useful to improve your program. One way to capture these insights and experiences is through an exit interview or mail-back questionnaire, accomplished as soon as you are aware that the volunteer is about to leave or has formally left the program. This procedure should not be followed in the case of forced resignations or devolunteering.

Two other features of a volunteer's departure of interest to the volunteer services manager are separation forms and letters of reference.

EXIT INTERVIEWS

An exit interview is a structured set of questions asked of volunteers when they leave library service. The purpose is to shed light on areas where the volunteer services program can be improved. You can learn about the quality of your program though questions about training and placement, the relationship between the volunteer and the supervising staff, the assigned tasks, suggestions for improving the program, and the reasons for leaving. The interviews are best given in person but can be conducted by telephone.

Initially, the process of developing questions for an exit interview is to look at your program from all angles (recruitment, placement, supervision, job duties, staff, and recognition) to decide on the type of data you want to collect. Staff volunteer supervisors often suggest questions to ask. Although this section is on exit interviews, it can also be useful to ask regular volunteers who are not leaving some of these questions; you might do this by uploading the volunteer services exit survey to the library intranet. In this case, it is good to provide confidentiality of the responses and state as much on the survey if it cannot be filled out in anonymity.

EXIT SURVEYS

An alternative to face-to-face interviews is a traditional mail, e-mail, or online exit questionnaire (see sample 34-1). Responses to mailed or e-mailed exit surveys are often quite low unless the volunteer has strong feelings either positive or negative about the library experience. Adding a personalized letter can help. Certainly enclosing a stamped, addressed envelope marked "confidential" also helps to increase mail-in responses. An e-mail reminder can also increase responses.

An easy-to-use form can be designed so that the questions are answered by a checkmark under a specific category, such as "very satisfied," "satisfied," or "unsatisfied." This type of survey can limit the scope of the response because the answers do not account for individual feelings or experiences. Therefore, to ensure getting a more informed picture, include spaces for written comments. The form should be easy to read and limited to one or two pages so that it takes five minutes or less to complete. You can ask that it be returned to you by a specific date.

The mailed or e-mailed survey should include the same set of questions as the formal exit interview so that you have some level of consistency when comparing the answers. If the survey is on the library intranet, volunteers who give notice can be asked to complete it online or you can conduct an exit interview, depending on time constraints and the number of volunteers and their locations. Volunteers who depart abruptly will not have access to the intranet and may not be willing to talk with you or complete a survey.

Dear_____ :

Thank you for your volunteering at the library. We are always trying to improve the volunteer services program and ask you to please take a couple of minutes to answer several questions about the program. Your comments are important and will be held in confidence.

Thank you in advance for your time.

Sincerely,

1. Were your personal needs met as a library volunteer? (Check one)

___ Yes, most of the time

___ Yes, some of the time

___ Seldom met

___ Not met

Your comments _____

2. In comparison with other volunteer experiences, how would you rate your volunteer time with the library? (Check one)

_____ Better

_____ Equal to

_____ Some what less positive

_____ Worse than

_____ I have had no other volunteer experience

Your comments _____

3. Did the library give you adequate training to perform your job(s)?

_____ Yes

_____ No

_____ Not always

Your comments _____

4. What additional type of training would you have liked?

Your comments _____

5. How effective was your staff supervisor in helping you become part of the library team?

___ Highly effective

___ Somewhat effective

Sample 34-1. **Volunteer Exit Survey**

___ Not very effective

___ I never felt part of the team

Your comments _____

6. Were you encouraged by your supervisor to offer suggestions on ways to do your volunteer job better?

___ Yes, most of the time

___ Only at times

___ Not too often

___ Never encouraged to make suggestions

Your comments _____

7. Did you feel you received recognition for your efforts?

___ I was well recognized

___ I had some positive comments

___ Rarely recognized

___ Never recognized

Your comments _____

8. Do you feel you were kept informed of changes in library policies and procedures that would impact your volunteer work?

___ Yes, all the time

___ Yes, most of the time

___ Only on rare occasions

___ Never

Your comments _____

9. Would you encourage your friends to become library volunteers?

___ Yes, definitely

___ Yes, with qualifications

___ Maybe

___ Not sure

Your comments _____

10. In what ways can the library volunteer program be better?

Your comments _____

Name (optional) _____

Thank you. Please return this survey in the stamped, preaddressed envelope, or by e-mail by _____

(Date)

INTERPRETATION OF DATA

Whether you use an exit interview, a written survey, or some combination, you need to know how to use the information you get to your best advantage in assessing the volunteer services program.

If your question response categories are, for example, "highly enjoyable," "very enjoyable," "not enjoyable," and "definitely not enjoyable," you are eliminating a neutral category (no opinion), which forces the volunteer to choose between opposite experiences. To interpret such answers, you can combine all the "highly enjoyable" and "very enjoyable" responses for a single positive total. Do the same for the negative experiences. Convert the respective totals into percentages by dividing them by all the exit interviews done over a three-month, six-month, or one-year period. If 60 percent, 70 percent, or even 80 percent of your former volunteers check off positive comments, you can take credit for having a program that meshes well with the volunteers' requirements and experiences.

Negative experiences, on the other hand, can provide you with information on changes you might consider in the program. Usually these comments fall into general categories, with specific complaints under each one. Serious comments need to be looked at immediately, including complaints such as "nowhere to store personal effects," "inflexible scheduling," "poor treatment by staff," "lack of volunteer identification," or "little appreciation." First, however, you must verify the validity of the remarks and the extent of the problem if it concerns a department, a particular branch, or a staff member. One of the simplest approaches in this case is to discuss the complaints with a few of your respected volunteers. They may have experienced the same feelings or situations, thereby validating the complaints. They may also make positive suggestions to improve the conditions.

Problems identified by complaints that indicate a lack of understanding or knowledge can be remedied more easily. For example, the complaints about recognition (i.e., "lack of identification" and "little appreciation") can be eliminated in the future by providing name badges with first names or volunteer identification cards. You can also encourage paid staff to be more attentive to the volunteers and their work, though at times this is easier said than done. Except for some focused time, neither of these actions is financially costly, yet both go a long way toward giving personal recognition to your volunteers for work well done.

Finally, make sure you discuss the results of your exit survey with your administrative supervisor. Comments that seem unrelated may actually be part of a larger problem.

Volunteer Separation Form

Volunteer Name _____ Date _____

Volunteered from _____ to _____

Volunteer position(s) held _____

Volunteer staff supervisor _____

Branch/Department _____

Reason for leaving

_____ Another volunteer position

_____ Personal travel

_____ Personal time for family

_____ Medical condition

_____ Paid employment

Other _____

Has the volunteer returned all library keys, equipment, and materials?

_____ Yes

_____ No

Did volunteer give notice?

_____ Yes

_____ No

Explanation _____

Overall how effective was the volunteer in performing duties for the library?

_____ Very effective

_____ Effective

_____ Not effective

Comments _____

Signature and Title _____

Sample 34-2. **Volunteer Separation Form**

SEPARATION FORMS

In a small community library, the use of a separation form may be administrative overkill. Merely shifting a volunteer's file folder from "active" to "separated" or "inactive" and adding the last date the volunteer left is all that is necessary. In larger programs with hundreds of volunteers in a year, using a separation form is a way to organize information (see sample 34-2). Separation forms are useful if you receive a call for a reference and need to refresh your memory quickly or find out which supervising staff member to ask for information.

LETTERS OF REFERENCE

One important benefit you can provide volunteers who are in career transition or meeting school requirements is a letter of reference. This is a low-cost benefit that requires no budgeted funds yet can go far to help a youth get into college or a job seeker get employment. To be sure, writing these letters increases your workload, but former volunteers often remember your letter as positive aid that assisted them along their journeys.

You can offer this benefit in conversations during an exit interview or in the cover letter sent with the exit survey. This gesture is also one way to increase your responses to exit surveys. It also ends volunteer time on a positive note.

There are two kinds of reference letters. One is the "neutral" letter written for the individual who was an average or below average volunteer; it simply acknowledges that the individual was a volunteer for the library. Be sure to include the dates of volunteering, the tasks performed for the library, and a general statement about how volunteers enhance library services. The second type of letter is written for the exceptional volunteer. Besides the factual information about dates and duties, you can amplify specific areas of excellence and add your personal comments that demonstrate your knowledge of the volunteer (see sample 34-3). After writing a few letters and storing them on your computer, you will have personal templates that can readily be used as a basis for other letters.

Ms. Patty Adams
Community Volunteers Inc.
3333 West Sunnyvale Drive
American City, OK 99999

Dear Ms. Adams:

It is my pleasure to recommend Molly Marygold for the position of administrative assistant to your nonprofit group. I have known Molly as a volunteer in our library for over three years. During that time she donated over 175 hours. Molly was an enthusiastic volunteer. She started with us cleaning books and DVDs in the Technical Services Department. Because of her computer and people skills, she was trained as a reference volunteer to help customers with ready reference questions. Over a period of three months, she became very proficient in helping with ready reference questions. Our head reference librarian has been pleased with her customer service skills and her ability to learn the ready reference sources quickly.

Molly is also skilled in word processing and several database programs. In fact, several months ago I asked her if she had extra volunteer time to develop a specialized volunteer database for capturing information on high school volunteers. I was extremely pleased with the way this project turned out. She and I worked closely over a three-week period to get the data prepared for an administrative report. She had the patience to make the numerous changes and then enter the data accurately. Molly did an outstanding job. Recently her personal circumstances have changed so that she is now seeking full-time employment.

Molly has excellent computer, office, and people skills as well as the enthusiasm to tackle the most challenging problems. She will be missed around here.

I give Molly my strongest recommendation and am sure she will be an outstanding employee for you because she was one of our best volunteers.

Please feel free to call me if you would like any additional information.

Sincerely,

Name
Title
Phone number

Sample 34-3. **Letter of Reference**

PART 6 | **VOLUNTEER RECORD KEEPING**

SECTION 35 | **VOLUNTEER HUMAN RESOURCE FILES**

A NEW VOLUNTEER services manager may start out with an odd assortment of names, telephone numbers, and e-mail addresses on scratch notes. There may be a box of obsolete files of former volunteers and volunteer forms that are no longer current, or there may be nothing at all. Organizing information on the active volunteers means setting up a minimum record system that keeps track of volunteer applicants and active volunteers.

Small libraries with few volunteers may find that volunteer records are easily maintained and accessible in a file cabinet. As the volunteer services program grows, it is useful to have computerized files, either on spreadsheets containing relevant information or a simple database of volunteers. Unless you have a computer-literate volunteer assistant, it is not likely you will have much time to develop spreadsheets or enter data into a database to track your volunteers. There are commercial volunteer software packages available; however, most of these are designed for organizations that have a large number of volunteers. These can prove beneficial if the financial and staffing resources are available. In most cases, the commercial software packages are not designed for smaller programs.

If you are thinking of buying a software package or change existing software, first seek advice from experienced volunteer services managers who are using commercial or customized software. Preferably seek out managers in other libraries or in nonprofit agencies that have about the same number of volunteers as you do. Ask a lot of questions. You need to know specifically what types of information will be most useful for your program. If the data requirements are too complex, you may not be able to maintain the files and the information will quickly become out of date unless you have a paid staff assistant assigned to the task. You need software that is intuitive, easy to use for an average volunteer administrative assistant, and easy to generate reports from.

When starting or updating a record-keeping system, whether manual or electronic, be sure to include the following key components as part of each volunteer's file: application forms; volunteer agreements; emergency contacts; references; performance evaluations; letters of reference; and separation forms.

APPLICATION FORMS

A volunteer application form is a key document in your file. It contains all the relevant information about an individual applying for a volunteer position. Depending on how sophisticated your program is, you may have as many as three types of volunteer applications: for the general community, court directed, and youth. Whether you keep separate physical files for each type of volunteer or combine them into a single alphabetical grouping depends on the number of volunteers in each category.

Not everyone who completes the application form becomes a library volunteer. You can keep the applications of individuals not selected for volunteering for six months in case any questions arise. There may be a separate file for special-event or one-day volunteers who are "active" but volunteer only for a particular library or foundation event such as the annual community fundraiser. There also may be an active pending file of applicants who have been screened and are willing and able to volunteer when the library has suitable openings.

The completed volunteer application forms for all of these categories must be kept confidential. These forms contain addresses, contact information, work information, and possibly social security numbers, so it is important that the information be secure.

If at all possible, have your own file cabinets. Be careful not to write interview notes on the application form. These should be kept in a separate location until the applicant is accepted as a volunteer, then discarded.

VOLUNTEER AGREEMENTS

The second most important set of documents in your files is the signed volunteer agreement forms. This may be just one document that formally states the rules the applicant agrees to abide by, or it may involve several forms. The form or forms, once signed, serve as the basis of a mutual agreement as well as providing a reason for devolunteering a person whose actions violate the rules.

Consent agreements include the forms that allow you to get a personal background check from the police department or a commercial firm that does background checks; a current copy of a driving record; and forms authorizing screening for drugs. All of these are types of documents that should be kept in the volunteer record files. These signed forms become important if information is discovered that prevents an individual from becoming a volunteer, if a formal complaint is made against you or the library, or if there are potential legal actions.

EMERGENCY CONTACTS

Your application form may have an emergency contact name and number for a volunteer, but in practice if the form is in your files and you are not around, the collected information becomes useless in the event of a medical emergency. One option is to have a separate, short form or card file that can be conveniently kept by the supervising staff. Then the emergency information is readily available if it is needed. Be sure to keep these secondary files up to date.

REFERENCES

Some volunteers bring with them letters of reference. These can be kept with the application form, but when you do reference checks on potential volunteers, whether by telephone or mail, keep this information separate from the application. You may receive negative or confidential information that should not be part of the volunteer's file. Your library administrative rules may state how long you can hold this information, but in general, once you make a decision, the letter of reference or any notes should be removed from the file.

For example, during a telephone reference check, you are told that an applicant had serious difficulties as a volunteer at a local school. The reference does not want to give you any details but suggests that you check for yourself. When you call the school, the principal politely states that information about staff or volunteers cannot be provided according to school policy. The principal does, however, verify that the person was a volunteer. At the moment, you have unsubstantiated information about a possible problem. Whatever you choose to do at this point should be based on library policy. Your written notes need to stay in your own file and not become part of the volunteer's application file.

PERFORMANCE EVALUATIONS

Whether a supervising staff member writes a short note about a volunteer's performance or you complete a formal evaluation form, these items become part of a volunteer's file. Similarly, if a customer writes a complimentary letter about a volunteer, this also becomes part of that file.

In most cases, performance comments serve as useful feedback to the volunteer. Most people want to know how well they are doing, and positive comments serve as personal rewards and motivators. These notes are useful reminders when you have volunteer recognition events and you want to say a few words about each volunteer.

When the comments are not positive, the forms serve to document a volunteer's performance that was not up to library standards and what action was taken. In either instance, these evaluative forms and notes become part of the volunteer's formal record.

LETTERS OF REFERENCE

You may be asked to write a letter of reference for a volunteer seeking full-time employment, a youth for high school graduation, or a service program. If you have had a long and close relationship, this is easy to do. In some cases, though, the volunteer may have worked in the library at odd times when you were usually not around. Ideally, the supervising staff member is willing to write either a letter or comments to you that you can use to write the letter of reference. Also useful are any evaluative notes, forms, or "notes to the file" for writing a letter of reference. Remember to put a copy of the letter in the volunteer's file so that you have a record of what you wrote and to whom you sent it.

SEPARATION FORMS

In a small volunteer program, you may have only a note saying that a volunteer is going to be doing something different and will no longer be volunteering after a specific date. In other cases, you may write a note that the volunteer has not come in or called for the past three weeks. You probably assume the volunteer quit. In a more formalized program, you may actually use a separation form indicating that a follow-up phone call was made, the dates of the person's volunteer activity, and why the volunteer is no longer volunteering.

Completed exit interview forms and exit surveys should be put in the volunteer file after you have used the data to do fact finding or produce a report. Again, this information should be held in confidence along with the rest of the volunteer file information.

RECORD RETENTION POLICY

How long should you retain your volunteer files? The easiest solution is to follow the retention policies of your human resources department that deal with staff files or jurisdictional rules that apply to your library. Recognize that these are still confidential records with a lot of personal and contact information. More often than not, there is usually a storage space problem in keeping numerous older volunteer records. If you do not have a formal retention policy, keep the volunteer applications of those not accepted into your program for six months. This enables you to respond to any questions, negative comments, or legal issues that might arise. These files should be shredded, a job a volunteer can do if you emphasize the confidentiality of the information being handled. In an active pending volunteer file, after six months many people have gone on to other adventures and you may want to make a follow-up call to see if they are still interested in volunteering. If not, their files can be shredded.

For people who have volunteered for any length of time, you may want to hold their files for at least one year in the event the individual wants you to verify volunteer time for a third party (e.g., an employer). Unless you have an excellent memory, you may not recall every volunteer and what they did. Unlike the records of paid staff, library volunteer records are not subject to wage and hour reviews or IRS inquiries, so there is no legal need to maintain the information beyond a year. You may want to seek guidance about your record retention plans with a library administrator or the director.

| # VOLUNTEER ADMINISTRATIVE RECORDS

THE MATERIALS THAT accumulate during a successful volunteer services program can be overwhelming. For this reason, you should identify which records, forms, and information you need to do your job effectively. Setting up general administrative files at the beginning is easier than trying to reorganize your files as your volunteer program expands. Decide how your computer files should fit in with hard copy files given your own time commitments and volunteer or paid staff assistance. By organizing your files according to the categories reviewed in this section, you can access the necessary information quickly and efficiently.

TIME AND ATTENDANCE RECORDS

Whether you use daily, weekly, or monthly volunteer sign-in sheets or individual time cards, e-mail reporting, or an electronic time form, you need to keep these time and attendance files for data reporting purposes. This information is used to reward volunteers on the basis of their number of donated hours and to report to the library administration the yearly community involvement by hours and numbers and types of volunteers. It also serves to demonstrate indirectly the success and value of your program.

Accessing the collected data from a software program streamlines your operations and enables you to produce various kinds of reports. Simplicity in collecting time data from volunteers and in creating routine reports is the key criterion for setting up your time and attendance files and reports.

Will you report data by library and department or aggregate all volunteer hours into one report? Will the different types of volunteers be separated in your monthly or yearly reports? Do you want the supervising staff to verify hours and dates of volunteering for those people who have required hours to meet their obligations?

JOB DESCRIPTIONS

Your files contain job description forms in electronic or hard copy formats that document the duties of the volunteer positions. These must be easy to update and available for volunteers to read. You can post them on the volunteer services web page or library intranet or just keep them in one or more notebooks available for volunteers to read who stop by your office. You also will likely have abbreviated job announcements that you use to post for volunteer positions on the website or in hard copy. These may be a short paragraph describing the key duties of each position.

DEPARTMENT REQUEST FORMS

In a formal program, you can design a form for use by supervising staff to request volunteers with specific skills or to fill particular positions. These completed forms become the basis for recruitment campaigns to fill the requested positions. In less formal programs, your file may contain notes or e-mail from staff requesting volunteers with specific skills or time requirements. This file is the counterpart to your "Active Pending Volunteer File" and, ideally, you will have a volunteer in the pending file who can be matched with your request form for specific kinds of volunteers.

Keeping your request forms organized makes it easier to remember the types of volunteers you currently need; however, the matching process is not always so simple. A library manager may want someone to shelve DVDs on Monday and Wednesday mornings when there is a staff member available to supervise, but none of your active pending volunteers has that time slot available. Now you need to reevaluate your available volunteer pool to see who is available to meet the departmental request. One way to set up your files so that this information is always at your fingertips is to use a volunteer tracking sheet (sample 36-1). Alternatively, having a computerized database available makes this matching process go quicker.

RECRUITMENT SOURCES

Although quite a few public libraries recruit volunteers through electronic postings on the library website or Facebook or send out e-mail blasts and tweets, numerous libraries still use traditional recruitment approaches. Whether you incorporate social networking sites or continue to use traditional recruitment postings, keeping an organized approach will make you more efficient. Further, if you establish procedures, they can be used to train an assistant.

One useful file, electronic or hard copy, is a list of individuals, community organizations, and local corporations that can serve as contacts and resources for potential volunteers. This file should include community skill-based volunteers who can use their core professional skills to assist the library: marketing experts, political consultants, project managers, accounting professionals, operations managers, and human resource managers.

Any file system should be convenient and easy to use. If you are working with an inherited list, you will need to refine it for your current library requirements. Contact lists get outdated quickly because people move from position to position through various career and lifestyle changes.

Volunteer Tracking Sheet

Name _____ Telephone _____

Street _____ City _____ Zip Code _____

Library or Department preference: _____

Days/Hours preferred per week: _____

Position/area desired: _____

Special skills mentioned: _____

Application mailed: _____ Returned: _____ Name tag ordered: _____
              (date)   (date)   (date)

Contacts, notes & action taken:

_____

_____

Sample 36-1. **Volunteer Tracking Sheet**

Cumulative Volunteer Services Report

Branch / Department	Community Volunteer		Friends of the Library		School Volunteer		Civic/Social Org. Vol.		Court-Directed Volunteer	
	Mo/Avg Persons	Hrs YTD	Mo/Avg Persons	Hrs YTD	Mo/Avg Persons	Hrs YTD	Mo/Avg Persons	Hrs YTD	Mo/Avg Persons	Hrs YTD
Circle City Library										
Tree City Library										
Plains City Library										
Children's Services										
Young Adult Services										
Tech. Services										
Reference Services										
Adult Literacy Program										
Local History										
Special Events										
LIBRARY TOTALS										

Sample 36-2. **Volunteer Services Report**

Library Quarterly Summary

	Mthly Avg Persons	Type of Vol %	Total Hours YTD	Type of Vol %	Monetary value to library - YTD
Community, Friends, School, Civic Volunteers					Hours $12.00/hr
Court-Directed Volunteers					Hours $7.25/hr

Compiled by _____

Sample 36-3. **Quarterly Summary of Volunteer Service**

Also include in your files successful examples of recruitment fliers, posters, and other recruitment ideas. If there are electronic versions, store them in electronic formats that can be accessed with current library technology. If you have a batch of old hard "floppies" that cannot be accessed by your current library computers, get them converted to read/write DVDs or stored online so that you can modify them in the future. There is little that is totally new, so by blending old with new creative elements you can arrive at novel recruitment graphics and postings that can work and look fresh.

SKILL INVENTORIES

Whether you use checklists of interest areas or formalized skill inventories, you need to know the skills and interests of your volunteers in order to match them with available positions. This type of information lends itself well to a database that can quickly match a volunteer's skills and interests to a job. It is this kind of "perfect" match that makes the volunteer services manager's job fulfilling.

MONTHLY/QUARTERLY/ANNUAL REPORTS

Your administrative files contain statistical reports about volunteers on a monthly, quarterly, or annual basis. These reports should contain the number of volunteers, their donated hours, projects, and any other information useful to you or your administration (see samples 36-2 and 36-3). Having a computer-literate and accurate volunteer assistant can make the routine reporting process go a lot smoother.

It is also important to keep a file for informal notes about particularly successful projects and events that you want to call attention to in your annual report. Trying to summarize a year's worth of work from memory is difficult. If you learn to put "memory reminders" in your file, it will help make the end-of-the-year reporting process easier.

As part of the regular routine quarterly process, it is useful to inventory your volunteer program forms (applications, agreements, time records, releases, etc.) and estimate how many hard copies you will need over the course of six months. If you increase the number of forms online that volunteers can access, and if they are used, you can reduce your physical inventory. Again, having a volunteer print or copy forms to build a small inventory saves you time over the course of the year.

GENERAL VOLUNTEER INFORMATION

There is a growing body of volunteer literature including general articles, books, and Internet sites. Some of this material is pertinent to library volunteer programs. One way to keep your enthusiasm growing and bring innovation to your program is by reading current material. For example, a hospital may use an idea to attract volunteers that you may like to try; a copy of a form used by a local museum can be modified to serve your needs; an idea for a guest speaker may be found in a local newspaper article. These ideas cover the whole realm of volunteerism and come from many sources. By drawing on others' ideas and experiences, you can develop your own individual volunteer resource file.

BIBLIOGRAPHY

Volunteers in Libraries

Beauregard, Sue-Ellen. *Volunteers: We Couldn't Do without Them!* Chicago: ALA/
Library Video Network, 1998. (Video)

Berry III, John N. "Worthington Libraries, OH." *Library Journal* 132 (June 15,
2007): 36–39.

Boatner, Debra K. "Volunteers: The Hope for Tomorrow's Library." Master's thesis,
George Fox College, 1992.

"Book Buddies Deliver to Homebound" (program for older adults at the Lexington
Public Library; reprinted from page 1, November/December 1995).
Unabashed Librarian, no. 98 (1996): 6.

Chadbourne, Robert. "Volunteers in the Library: Both Sides Must Give in Order to
Get." *Wilson Library Bulletin* (June 1993): 26–27.

Childs, Catherine C. "Cunning Passages, Contrived Corridors: Mobilizing Volunteers
for a Public Library Tour." *Public Libraries* 32, no. 3 (May 1, 1993): 143–146.

Childs, Catherine C., and John Waite Bowers. "Introducing the Colorado Libraries
Volunteer Managers Council." *Colorado Libraries* 23 (Summer 1997): 36–39.

Conway, P. S. "Examining the Basics: Work, Jobs and Income (Economic Impact of
the Volunteer Labor Market)." *Public Library Journal* 15, no. 1 (Spring 2000):
17–18.

Driggers, P. F. "Risk Management for Volunteer Programs." *Colorado Libraries* 26, no. 1 (Spring 2000): 45–46.

Fister, Barbara, and Barry Trott. "Reading as a Contact Sport." *Reference and User Services Quarterly* 44 (Summer 2005): 303–309.

Gillespie, Kellie M. *Teen Volunteer Services in Libraries.* Lanham, Md.: Scarecrow Press, 2004.

Heiserman, Jo Ann. "Library Directors and Volunteer Programs." *Colorado Libraries* 17, no. 2 (June 1991): 16–17.

Hyland, Penelope. "The Value of Volunteers." *Colorado Libraries* 32 (Spring 2006): 45–46.

Jervis, B. "Unpaid Volunteers: Burden or Bonus? (in Public Libraries in Great Britain; Survey Results)." *Public Library Journal* 15, no. 1 (Spring 2000): 15–16.

Karp, Rashelle. *Volunteers in Libraries.* Small Libraries Publications, no. 20. Chicago: ALA, 1993.

Manning, Mary. "Public Library Volunteers: Ya Gotta Love 'Em . . . or Do You?" *Public Libraries* 35 (November/December 1996): 336–372.

McCune, Bonnie F. "The New Volunteerism: Making It Pay Off for Your Library." *American Libraries* 24, no. 9 (October 1993): 822–824.

———. "Marketing to Find Volunteers." *Colorado Libraries* 26, no. 3 (Fall 2000): 40–41.

———. "Diversity and Volunteers." *Colorado Libraries* 31 (Fall 2005): 43–44.

McCune, Bonnie F., and Charleszine Nelson. *Recruiting and Managing Volunteers in Libraries: A How-to-Do It Manual.* New York: Neal-Schuman, 1995.

McGrath, Marsha. "Teen Volunteers in the Library." *Public Libraries* 29, no. 1 (January 1, 1990): 24–29.

Nicely, Connie. "Rural Library Volunteers." *Colorado Libraries* 17, no. 2 (June 1, 1991): 11.

OCLC Online Computer Library Center. "*Volunteers.*" www.Webjunction.org/volunteers (2008).

Reed, Sally Gardner. *Library Volunteers Worth the Effort! A Program Manager's Guide.* Jefferson, N.C.: McFarland, 1994.

Rogers, Michael. "Californialibaries.Volunteermatch.Org Site Will Help Baby Boomers and Other Skilled Volunteers Sign Up." *Library Journal* (May 11, 2009). www.libraryjournal.com/article/CA6657556.html?q=California+State+Library+and+volunteers/.

Ross, Janet. "Success with Volunteers." *Library Mosaics* 6, no. 4 (July 1, 1995): 19.

Schmidt, David. "Wanted: Library Volunteers." *Colorado Libraries* 20, no. 1 (Spring 1994): 15.

"Self-service at Montgomery City: If Budget Gets Cut, Branches May Be Staffed Primarily by Volunteers." *Library Journal* 117 (April 1, 1992): 24.

Senior Net. "Book Donation Initiative." http://seniornet.org.

Sherman, G. W. "How One Library Solved the Overcrowded Storytime Problem (Marshall Public Library Uses Volunteers)." *School Library Journal* 44, no. 11 (November 1998): 36–38.

Smith, Marsha Anderson. "The Library Volunteer Program in Recessionary Times: An Interview with Bernie Margolis and Debbra Buerkle at Pikes Peak Library District." *Colorado Libraries* 17, no. 2 (June 1991): 9–10.

Suellentrop, Tricia. "Step Right Up." *School Library Journal* 53 (December 2007): 24.

Tuccillo, Diane P. *Library Teen Advisory Groups.* Lanham, Md.: Scarecrow Press, 2004.

Victim Assistance On-Line. "Research Volunteer Program." www.vaonline.org/rvolunteers.html (2008).

Wakefield, Barbara. "Court-Ordered Volunteers." *Colorado Libraries* 17, no. 2 (June 1991): 18.

"Ways to Recognize Volunteer Service." *Unabashed Librarian,* no. 113 (1999): 17.

Wells, L. B. "Volunteers in the Libraries." In *The Library Trustee.* 5th ed. Chicago: ALA, 1995, 172–180.

White, Herbert S. "The Double-Edged Sword of Library Volunteerism." *Library Journal* 118 (April 15, 1993): 66–67.

General Works on Volunteerism

Allen, Ken. *Creating More Effective Volunteer Involvement.* Washington, D.C.: Points of Light Foundation, 1996.

American Association of Retired Persons. *Bringing Lifetimes of Experience: A Guide for Involving Older Volunteers.* Washington, D.C.: AARP, 1994.

Burt, Eleanor, and John Taylor. "When 'Virtual' Meets Values: Insights from the Voluntary Sector." *Information, Communication and Society* 4 (March 2001): 54–73.

Campbell, Katherine Noyce, and Susan Ellis. *The (Help!) I Don't Have Enough Time Guide to Volunteer Management.* Philadelphia: Energize, 1995.

Conhaim, Wallys W. "Virtual Volunteering." *Information Today* 20 (March 2003).

Cravens, Jayne. "Studies and Research Regarding Online Volunteering/Virtual Volunteering." www.coyotecom.com/volunteer/ovresearch.html (2008).

———. "Myths about Online Volunteering (Virtual Volunteering)." www.coyote com.com/volunteer/ovmyths.html (2009).

Ellis, Susan. *The Volunteer Recruitment Book.* Philadelphia: Energize, 1994.

———. *From the Top Down: The Executive Role in Volunteer Program Success.* Rev. ed. Philadelphia: Energize, 1996.

———. *Focus on Volunteering Kopy Kit.* 2nd ed. Philadelphia: Energize/Parlay International, 1998.

Ellis, Susan, and Jayne Cravens. *The Virtual Volunteering Guidebook: How to Apply the Principles of Real-World Volunteer Management.* Palo Alto, Calif.: Energize. 2000. www.serviceleader.org/new/virtual/2003/04/000109.php.

Ellis, Susan, and Katherine H. Noyes. *No Excuses: The Team Approach to Volunteer Management.* Philadelphia: Energize, 1981.

Eystad, Melissa, ed. *Measuring the Difference Volunteers Make: A Guide to Outcome Evaluation for Volunteer Program Managers.* St. Paul: Minnesota Department of Human Services, 1997.

Fischer, Lucy Rose, and Kay Banister. *Older Volunteers: A Guide to Research and Practice.* Thousand Oaks, Calif.: Sage, 1993.

Glasrud, Bruce. "Volunteerism Vectors." *Nonprofit World* 25 (May/June 2007): 25–27.

Graff, Linda. *By Definition: Policies for Volunteer Programs.* 2nd ed. Etobicoke, Ont.: Volunteer Ontario, 1997.

———. *Beyond Police Checks: The Definitive Employee and Volunteer Screening Guidebook.* Dundas, Ont.: Graff and Associates, 1999.

Indiana State Library. "Virtual Volunteering." www.in.gov/library/2363.htm.

Lee, Jarene Frances, Julia M. Catagnus, and Susan J. Ellis, eds. *What We Learned (the Hard Way) about Supervising Volunteers.* Collective Wisdom Series. Philadelphia: Energize, 1998.

McCurley, Steve, and Rick Lynch. "Supervising the Silent Volunteer." *Grapevine,* May/June, 1995.

———. *Volunteer Management: Mobilizing All the Resources of the Community.* Downers Grove, Ill.: Heritage Arts, 1996.

McKaughan, Molly. *Corporate Volunteerism: How Families Make a Difference.* New York: The Conference Board, 1997.

Minnesota Office of Citizenship and Volunteer Services. *Playing It Safe: How to Control Liability and Risk in Volunteer Programs.* Rev. ed. St. Paul: Minnesota Office of Citizenship and Volunteers, 1998.

No Surprises Controlling Risks in Volunteer Programs. Washington, D.C.: Points of Light Foundation, Nonprofit Risk Management Center, and the American Bar Association, 1993.

Pidgeon, Walter P. *The Universal Benefits of Volunteering.* Somerset, N.J.: John Wiley, 1997.

Scheier, Ivan. *Building Staff/Volunteer Relations: A Positive Approach to a Universal Challenge.* Philadelphia: Energize, 1993.

Stallings, Betty. *Resources Kit for Managers of Volunteers.* Pleasanton, Calif.: Building Better Skills, 1992.

———. *Training Busy Staff to Succeed with Volunteers.* Pleasanton, Calif.: Building Better Skills, 1996.

Sutton, Charyn D. *Pass It On: Outreach to Minority Communities.* Philadelphia: Energize, 1992.

University of Texas, LBJ School of Public Affairs, RGK Center for Philanthropy and Community Service. "Virtual Volunteering Resources." www.serviceleader.org/new/virtual/index.php (2007).

Vineyard, Sue. *New Competencies for Volunteer Administrators, Self-Study Guide.* Washington, D.C.: Points of Light Institute, 1998.

Volunteer South Simcoe. "VSS Library: Virtual Volunteering." www.volunteer southsimcoe.ca/resource_library (2008).

Useful Volunteer Websites

Association of Leaders in Volunteer Engagement, http://cvacert.org.

Corporation for National and Community Service, www.serve.gov.

Council for Certification in Volunteer Management, http://cvacert.org.

Energize, Inc., www.Energize.com.

Free Management Library "Volunteers," www.managementhelp.org.

Idealist.Org, www.idealist.org/vmrc/index.html.

National Association of Volunteer Programs in Local Government, www.navplg.org.

Points of Light Institute, www.pointsoflight.org.

TechSoup, http://home.techsoup org./pages/default.aspx.

Thanks Company, www.Thankscompany.com.

Volunteergifts.com, www.volunteergifts.com.

VolunteerMatch, www.volunteerMatch.org.

Volunteer Today, www.VolunteerToday.com.

Newsletters

DOVIA (Directors of Volunteers in Associations). Over 360 groups located throughout the United States.

Grapevine. CAHHS, Volunteer Sales Center, P.O. Box 2038, Sacramento, CA 95812-2038.

Points of Light Foundation, 1400 I Street, NW, Suite 800, Washington, DC 20005, info@pointsoflight.org.

ILLUSTRATION CREDITS

SAMPLE 18.3   City of Tuscon. Teen Volunteer Application Form. Tucson, Arizona. www.library.pima.gov/pdf/teen-vol-app.pdf.

SAMPLE 18.4   City of Oklahoma. Court Appointed Community Service. Oklahoma City, Oklahoma. www.mls.lib.ok.us/mls/mls_volunteer/ volapp_courtappoint_2004.pdf.

SAMPLE 18.6   City of Carlsbad. One-Day Volunteer Application. Carlsbad, California. www.carlsbadca/residents/volunteer/Documents/ Vol-Application-one-day.pdf.

SAMPLE 20.1   City of Oklahoma. Authorization for Background Check. Oklahoma City, Oklahoma. www.mls.lib.ok.us/mls/mls_volunteer/ dvs_volapp_adult_2004.pdf.

SAMPLE 20.2   Alachua County Library District. Youth Reference Form. Gainesville, Florida. www.aclib.us/files/nodeimages/Reference_ Form.pdf.

SAMPLE 21.2   City of Carlsbad. Service Agreement and Release. Carlsbad, California. www.carlsbadca/residents/volunteer/Documents/ Library-vol-packet.pdf.

SAMPLE 21.2   Nashville Public Library. Young Adult Program Parent/Guardian Agreement. Nashville, Tennessee. www.library.nashville.org/Info/ gen_giving_volunteer.asp.

SAMPLE 31.1   Mesa County Public Library District. Volunteer Guidelines. Grand Junction, Colorado. www.mcpld.org.

INDEX

Page numbers in bold indicate sample documents.